Crosswalk Coach for the Common Core State Standards, English Language Arts, Grade 7

Coach™

Triumph Learning®

Crosswalk Coach for the Common Core State Standards, English Language Arts, Grade 7
314NA
ISBN-13: 978-0-7836-7881-8

Contributing Writer: Norma Brenes
Cover Image: © Veer/Image Source Photography

Triumph Learning® 136 Madison Avenue, 7th Floor, New York, NY 10016

© 2011 Triumph Learning, LLC
Coach is an imprint of Triumph Learning®

Printed in the United States of America.

10 9 8 7 6 5 4 3 2 1

The National Governors Association Center for Best Practices and Council of Chief State School Officers are the sole owners and developers of the Common Core State Standards, ©Copyright 2010. All rights reserved.

Frequently Asked Questions about the Common Core State Standards

What are the Common Core State Standards?

The Common Core State Standards for mathematics and English language arts, grades K–12, are a set of shared goals and expectations for the knowledge and skills that will help students succeed. They allow students to understand what is expected of them and to become progressively more proficient in understanding and using mathematics and English language arts. Teachers will be better equipped to know exactly what they must do to help students learn and to establish individualized benchmarks for them.

Will the Common Core State Standards tell teachers how and what to teach?

No. Because the best understanding of what works in the classroom comes from teachers, these standards will establish *what* students need to learn, but they will not dictate *how* teachers should teach. Instead, schools and teachers will decide how best to help students reach the standards.

What will the Common Core State Standards mean for students?

The standards will provide a clear, consistent understanding of what is expected of student learning across the country. Common standards will not prevent different levels of achievement among students, but they will ensure more consistent exposure to materials and learning experiences through curriculum, instruction, teacher preparation, and other supports for student learning. These standards will help give students the knowledge and skills they need to succeed in college and careers.

Do the Common Core State Standards focus on skills and content knowledge?

Yes. The Common Core State Standards recognize that both content and skills are important. They require rigorous content and application of knowledge through higher-order thinking skills. The English language arts standards require certain critical content for all students, including classic myths and stories from around the world, America's founding documents, foundational American literature, and Shakespeare. The remaining crucial decisions about content are left to state and local determination. In addition to content coverage, the Common Core State Standards require that students systematically acquire knowledge of literature and other disciplines through reading, writing, speaking, and listening.

In mathematics, the Common Core State Standards lay a solid foundation in whole numbers, addition, subtraction, multiplication, division, fractions, and decimals. Together, these elements support a student's ability to learn and apply more demanding math concepts and procedures.

The Common Core State Standards require that students develop a depth of understanding and ability to apply English language arts and mathematics to novel situations, as college students and employees regularly do.

Will common assessments be developed?

It will be up to the states: some states plan to come together voluntarily to develop a common assessment system. A state-led consortium on assessment would be grounded in the following principles: allowing for comparison across students, schools, districts, states and nations; creating economies of scale; providing information and supporting more effective teaching and learning; and preparing students for college and careers.

Table of Contents

Common Core State Standards Correlation Chart

Common Core State Standard	Grade 7	Crosswalk Coach Lesson(s)
Reading Standards for Literature		
Key Ideas and Details		
RL.7.1	Cite several pieces of textual evidence to support analysis of what the text says explicitly as well as inferences drawn from the text.	8
RL.7.2	Determine a theme or central idea of a text and analyze its development over the course of the text; provide an objective summary of the text.	6
RL.7.3	Analyze how particular elements of a story or drama interact (e.g., how setting shapes the characters or plot).	2, 4
Craft and Structure		
RL.7.4	Determine the meaning of words and phrases as they are used in a text, including figurative and connotative meanings; analyze the impact of rhymes and other repetitions of sounds (e.g., alliteration) on a specific verse or stanza of a poem or section of a story or drama.	3, 7
RL.7.5	Analyze how a drama's or poem's form or structure (e.g., soliloquy, sonnet) contributes to its meaning.	2, 3
RL.7.6	Analyze how an author develops and contrasts the points of view of different characters or narrators in a text.	5
Integration of Knowledge and Ideas		
RL.7.7	Compare and contrast a written story, drama, or poem to its audio, filmed, staged, or multimedia version, analyzing the effects of techniques unique to each medium (e.g., lighting, sound, color, or camera focus and angles in a film).	2
RL.7.8	(Not applicable to literature.)	
RL.7.9	Compare and contrast a fictional portrayal of a time, place, or character and a historical account of the same period as a means of understanding how authors of fiction use or alter history.	1
Range of Reading and Level of Text Complexity		
RL.8.10	By the end of the year, read and comprehend literature, including stories, dramas, and poems, in the grades 6–8 text complexity band proficiently, with scaffolding as needed at the high end of the range.	1–8
Reading Standards for Informational Text		
Key Ideas and Details		
RI.7.1	Cite several pieces of textual evidence to support analysis of what the text says explicitly as well as inferences drawn from the text.	8, 11
RI.7.2	Determine two or more central ideas in a text and analyze their development over the course of the text; provide an objective summary of the text.	9, 10
RI.7.3	Analyze the interactions between individuals, events, and ideas in a text (e.g., how ideas influence individuals or events, or how individuals influence ideas or events).	9, 12
Craft and Structure		
RI.7.4	Determine the meaning of words and phrases as they are used in a text, including figurative, connotative, and technical meanings; analyze the impact of a specific word choice on meaning and tone.	7
RI.7.5	Analyze the structure an author uses to organize a text, including how the major sections contribute to the whole and to the development of the ideas.	14

Common Core State Standard	Grade 7	Crosswalk Coach Lesson(s)
	**Reading Standards for Informational Text (continued)**	
	**Craft and Structure (continued)**	
RI.7.6	Determine an author's point of view or purpose in a text and analyze how the author distinguishes his or her position from that of others.	10, 12
	**Integration of Knowledge and Ideas**	
RI.7.7	Compare and contrast a text to an audio, video, or multimedia version of the text, analyzing each medium's portrayal of the subject (e.g., how the delivery of a speech affects the impact of the words).	14
RI.7.8	Trace and evaluate the argument and specific claims in a text, assessing whether the reasoning is sound and the evidence is relevant and sufficient to support the claims.	10
RI.7.9	Analyze how two or more authors writing about the same topic shape their presentations of key information by emphasizing different evidence or advancing different interpretations of facts.	12
	**Range of Reading and Level of Text Complexity**	
RI.7.10	By the end of the year, read and comprehend literary nonfiction in the grades 6–8 text complexity band proficiently, with scaffolding as needed at the high end of the range.	9–15
	**Writing Standards**	
	**Text Types and Purposes**	
W.7.1	Write arguments to support claims with clear reasons and relevant evidence.	16
W.7.1.a	Introduce claim(s), acknowledge alternate or opposing claims, and organize the reasons and evidence logically.	16
W.7.1.b	Support claim(s) with logical reasoning and relevant evidence, using accurate, credible sources and demonstrating an understanding of the topic or text.	16
W.7.1.c	Use words, phrases, and clauses to create cohesion and clarify the relationships among claim(s), reasons, and evidence.	16
W.7.1.d	Establish and maintain a formal style.	16
W.7.1.e	Provide a concluding statement or section that follows from and supports the argument presented.	16
W.7.2	Write informative/explanatory texts to examine a topic and convey ideas, concepts, and information through the selection, organization, and analysis of relevant content.	17
W.7.2.a	Introduce a topic clearly, previewing what is to follow; organize ideas, concepts, and information, using strategies such as definition, classification, comparison/contrast, and cause/effect; include formatting (e.g., headings), graphics (e.g., charts, tables), and multimedia when useful to aiding comprehension.	17
W.7.2.b	Develop the topic with relevant facts, definitions, concrete details, quotations, or other information and examples.	17
W.7.2.c	Use appropriate transitions to create cohesion and clarify the relationships among ideas and concepts.	17
W.7.2.d	Use precise language and domain-specific vocabulary to inform about or explain the topic.	17
W.7.2.e	Establish and maintain a formal style.	17
W.7.2.f	Provide a concluding statement or section that follows from and supports the information or explanation presented.	17

Common Core State Standard	Grade 7	Crosswalk Coach Lesson(s)
	**Writing Standards** (*continued*)
	**Text Types and Purposes** (*continued*)
W.7.3	Write narratives to develop real or imagined experiences or events using effective technique, relevant descriptive details, and well-structured event sequences.	18
W.7.3.a	Engage and orient the reader by establishing a context and point of view and introducing a narrator and/or characters; organize an event sequence that unfolds naturally and logically.	18
W.7.3.b	Use narrative techniques, such as dialogue, pacing, and description, to develop experiences, events, and/or characters.	18
W.7.3.c	Use a variety of transition words, phrases, and clauses to convey sequence and signal shifts from one time frame or setting to another.	18
W.7.3.d	Use precise words and phrases, relevant descriptive details, and sensory language to capture the action and convey experiences and events.	18
W.7.3.e	Provide a conclusion that follows from and reflects on the narrated experiences or events.	18
	**Production and Distribution of Writing**
W.7.4	Produce clear and coherent writing in which the development, organization, and style are appropriate to task, purpose, and audience. (Grade-specific expectations for writing types are defined in standards 1–3 above.)	16–18
W.7.5	With some guidance and support from peers and adults, develop and strengthen writing as needed by planning, revising, editing, rewriting, or trying a new approach, focusing on how well purpose and audience have been addressed. (Editing for conventions should demonstrate command of Language standards 1–3.)	16–19
W.7.6	Use technology, including the Internet, to produce and publish writing and link to and cite sources as well as to interact and collaborate with others, including linking to and citing sources.	19
	**Research to Build and Present Knowledge**
W.7.7	Conduct short research projects to answer a question, drawing on several sources and generating additional related, focused questions for further research and investigation.	20
W.7.8	Gather relevant information from multiple print and digital sources, using search terms effectively; assess the credibility and accuracy of each source; and quote or paraphrase the data and conclusions of others while avoiding plagiarism and following a standard format for citation.	20
W.7.9	Draw evidence from literary or informational texts to support analysis, reflection, and research.	20
W.7.9.a	Apply grade 7 Reading standards to literature (e.g., "Compare and contrast a fictional portrayal of a time, place, or character and a historical account of the same period as a means of understanding how authors of fiction use or alter history").	20
W.7.9.b	Apply grade 7 Reading standards to literary nonfiction (e.g. "Trace and evaluate the argument and specific claims in a text, assessing whether the reasoning is sound and the evidence is relevant and sufficient to support the claims").	20
	**Range of Writing**
W.7.10	Write routinely over extended time frames (time for research, reflection, and revision) and shorter time frames (a single sitting or a day or two) for a range of discipline-specific tasks, purposes, and audiences.	16–18

Common Core State Standard	Grade 7	Crosswalk Coach Lesson(s)
	Language Standards	
Conventions of Standard English		
L.7.1	Demonstrate command of the conventions of standard English grammar and usage when writing or speaking.	21–22
L.7.1.a	Explain the function of phrases and clauses in general and their function in specific sentences.	22
L.7.1.b	Choose among simple, compound, complex, and compound-complex sentences to signal differing relationships among ideas.	22
L.7.1.c	Place phrases and clauses within a sentence, recognizing and correcting misplaced and dangling modifiers.	21
L.7.2	Demonstrate command of the conventions of standard English capitalization, punctuation, and spelling when writing.	23
L.7.2.a	Use a comma to separate coordinate adjectives (e.g., *It was a fascinating, enjoyable movie* but not *He wore an old[,] green shirt*).	23
L.7.2.b	Spell correctly.	23
Knowledge of Language		
L.7.3	Use knowledge of language and its conventions when writing, speaking, reading, or listening.	24
L.7.3.a	Choose language that expresses ideas precisely and concisely, recognizing and eliminating wordiness and redundancy.	24
Vocabulary Acquisition and Use		
L.7.4	Determine or clarify the meaning of unknown and multiple-meaning words and phrases based on *grade 7 reading and content*, choosing flexibly from a range of strategies.	25, 26
L.7.4.a	Use context (e.g., the overall meaning of a sentence or paragraph; a word's position or function in a sentence) as a clue to the meaning of a word or phrase.	25
L.7.4.b	Use common, grade-appropriate Greek or Latin affixes and roots as clues to the meaning of a word (e.g., *belligerent, bellicose, rebel*).	26
L.7.4.c	Consult general and specialized reference materials (e.g., dictionaries, glossaries, thesauruses), both print and digital, to find the pronunciation of a word or determine or clarify its precise meaning or its part of speech.	26
L.7.4.d	Verify the preliminary determination of the meaning of a word or phrase (e.g., by checking the inferred meaning in context or in a dictionary).	25
L.7.5	Demonstrate understanding of figurative language, word relationships, and nuances in word meanings.	7, 27
L.7.5.a	Interpret figures of speech (e.g., literary, biblical, and mythological allusions) in context.	7
L.7.5.b	Use the relationship between particular words (e.g., synonym/antonym, analogy) to better understand each of the words.	27
L.7.5.c	Distinguish among the connotations (associations) of words with similar denotations (definitions) (e.g., *refined, respectful, polite, diplomatic, condescending*).	27
L.7.6	Acquire and use accurately grade-appropriate general academic and domain-specific words and phrases; gather vocabulary knowledge when considering a word or phrase important to comprehension or expression.	25

Common Core State Standard	Grade 7	Crosswalk Coach Lesson(s)
	**Reading Standards for Literacy in History/Social Studies**	
	**Key Ideas and Details**	
RH.7.1	Cite specific textual evidence to support analysis of primary and secondary sources.	11
RH.7.2	Determine the central ideas or information of a primary or secondary source; provide an accurate summary of the source distinct from prior knowledge or opinions.	9, 11
RH.7.3	Identify key steps in a text's description of a process related to history/social studies (e.g., how a bill becomes law, how interest rates are raised or lowered).	13
	**Craft and Structure**	
RH.7.4	Determine the meaning of words and phrases as they are used in a text, including vocabulary specific to domains related to history/social studies.	25
RH.7.5	Describe how a text presents information (e.g., sequentially, comparatively, causally).	13
RH.7.6	Identify aspects of a text that reveal an author's point of view or purpose (e.g., loaded language, inclusion or avoidance of particular facts).	10
	**Integration of Knowledge and Ideas**	
RH.7.7	Integrate visual information (e.g., in charts, graphs, photographs, videos, or maps) with other information in print and digital texts.	14
RH.7.8	Distinguish among fact, opinion, and reasoned judgment in a text.	15
RH.7.9	Analyze the relationship between a primary and secondary source on the same topic.	11
	**Range of Reading and Level of Text Complexity**	
RH.7.10	By the end of grade 8, read and comprehend history/social studies texts in the grades 6–8 text complexity band independently and proficiently.	9–15
	**Reading Standards for Literacy in Science and Technical Subjects**	
	**Key Ideas and Details**	
RST.7.1	Cite specific textual evidence to support analysis of science and technical texts.	9, 11
RST.7.2	Determine the central ideas or conclusions of a text; provide an accurate summary of the text distinct from prior knowledge or opinions.	11
RST.7.3	Follow precisely a multistep procedure when carrying out experiments, taking measurements, or performing technical tasks.	13
	**Craft and Structure**	
RST.7.4	Determine the meaning of symbols, key terms, and other domain-specific words and phrases as they are used in a specific scientific or technical context relevant to *grades 6–8 texts and topics*.	25
RST.7.5	Analyze the structure an author uses to organize a text, including how the major sections contribute to the whole and to an understanding of the topic.	9, 13
RST.7.6	Analyze the author's purpose in providing an explanation, describing a procedure, or discussing an experiment in a text.	13
	**Integration of Knowledge and Ideas**	
RST.7.7	Integrate quantitative or technical information expressed in words in a text with a version of that information expressed visually (e.g., in a flowchart, diagram, model, graph, or table).	14
RST.7.8	Distinguish among facts, reasoned judgment based on research findings, and speculation in a text.	15
RST.7.9	Compare and contrast the information gained from experiments, simulations, video, or multimedia sources with that gained from reading a text on the same topic.	12

Common Core State Standard	Grade 7	Crosswalk Coach Lesson(s)
	**Reading Standards for Literacy in Science and Technical Subjects** (*continued*)
	**Range of Reading and Level of Text Complexity**
RST.7.10	By the end of grade 8, read and comprehend science/technical texts in the grades 6–8 text complexity band independently and proficiently.	9–15
	**Writing Standards for Literacy in History/Social Studies, Science, and Technical Subjects**
	**Text Types and Purposes**
WHST.7.1	Write arguments focused on *discipline-specific content*.	16
WHST.7.1.a	Introduce claim(s) about a topic or issue, acknowledge and distinguish the claim(s) from alternate or opposing claims, and organize the reasons and evidence logically.	16
WHST.7.1.b	Support claim(s) with logical reasoning and relevant, accurate data and evidence that demonstrate an understanding of the topic or text, using credible sources.	16
WHST.7.1.c	Use words, phrases, and clauses to create cohesion and clarify the relationships among claim(s), counterclaims, reasons, and evidence.	16
WHST.7.1.d	Establish and maintain a formal style.	16
WHST.7.1.e	Provide a concluding statement or section that follows from and supports the argument presented.	16
WHST.7.2	Write informative/explanatory texts, including the narration of historical events, scientific procedures/ experiments, or technical processes.	17
WHST.7.2.a	Introduce a topic clearly, previewing what is to follow; organize ideas, concepts, and information into broader categories as appropriate to achieving purpose; include formatting (e.g., headings), graphics (e.g., charts, tables), and multimedia when useful to aiding comprehension.	17
WHST.7.2.b	Develop the topic with relevant, well-chosen facts, definitions, concrete details, quotations, or other information and examples.	17
WHST.7.2.c	Use appropriate and varied transitions to create cohesion and clarify the relationships among ideas and concepts.	17
WHST.7.2.d	Use precise language and domain-specific vocabulary to inform about or explain the topic.	17
WHST.7.2.e	Establish and maintain a formal style and objective tone.	17
WHST.7.2.f	Provide a concluding statement or section that follows from and supports the information or explanation presented.	17
WHST.7.3	(Not applicable as a separate requirement.)	
	**Production and Distribution of Writing**
WHST.7.4	Produce clear and coherent writing in which the development, organization, and style are appropriate to task, purpose, and audience.	18
WHST.7.5	With some guidance and support from peers and adults, develop and strengthen writing as needed by planning, revising, editing, rewriting, or trying a new approach, focusing on how well purpose and audience have been addressed.	19
WHST.7.6	Use technology, including the Internet, to produce and publish writing and present the relationships between information and ideas clearly and efficiently.	19
	**Research to Build and Present Knowledge**
WHST.7.7	Conduct short research projects to answer a question (including a self-generated question), drawing on several sources and generating additional related, focused questions that allow for multiple avenues of exploration.	20

Common Core State Standard	Grade 7	Crosswalk Coach Lesson(s)
	Writing Standards for Literacy in History/Social Studies, Science, and Technical Subjects *(continued)*	
Research to Build and Present Knowledge *(continued)*		
WHST.7.8	Gather relevant information from multiple print and digital sources, using search terms effectively; assess the credibility and accuracy of each source; and quote or paraphrase the data and conclusions of others while avoiding plagiarism and following a standard format for citation.	20
WHST.7.9	Draw evidence from informational texts to support analysis, reflection, and research.	20
Range of Writing		
WHST.7.10	Write routinely over extended time frames (time for reflection and revision) and shorter time frames (a single sitting or a day or two) for a range of discipline-specific tasks, purposes, and audiences.	16–20

CHAPTER 1

Reading Literature

Chapter 1: Diagnostic Assessment for Lessons 1–8

Lesson 1 Fiction
RL.7.9, RL.7.10, W.7.9.a

Lesson 2 Drama
RL.7.3, RL.7.4, RL.7.5,
RL.7.10, W.7.9.a

Lesson 3 Poetry
RL.7.4, RL.7.5, W.7.9.a

Lesson 4 Plot
RL.7.3, RL.7.10, W.7.9.a

Lesson 5 Character
RL.7.6, RL.7.10, W.7.9.a

Lesson 6 Theme
RL.7.2, RL.7.10, W.7.9.a

Lesson 7 Figurative Language
RL.7.4, RL.7.10, RI.7.4,
RI.7.10, W.7.9.a–b, L.7.5.a

Lesson 8 Make Inferences
RL.7.1, RL.7.10, RI.7.1,
RI.7.10, W.7.9.a–b

Chapter 1: Cumulative Assessment for Lessons 1–8

1 Diagnostic Assessment for Lessons 1–8

Read the poem and answer the questions that follow.

The Wind's Visit
by Emily Dickinson

The wind tapped like a tired man,
And like a host, "Come in,"
I boldly answered; entered then
My residence within

5   A rapid, footless guest,
To offer whom a chair
Were as impossible as hand
A sofa to the air.

No bone had he to bind him,
10   His speech was like the push
Of numerous humming-birds at once
From a superior bush.

His countenance a billow,
His fingers, if he pass,
15   Let go a music, as of tunes
Blown tremulous in glass.

He visited, still flitting;
Then, like a timid man,
Again he tapped—'twas flurriedly—
20   And I became alone.

countenance: face
billow: a high wave
tremulous: trembling

1. Which line from the poem contains alliteration?

   A. "His countenance a billow"

   B. "His speech was like the push"

   C. "A rapid, footless guest"

   D. "No bone had he to bind him"

2. Which lines from the poem rhyme?

   A. lines 1 and 2

   B. lines 7 and 8

   C. lines 10 and 12

   D. lines 14 and 15

3. From this poem, you can infer that the speaker

   A. is puzzled by the wind.

   B. has an appreciation for nature.

   C. prefers to be alone.

   D. is not very observant.

4. Read these lines from the poem.

   His speech was like the push
   Of numerous humming-birds
   at once

   Which kind of figurative language does the poet use to describe the sound of the wind?

   A. metaphor

   B. simile

   C. allusion

   D. alliteration

5. Explain how the poet uses personification in the poem.

   _____

   _____

   _____

   _____

   _____

   _____

   _____

   _____

Read the passage and answer the questions that follow.

A Surprise for Rosie

Rosie crossed the street and walked up the block to her building. It was a hot afternoon in August 1876, and the neighborhood streets were filled with people. Children played jump rope and jacks. Street vendors in wagons or on foot advertised their wares. A woman was trying to sell some wilted flowers she had probably picked from a park, but she was not having much success. Rosie knew the woman lived in the building next to hers. She also knew the woman would probably not be eating supper that night if she could not sell some flowers.

Rosie wondered what her family would be eating for supper. She was tired of potatoes, but, when she complained, her mother would remind her to be grateful to have any food in her belly at all. Rosie was well aware that they were lucky to eat regularly. Still, sometimes she stayed up in bed, staring longingly at the pictures in a magazine her brother had found in the alley. The pages were still in good condition, and the colorful photographs fascinated Rosie. Women dressed in fancy clothes and hats stared back at her with frozen smiles. There were advertisements for the newest household appliances that would never find their way into her mother's kitchen. But what really captivated Rosie were the recipes with pictures of tender steaks, lobster, cakes, and pies. Rosie could only imagine what they tasted like as she salivated over the glossy pages.

As she climbed up the steps to their fourth-floor apartment, Rosie paused to greet her neighbor, Mrs. Rizzio. Like many tenants in the building, Mrs. Rizzio kept her front door open on hot days.

"Hard day at work?" Mrs. Rizzio asked.

Rosie smiled. "It was not so bad today. Mr. Henderson was out, so his wife ran the floor. She's much nicer."

Rosie's aunt had found a job for her at the clothing factory. Rosie was only 11 years old, but she worked three days a week, sewing buttonholes and pockets on shirts. The hours were long and the work was tedious, but her family needed the money. Still, Rosie would give up the job in a second for the opportunity to go to school in September. She had attended school in Ireland before her family had immigrated to America a year ago. The family had expected life to be wonderful here, but in many ways they were worse off than before.

Rosie climbed the last step and opened the door to her apartment. As soon as she entered, she smelled potatoes cooking in the kitchen. Rosie sighed and closed the door.

"Is that you, Rosie?" her mother called as she came out of the kitchen. She pushed a strand of hair out of Rosie's eyes and kissed her cheek.

"You look tired. Go have a lie-down before supper."

Rosie nodded and entered the room that served as bedroom for her parents, her brother, and herself. Her mother had set up curtains to divide the room and create the illusion of privacy, but in reality there was very little of it. It was such a small space that there was barely room to walk around the cots they used for beds. Rosie kicked off her shoes and stretched out on her bed. The thin mattress provided little comfort, but it was better than sleeping on the floor.

Rosie closed her eyes and began to drift into a pleasant sleep. Suddenly, she felt something crawling in her hair. She screamed and sat up, running her fingers through her hair in a panic. Then, she heard a laugh.

"Did I scare you, Sleeping Beauty?" her brother asked, rising from behind the cot.

"Kevin! I've told you not to do that! Mom!"

Their mother yelled back from the kitchen, "Whatever it is, I don't want to know about it! Your father will be home soon, and I don't want any more shenanigans. Both of you run downstairs and wash up. Supper is almost ready. If you see your father, tell him I said to wash up before he comes upstairs or we shall have words!"

Rosie and her brother knew that hardly anything scared their father more than the threat of having words with their mother. They followed her into the kitchen and retrieved the metal bucket in the corner. They left the apartment and walked down the stairs. They had to get water from the faucet at the back of the building. On the third floor, they saw Mrs. Rizzio hugging another neighbor. Mrs. Kowalski appeared to be crying.

"I wonder what's wrong," Rosie whispered.

"You didn't hear? Mrs. Kowalski is getting evicted." It seemed that Mrs. Kowalski could no longer afford to pay the rent in their building. She had to move to a cheaper apartment.

At the faucet, they found their father, washing his hands and face. Despite his obvious fatigue, he beamed at the sight of his children. They ran into his arms and embraced him.

At supper, Rosie's father said, "So, tomorrow our little girl is one year older."

Rosie kept her eyes on her plate. She knew there was no money for her present. She glanced up to see her parents smiling at each other.

The next day, Rosie tried to forget it was her birthday. When her father got home from work, he held out a package wrapped in paper. Rosie opened it. Then her mouth dropped open.

"The boss let me have this for two extra hours of work next week," her father said. "Sometimes it is good to work at a slaughterhouse. I could only get one, but it is all for the birthday girl."

"I'll get this in the pan right away," her mother said, taking the package.

Rosie was so happy she burst into tears. "Thank you so much!" she managed to say. "But you will need to cut it into four pieces so that we can all enjoy it."

Her brother grinned from ear to ear when he heard that.

6. This passage is an example of

   A. a fable.

   B. a myth.

   C. a novel.

   D. historical fiction.

7. How does Rosie feel about having to work?

   A. She is angry that she is expected to earn money.

   B. She accepts that it is something she must do.

   C. She resents being underpaid for her labor.

   D. She is happy that work allows her to skip school.

8. Why is the magazine Rosie reads important to the plot?

   A. It illustrates that some people live better than others.

   B. It shows that Rosie can read and would do well in school.

   C. It explains the significance of Rosie's birthday present.

   D. It proves that people should not wish for things they cannot have.

9. What is the theme of the passage?

   A. Life is hard, and then it gets worse.

   B. People can make the best of a bad situation.

   C. Money is only important to rich people.

   D. Don't waste time on foolish dreams.

Read the passage and answer the questions that follow.

Immigration in the Gilded Age

For decades, people had been leaving their home countries and sailing to America. After all, our country was built by immigrants. But during the Gilded Age, near the beginning of the twentieth century, more people came than ever before.

Why They Came

In 1876, America's industrial strength was growing. Newspapers spread the word around the globe. Sometimes, the stories were exaggerated as people retold them. Yes, railroads crisscrossed the country, and factories were springing up in cities and towns. Companies needed workers. Some businessmen became extremely wealthy and lived lives of great luxury. Their fancy homes and glamorous lifestyle gave the era its name, the Gilded Age. But there was no guarantee that everyone would become rich—or even get a job.

Still, thousands of people were lured by the possibility of finding something better than they had. Many people from rural parts of our country left their farms to head to the cities. Thousands more people arrived from other countries. Many countries in Europe and Asia were going through hard times. Crops were failing. Taxes were high. And many people were eager to join family members who were already living in the United States.

When the immigrants arrived, however, they learned that there were two sides to the story. There were jobs, but so many people wanted work that there weren't enough good jobs to go around. Many workers made barely enough money to live on. Some immigrants washed filthy rags they had found in the garbage and sold them for a few cents. Others worked in grim meat factories called slaughterhouses, washing blood from the floor for five dollars a week.

Gloomy—Not Gilded

Without good jobs, immigrants couldn't earn enough money to live in comfortable homes. They mainly moved into tenements. These apartment buildings were crowded, dirty, and unsafe. Often staircases were falling apart and ceilings were crumbling. Unfortunately, many landlords were Scrooges. They didn't want to pay to have them fixed.

To collect more rent, landlords often squeezed more than one family into a single apartment. The landlord rented each room to a different family. Three families might have lived in an apartment that would normally house only one.

A little household usually had a stove, but it probably didn't have water. Most tenements had no indoor plumbing. People got their water from a faucet in back of the house.

If your parents had been immigrants during the Gilded Age, your family might have lived in one or two small, dark rooms. You would have played ball in the back alleys or picked coal off the streets for your family's stove. You might have gone to school, unless it was winter and your shoes were completely worn out.

Children Making a Living

A pair of worn-out shoes may not sound like a big problem today. But for an immigrant family during the Gilded Age, buying a new pair of shoes might mean the family couldn't pay the rent. Most landlords would evict people who couldn't pay.

Making enough money to buy food and pay rent was a major struggle for many immigrant families. That's the main reason many children didn't go to school or only went part of the time—they had to work to help their families survive. Children often worked at home, where families would set up shop in their room.

Everyone except babies helped out—making candy to sell, rolling cigars, or doing extra sewing for a clothing factory. As children got older, they often worked outside the home. A girl might do finishing work, such as sewing pockets or buttonholes for a company that made clothing. A boy might work on a cotton-spinning machine in a textile factory.

In some states, laws said that no one could hire a child under the age of 14. Still, many companies ignored the laws. Landlords were supposed to keep their buildings repaired, but most wouldn't spend the money. Sanitation laws said that cities had to keep the streets clean. However, tenement streets were usually filled with garbage and dirty sewer water. The problem was that many city governments didn't enforce the laws.

Many people tried to ignore the miserable conditions in the tenements. However, like the workers who went on strike to fight for their rights, this was a problem that couldn't be ignored for very long. Through powerful words and pictures, journalists and photographers began to reveal the truth: Beneath the glamour of the Gilded Age lay a lot of problems.

Muckrakers and the Progressive Movement

Muckraking was a way of exposing problems to the public and of getting the public to demand change. In other words, it was a way of "raking or stirring up the muck" that lay beneath the shiny exterior of the Gilded Age.

One of the most famous muckrakers was Jacob Riis. Riis photographed and wrote about the wretched conditions of immigrants in New York City. He published a famous book in 1890 titled *How the Other Half Lives*. The book's success helped to initiate calls for better housing, improved sanitation, and fairer landlord practices.

As the Gilded Age was coming to an end, a new movement emerged: the Progressive movement. The Progressives were activists who sought to reform and improve the conditions of the city slums and tenements. They also worked to improve the working conditions of immigrants. The Progressives encouraged government to pass new laws and restrictions protecting workers. In 1874, Massachusetts passed the nation's first law limiting the number of hours that women and children could work in factories. Other labor laws were passed restricting children from working in coal mines and other dangerous conditions.

At the urging of Jane Addams, a Progressive activist, child labor laws were strengthened even further, raising age limits, restricting night work, and requiring school attendance. By the early 1900s, the Progressives had considerably improved immigrant conditions in our cities and factories.

10. Read this sentence from the passage.

Unfortunately, many landlords were Scrooges.

Why does the author MOST LIKELY make an allusion to Scrooge?

A. to suggest that wealth is not the key to happiness

B. to indicate that landlords were old and rich

C. to show that landlords had read *A Christmas Carol*

D. to emphasize that landlords were stingy

11. Why did some city governments MOST LIKELY not enforce sanitation laws in poor neighborhoods?

A. They did not think poor immigrants were important.

B. They thought the neighborhoods were not so dirty.

C. No one wanted to pick up garbage for a living.

D. The laws did not specify which neighborhoods to clean.

Use "A Surprise for Rosie" and "Immigration in the Gilded Age" to answer questions 12–13.

12. Both "A Surprise for Rosie" and "Immigration in the Gilded Age" illustrate that

   A. people struggled to put food on the table.

   B. laws were instituted to protect children.

   C. working at slaughterhouses paid well.

   D. many people moved from farms to the cities.

13. Which details in "A Surprise for Rosie" support information about children in "Immigration in the Gilded Age"?

   _____

   _____

   _____

   _____

   _____

   _____

   _____

1 Fiction

RL.7.9, RL.7.10, W.7.9.a

Getting the Idea

Fiction is a literary work produced from a writer's imagination. A **genre** is a category, or type, of literature. The chart below lists some of the major genres of fiction.

Type of Fiction	Definition	Example
contemporary fiction	a narrative set in modern times	*Holes*
historical fiction	a narrative set in the past that gives a fictional account of historical figures or events	*Number the Stars*
novel	a long narrative, usually divided into chapters	*My Side of the Mountain*
short story	a short narrative with a plot and characters	"The Ransom of Red Chief"
fable	a short story with a moral or lesson; often has animal characters	"The Ant and the Grasshopper"
myth	a traditional story that tells about a culture's heroes, ancestors, or gods; may explain how the natural world was created or how it works	"How Sun and Moon Came to Be"

A work of fiction may be very long or very short. It may deal with familiar scenes from everyday life or describe events that would never happen in the real world. It may tell about serious issues or be lighthearted and comical. While there are many different ways in which authors shape their works, fictional texts include the same basic elements: characters, a setting, and a plot.

You will learn more about the elements of fiction later in this chapter. The important thing to remember is that fiction is a work of invention, even when the story includes facts or realistic events.

A good example of this is historical fiction, which blends fact and fiction. In *The Autobiography of Miss Jane Pittman*, author Ernest James Gaines chronicles the life of the fictional title character. Told mostly from Jane's point of view, the novel describes events from Jane's childhood until she is about 110 years old. Although Jane is a fictional character, the context of her experiences is real. A former slave, she tells about her life before and after the end of the American Civil War. She is a personal witness to the cruelty of slavery and the injustice of racial discrimination. She lives through the turmoil of the civil rights movement in the 1960s. The reader experiences these events through Jane's eyes. In that way, the reader gains insight into what life was like for many African Americans during specific periods in our country's history.

When authors set out to write historical fiction, they begin by immersing themselves in the time period in which their novel will be set. This involves reading a great many different books and studying other relevant source materials. An author will especially want to read first-hand accounts of the period written by the people who actually lived at the time, such as letters, diary entries, autobiographies, personal essays, and newspaper articles.

In the end, though, historical fiction is fiction. Sometimes, authors will change the facts in order to make the narrative more interesting. They may gloss over the flaws of real-life characters in order to make them appear more heroic. The dialogue of the characters will almost certainly be made up by the author, though it may be based on a first-hand source. Well-written and well-researched historical novels are enlightening and educational. However, if you read historical fiction and become interested in a particular time period, seek out authoritative historical accounts. It is the best way to learn about the real characters and events.

Thinking It Through

Read the following paragraph, and then answer the question that follows.

One day, long ago, a dog found a bone while digging in a forest. "What luck!" thought the dog, snatching up the bone to carry home. As the dog crossed the bridge over a stream, he glanced into the water and spotted his own shadow. "What's this?" he thought. "Another dog is carrying a bone twice as large as mine!" Immediately, the dog jumped into the stream and began to struggle with his own shadow, attempting to take the bigger bone. As he opened his mouth, the bone slipped out. It fell into the stream and floated away before he could retrieve it. Thus, he was left without either bone.

What type of fiction is this paragraph? Explain how you know.

_____

_____

_____

_____

_____

HINT Think about what the main character learns from his experience.

Coached Example

Read the passages and answer the questions.

When Spring Comes, Winter Must Leave

Many years ago, when the world was new, a fellow named Old Man Winter lived in a lodge made of ice and snow. Wherever he walked, the ground turned hard and cold. When he breathed, the rivers froze, and the lakes became solid.

One day, Old Man Winter noticed that the snowdrifts were growing smaller, and the ice on the lake was cracking. One afternoon, as he was dozing off, there was a knock on the door of his lodge. "Go away!" he shouted. Suddenly, the door fell down and a young man rushed into the lodge. "Who are you? And how dare you burst into my home?" Old Man Winter shouted. "I am the one who makes birds fly away!"

"I am young and strong, and you do not frighten me," the young man responded. "When I walk over the land, the snow melts, and the birds and animals come to see me. You cannot stay. It is time now for you to go."

The old man opened his mouth to speak, but no words came out. Sweat poured from his brow, and he grew smaller and smaller. Before long, he was gone. His lodge melted away, and where it once had been, flowers began to grow. Once again, Young Spring had chased away Old Man Winter.

Walking to School

It was a cold, windy morning. Ryan walked along the snowy sidewalk with his best friend, Jake. Snowflakes carried on the wind flew briskly into their faces. "As if getting up at the crack of dawn to go to school wasn't bad enough, we have to do it through a snowstorm," Ryan grumbled.

Jake laughed. "This isn't a snowstorm! This is awesome! I hope it builds up so I can go sledding this afternoon. Want to come?"

Ryan shook his head and buried his face in his wool scarf. "No thanks! Right now I'm trying to imagine myself on the beach, catching a serious tan."

"Oh, come on. Don't tell me you're afraid of a little snow. I mean, summer's fun, but winter is great. Sledding, skiing, skating, snowball fights—that's what winter's all about."

Ryan shivered. "I'm just glad spring is around the corner. Walk a little faster, will you? I can't wait to get indoors where it's warm and dry."

1. The first passage is an example of

   A. a myth.

   B. a novel.

   C. historical fiction.

   D. contemporary fiction.

   HINT The passage explains an occurrence in nature.

2. How are the two passages similar?

   A. They are both contemporary fiction.

   B. They both focus on the change of seasons.

   C. They both illustrate that summer is the best season.

   D. They both suggest that it should be winter all year round.

   HINT The correct answer is true for both passages.

3. Which character in "When Spring Comes, Winter Must Leave" would Ryan MOST LIKELY relate to? Explain your answer.

   _____

   _____

   _____

   _____

   _____

   HINT Choose the character that would most appeal to Ryan.

4. Explain one key difference between the two passages.

   _____

   _____

   _____

   _____

   _____

   HINT Think about the major elements in the passages, and choose one to contrast.

Lesson Practice

Use the Reading Guides to help you understand the passages.

Reading Guide

What period in history is this historical account about?

Why do some people describe the relocation centers as concentration camps?

Why do you think it would be important for an author writing a fiction story based on this period to read Executive Order 9066?

After the Japanese bombed Pearl Harbor, the United States forced Japanese Americans to live in internment camps, believing this action was necessary to protect national security. Years later, the United States issued an official apology and gave compensation to the citizens involved.

Executive Order 9066

On December 7, 1941, the Japanese bombed Pearl Harbor on the coast of Oahu Island in Hawaii. The surprise attack resulted in the death or wounding of over 3,000 Americans. In addition, nineteen U.S. naval vessels, including eight battleships, were sunk or badly damaged. The next day, the United States declared war on Japan.

On February 19, 1942, President Franklin D. Roosevelt issued Executive Order 9066. The Order authorized the government to "prescribe military areas from which people may be excluded, and with respect to which, the right of any person to enter, remain in, or leave shall be subject to whatever restrictions the Secretary of War or the appropriate military commander may impose in his discretion."

The Order allowed about 120,000 people of Japanese ancestry living on the West Coast to be excluded from certain areas and to be evacuated and imprisoned in ten relocation centers, which by many accounts were more accurately described as concentration camps.

Although most of the people were American citizens or in the country legally, they were forced out of their homes and jobs. They could take with them only what they could carry, and then were placed in camps surrounded by guards and barbed wire. About half of those incarcerated were children, who were sometimes separated from their families. Camps were often overcrowded and unsanitary. Medical care was not always adequate, contributing to the death of some of the prisoners.

Many believe that Order 9066 was necessary to protect against espionage and sabotage after the United States declared war on Japan. However, others say that imprisoning people this way without any evidence or due process of law was a grave injustice.

A World Turned Upside Down

What type of fiction is this passage?

Some of the events in this passage actually happened.

How do the two passages relate to each other? How do they complement each other? What can you learn about the time period from each passage?

Michiko opened her eyes and stared at the fly buzzing around her sleeping baby brother. She waved it away, and then followed its path over the neighboring beds in the barracks. She almost envied the fly, for it was free to go where it wished. Michiko shut her eyes and fought the urge to cry.

Only weeks ago her life had been so different. She still remembered the day that her father rushed home from work. He had called for Michiko's mom, and the two of them had talked in low, urgent tones. Then, they had turned on the radio and listened to news reports.

Michiko knew when her parents did not wish to be disturbed. She had taken her brother outside to sit on the front porch. Her friend Annie had walked by with her father, but when Michiko had waved hello, Annie had quickly turned her head. Annie's father had glared at Michiko as if she had personally wronged him.

Finally, her parents had called her inside. Her mother said, "Japan bombed a naval station in Hawaii. The United States will probably declare war on Japan. Life may become difficult for us, Michiko."

"But we have nothing to worry about!" she had cried, wishing her words would make it true. "We're American citizens!"

Within a few months, Michiko's father had lost his job. Then, they had received notice that they had to evacuate their home.

"This is our house! What about all my things? They can't make us leave!" A few days later, they had boarded a bus to a relocation center in Poston, Arizona.

And here she was, living among strangers and surrounded by armed guards as if she were a criminal. Her grandmother had been sent to a camp in Idaho, and Michiko missed her terribly.

Answer the following questions.

1. What distinguishes "Executive Order 9066" from works of fiction?

   A. It is a factual account about real people and real events.

   B. It describes events that happened in the past.

   C. It focuses on a particular group of people.

   D. It has a historical context.

2. "A World Turned Upside Down" is BEST described as

   A. a fable.

   B. a novel.

   C. historical fiction.

   D. contemporary fiction.

3. Which element from "A World Turned Upside Down" BEST helps the reader identify its genre?

   A. the relationship between Michiko's parents

   B. details about the bombing of Pearl Harbor

   C. how Michiko treats her brother

   D. Michiko's unhappiness

4. The author of "A World Turned Upside Down" MOST LIKELY

   A. thinks that Executive Order 9066 was justified.

   B. believes that Executive Order 9066 was unjust.

   C. thinks that the United States should not have entered the war.

   D. did not do research on Japanese relocation centers.

5. Write three details from "A World Turned Upside Down" that support ideas stated in "Executive Order 9066."

   _____

   _____

   _____

   _____

   _____

   _____

2 Drama

RL.7.3, RL.7.4, RL.7.5, RL.7.10. W.7.9.a

Getting the Idea

A **drama** is a literary work intended to be performed by actors for an audience. Plays, films, and television shows are types of dramas. The author of a play is called a **playwright**, which literally means "one who crafts plays."

Most plays are divided into sections. An **act** is a major division of a play. Three- and five-act plays are very common. Each act is made up of scenes. A **scene** is a subdivision of an act with a fixed setting and continuous time frame. When the action of the play moves to a different setting or a different time, the scene ends and the next one begins.

A drama includes **dialogue**, or the words spoken by characters to each other. Some plays include soliloquies. A **soliloquy** is a speech delivered by one character while he or she is alone onstage. Soliloquies allow the audience to know what a character is feeling or thinking. A good example is the soliloquy in Shakespeare's play *Hamlet* that begins, "To be or not to be." As Hamlet recites the words, his inner torment is revealed to the audience.

Typically, the way that characters speak reflects the time period in which the play was written or the time and place in which the play takes place. Sometimes dialogue may include rhyme. The rhyming may elevate the dialogue, making it more formal and sophisticated, or it may make it lighthearted and fun.

Stage directions tell actors what to do. For example, they tell actors what actions to perform, how to speak their lines, and when to enter and exit the stage. When you read a play, you will see the stage directions in *italic* print; for example: *Nathan opens the box and peeks inside. He smiles broadly*. Sometimes, stage directions are shown in parentheses.

Reading a play is very different from seeing it performed onstage. For one thing, a staged play uses lighting and sound effects. The written play may say: A *clap of thunder startles the children*. During a performance, you will actually *hear* the thunder and may be startled yourself. Dramas also include music to set the mood. As you may know, a movie becomes a lot scarier when you hear spooky music in the background.

The elements of a drama interact to create meaning. For example, a drama about a family lost in the wilderness focuses on the characters' struggle to survive in a harsh environment. The setting shapes the characters and plot, forcing the characters to deal with challenges they would not normally face.

Thinking It Through

Read the following stage directions from a play, and then answer the question that follows.

Aisha slams the phone receiver down and bangs her fist on the table. The phone rings, but she ignores it. She stands up and storms out of the room.

Explain what the stage directions reveal about Aisha.

_____

_____

_____

_____

_____

 How does someone who acts like Aisha most likely feel?

Coached Example

Read the passage and answer the questions.

Bernard enters his bedroom on crutches and carefully lowers himself onto his bed. His left foot is in a cast. He leans the crutches against the wall. He looks at his trophies on the bookshelf, and then picks up the picture frame on his nightstand. He stares at the picture for a long moment.

BERNARD: (*after a deep sigh*) Hey, Dad. The doctors say I may not play again for a year. This morning I didn't even want to get out of bed. I can't believe this happened to me. The scout from the university is going to be at the big game next month. Coach says I'm a shoo-in for a scholarship. But now the scout won't get to see me play. I really wish you were here. I need your advice. The cast comes off next week, and I know I can be ready for the game. I know it! I just have to push myself and convince the doctors and Coach. But what if I make a mistake, pushing myself to heal too quickly? I could damage my foot for life. What do I do, Dad? What do I do?

1. This passage is a soliloquy because

   A. the audience cannot hear it.

   B. it takes place in one scene.

   C. Bernard is speaking with his father.

   D. Bernard is really speaking to himself.

   HINT Think about the definition of a soliloquy.

2. If this scene included background music, what kind of mood should the music set?

   A. mysterious

   B. excited

   C. happy

   D. sad

   HINT The music should reflect the feelings that the scene conveys to the audience.

Lesson Practice

Use the Reading Guide to help you understand the passage.

Reading Guide

Who is the playwright?

How does the first stage direction at the start of the passage help you visualize the setting?

The dialogue is the conversation between characters in a drama. This drama takes place in London. Where do you see English dialect being used?

Which key details do you learn from the first 15–20 lines of dialogue?

excerpted and adapted from

Pygmalion

by George Bernard Shaw

Act I

Covent Garden at 11:15 p.m. Torrents of heavy summer rain. Cab whistles blowing frantically. Pedestrians running for shelter into the market and under the portico of St. Paul's Church, where there are already several people, among them a lady and her daughter in evening dress. They are all staring gloomily at the rain, except one man, who seems preoccupied with a notebook in which he is writing busily.

THE DAUGHTER: (*in the space between the central pillars*) I'm getting chilled to the bone. What can Freddy be doing all this time? He's been gone twenty minutes.

THE MOTHER: (*on her daughter's right*) Not so long. But he ought to have got us a cab by this time.

A BYSTANDER: (*on the lady's right*) He won't get no cab until half-past eleven, missus, when they come back after dropping their theatre fares.

THE MOTHER: But we must have a cab. We can't stand here until half-past eleven. The weather's too foul.

THE DAUGHTER: If Freddy had a bit of boldness, he would have got one at the theatre door.

THE MOTHER: What could he have done, poor boy?

THE DAUGHTER: Others got cabs. Why couldn't he?

Freddy rushes in out of the rain and comes between them, closing a dripping umbrella. He is a young man of twenty, in evening suit, very wet around the ankles.

THE DAUGHTER: Well, haven't you got a cab?

FREDDY: There's not one to be had for love or money.

THE MOTHER: Oh, Freddy. You can't have tried.

THE DAUGHTER: It's too tiresome. Do you expect us to go and get one ourselves?

FREDDY: I tell you they're all engaged. The rain was so sudden: nobody was prepared; and everybody had to take a cab. I've been to Charing Cross one way and nearly to Ludgate Circus the other; and they were all taken.

THE MOTHER: Did you try Trafalgar Square?

FREDDY: There wasn't one at Trafalgar Square.

THE DAUGHTER: Did you try?

FREDDY: I tried as far as Charing Cross Station. Did you expect me to walk to Hammersmith, sister?

THE DAUGHTER: You haven't tried at all.

THE MOTHER: You really are very helpless, Freddy. Go again.

FREDDY: I shall simply get soaked for nothing.

THE DAUGHTER: And what about us? Are we to stay here all night in this weather, with next to nothing on? You selfish pig—

FREDDY: Oh, very well: I'll go, I'll go.

He opens his umbrella and dashes off, but collides with a flower girl, who is hurrying in for shelter, knocking her basket out of her hands. A blinding flash of lightning, followed instantly by a rattling peal of thunder, orchestrates the incident.

THE FLOWER GIRL: Nah then, Freddy: look where ya gowin', deah.

FREDDY: Sorry (*he rushes off*).

THE FLOWER GIRL: (*picking up her scattered flowers and replacing them in the basket*) There's manners for yer! Two bunches o voylets trod into the mud.

She sits down, sorting her flowers. She is not at all an attractive person. She is perhaps eighteen, perhaps twenty. She wears a little sailor hat of black straw that has long been exposed to the dust and soot of London. Her hair needs washing. She wears a shoddy black coat that reaches nearly to her knees and a brown skirt with a coarse apron. Her boots are much the worse for wear. She is as clean as she can afford to be, but compared to the ladies she is very dirty. She needs the services of a dentist.

Answer the following questions.

1. Which element of the setting has the MOST impact on the characters?

   A. the rain

   B. the time of day

   C. the market

   D. the theater

2. Which detail in the stage directions at the beginning of the play will MOST LIKELY prove to be important to the plot?

   A. the garden

   B. the cab whistles

   C. the man writing

   D. the church

3. Which of the following would happen only if a new scene has begun?

   A. It suddenly stops raining.

   B. The bystander exits the stage.

   C. Freddy returns to say he found a cab.

   D. The flower girl is drinking tea in a character's house.

4. Which detail in the stage directions BEST suggests that Freddy and the flower girl's collision is important?

   A. Their collision is accompanied by lightning and thunder.

   B. The collision knocks the girl's flowers out of her hands.

   C. Freddy opens his umbrella before he runs into her.

   D. The flower girl is in need of a dentist.

5. What does the dialogue suggest about the daughter?

   _____

   _____

   _____

   _____

   _____

   _____

3 Poetry

RL.7.4, RL.7.5, W.7.9.a

Getting the Idea

Poetry is literature written in verse, or in short lines. Poems are usually divided into **stanzas**, or groups of lines within a poem.

Poems are typically shorter than other works of literature, so poets have fewer words to create meaning and express their thoughts and feelings. This requires an imaginative and careful use of words. For example, most poets use figurative language to create images in the reader's mind.

Poems often include rhyme. **Rhyme** is the repetition of sounds at the ends of lines. Read this stanza from "The Dumb Soldier" by Robert Louis Stevenson."

> In the silence he has heard
> Talking bee and ladybird,
> And the butterfly has flown
> O'er him as he lay alone.

This stanza has two pairs of rhyming lines. The words *heard* and *ladybird* rhyme in the first two lines. The words *flown* and *alone* rhyme in the last two lines. So, the rhyme pattern in this poem can be expressed as AABB. Each new letter represents a new rhyming sound.

Notice, too, that the poem has a **rhythm**, or musical quality. This is a result of the meter. **Meter** is the pattern of stressed and unstressed syllables in a line of poetry. Read the poem aloud and note where the beats, or stressed syllables, fall in each line. The beats are the syllables you say more loudly as you read.

In the example below, the stressed syllables are shown in boldfaced print to help you "hear" the rhythm.

> I **climbed** a **steep** and **rock**y **cliff**
> That **over**looked a **shin**ing **sea**
> Then **sat** up**on** a **nar**row **ledge**
> And **lis**tened **to** the **wind** blow **free.**

Another way that poets create rhythm is through alliteration. **Alliteration** is the repetition of consonant sounds at the beginning of words. You've probably come across alliteration in nursery rhymes: *sing a song of sixpence* (repeated *s* sound). This literary device is also common in limericks: *A tutor who tooted a flute tried to tutor two tooters to toot* (repeated *t* sound).

As you read this stanza from "The Sea Wind" by Sara Teasdale, listen for alliteration.

> I am a pool in a peaceful place,
>
> I greet the great sky face to face,
>
> I know the stars and the stately moon
>
> And the wind that runs with rippling shoon—
>
> But why does it always bring to me
>
> The far-off, beautiful sound of the sea?

Several lines have two or more words that begin with the same sound. For example: *a pool in a peaceful place; greet the great sky face to face*. Alliteration enhances the rhythm and flow of a poem, thus making the poem sound more pleasant for the reader. Alliteration is also used to make certain words stand out to the reader. See if you can find other examples of alliteration in the stanza.

Some poems follow specific forms or structures. A **sonnet** is a fourteen-line poem with a precise rhyme scheme and meter. Because of their structure, sonnets are considered formal poems. Their formal quality makes them especially appropriate to deal with serious themes, such as love, death, and nature.

Thinking It Through

Read the following stanzas from "The Fossil Raindrops" by Harriet Prescott Spofford, and then answer the question that follows.

Over the quarry the children went rambling,
Hunting for stones to skip.
Into the clefts and the crevices scrambling,
Searching the quarrymen's chip.

Sweet were their voices and gay was their laughter,
That holiday afternoon,
One tumbled down and the rest tumbled after,
All of them singing one tune.

Explain how the author creates rhythm in this poem.

_____

_____

_____

_____

_____

_____

 HINT   Read the poem aloud and listen for the number of beats in each line. Do you detect a pattern?

Coached Example

Read the poem and answer the questions.

The Evening Comes
by Lloyd Mifflin

The evening comes: the boatman lifts the net,
Poles his canoe and leaves it on the shore;
So low the stream he does not use the oar;
The umber rocks rise like a parapet
5   Up through the purple and the violet,
And the faint-heard and never-ending roar
Of moving waters lessens more and more,
While each vague object looms a silhouette.
The light is going; but low overhead
10 Poises the glory of the evening star;
The fisher, silent on the rocky bar,
Drops a still line in pools of fading red;
And in the sky, where all the day lies dead,
Slowly the golden crescent sinks afar.

umber: brown
parapet: a wall-like structure for defense

---

1. This poem can be described as a sonnet because

   A. every line rhymes with another.

   B. it has fourteen lines and a rhyme scheme.

   C. it describes a scene in nature.

   D. the poet uses some difficult words.

HINT Choose the answer that most specifically applies to sonnets.

2. What is the rhyme scheme of the first four lines?

   A. AABB

   B. ABCD

   C. ABAB

   D. ABBA

HINT Different letters stand for different sounds. Compare each answer choice to the rhymes you see in the poem.

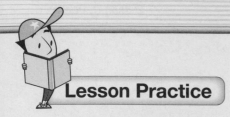

Lesson Practice

Use the Reading Guide to help you understand the poem.

Reading **Guide**

Rhyme is the repetition of sounds at the ends of lines.

How many lines does each stanza have?

Notice how the use of alliteration enhances the rhythm of the poem.

I Wandered Lonely as a Cloud
by William Wordsworth

I wandered lonely as a cloud
That floats on high o'er vales and hills,
When all at once I saw a crowd,
A host, of golden daffodils;
5   Beside the lake, beneath the trees,
Fluttering and dancing in the breeze.

Continuous as the stars that shine
And twinkle on the milky way,
They stretched in never-ending line
10   Along the margin of a bay:
Ten thousand saw I at a glance,
Tossing their heads in sprightly dance.

The waves beside them danced; but they
Out-did the sparkling waves in glee:
15   A poet could not but be gay,
In such a jocund company:
I gazed—and gazed—but little thought
What wealth the show to me had brought:

For oft, when on my couch I lie
20   In vacant or in pensive mood,
They flash upon that inward eye
Which is the bliss of solitude;
And then my heart with pleasure fills,
And dances with the daffodils.

vales: valleys
jocund: lighthearted
pensive: thoughtful

Answer the following questions.

1. How many stressed syllables does each line in the poem have?

    A. seven

    B. six

    C. five

    D. four

2. Read this line from the poem.

    When all at once I saw a crowd

    On which words do the stressed syllables fall in this line?

    A. when, all, at, once

    B. I, saw, a, crowd

    C. when, at, I, a

    D. all, once, saw, crowd

3. Which lines from the poem rhyme?

    A. lines 4 and 6

    B. lines 8 and 11

    C. lines 14 and 16

    D. lines 19 and 20

4. Which line from the poem does NOT contain alliteration?

    A. "And then my heart with pleasure fills"

    B. "What wealth the show to me had brought"

    C. "And dances with the daffodils"

    D. "Beside the lake, beneath the trees"

5. What is the effect of the daffodils on the speaker?

    _____

    _____

    _____

    _____

    _____

4 Plot

RL.7.3, RL.7.10, W.7.9.a

Getting the Idea

Plot is the sequence of events, or what happens, in a work of fiction or a drama. Elements of a plot are connected and unfold logically as the story progresses. The chart below lists the major elements of plot.

Elements of Plot	
exposition	the beginning of the story, when the setting and characters are established
conflict	a problem that a character must resolve
rising action	the bulk of the story, during which the character works to resolve the problem
climax	the turning point, usually the most exciting part
falling action	the events after the climax, leading to the solving of the problem
resolution	the ending of the story, when the conflict has been resolved

You will see this type of structure in most stories and books. For example, imagine an adventure story about a boy named Vinay. In the exposition, Vinay travels to a rainforest with his uncle during summer vacation. The conflict arises when Vinay finds a treasure map pinpointing the location of a large diamond. Vinay decides to find the diamond, but he must find it fast because a group of criminals knows he has the map. The rising action happens as Vinay and the criminals search for the diamond. The climax occurs when Vinay is caught by the criminals but outwits them and takes the diamond. During the falling action, Vinay finds his way back to his uncle, leaving the criminals far behind. In the resolution, Vinay and his uncle fly back home with the diamond.

Setting is where and when a story takes place. Usually, authors state the setting directly. Sometimes you have to figure it out. Look for clues, such as description of the climate, the available technology, or the ways people dress or talk. A book about using flying cars to travel on Earth would be set in the future. If the story is about knights fighting a battle over rights to a kingdom, it is most likely set in the Middle Ages.

The elements of a story often interact, or work together. The setting, for example, can have a major impact on the characters and plot. In the novel *Roll of Thunder, Hear My Cry*, the Logans, an African American family, live on a farm in rural Mississippi in the early 1930s. The setting plays a key role in the racism and violence that they endure. How characters interact with each other can lead to events that create or solve conflicts and shape the plot.

Thinking It Through

Read the following paragraph, and then answer the question that follows.

Rachel was the star of her school track team. She had set the school record in the 400-meter hurdle. A month before a track meet against a rival school, Rachel twisted her ankle jumping over a hurdle. She would have to walk with crutches so it would heal. Rachel returned to the track a month later.

Which sentence in the story states the conflict?

_____

_____

_____

_____

HINT The conflict is a problem a character faces.

Coached Example

Read the passage and answer the questions.

Dean felt Miranda grab his arm as he stumbled over a particularly rocky part of the trail. "Careful there," she said. "We wouldn't want you to fall when you're so close."

"Are we really almost there?" Dean asked, wiping the sweat from his brow. The climb to the top of the mountain had taken six days. It had been rough going at times. The other hikers had tried to talk Dean out of it many times, but Dean had refused to turn back. This was something he had to prove to himself.

"Yes! Can you believe it? I'm so proud of you!"

"Tell me that when we reach the top," Dean said with a smile.

Their ascent continued for another half hour. Finally, they reached the top. As his friends watched, Dean stretched out his arms and stood like a conquering warrior on the summit.

"Where are you, Miranda?" he asked.

"Right here," she said, moving to his side.

"Tell me what it looks like," Dean asked, his eyes tearing behind the dark sunglasses. Miranda described the view. Then, the hikers headed back down the mountain.

---

1. Which event is the climax?

   A. Dean stumbles over rocks.

   B. The hikers climb for six days.

   C. Dean reaches the top.

   D. Miranda describes the view.

   HINT The climax is the most exciting part.

2. What is the resolution of the story?

   A. Dean wipes his brow.

   B. The hikers reach the top of the mountain.

   C. Miranda describes the view.

   D. The hikers walk back down the mountain.

   HINT The resolution occurs closest to the end.

Lesson Practice

Use the Reading Guide to help you understand the passage.

Duplicating any part of this book is prohibited by law.

Reading Guide

Where does the passage take place? Find the words in paragraph 1 that tell you the setting.

As you read, think about how the story develops. The rising action begins with the magistrate's riddle.

Who are the main characters in the passage?

The Clever Daughter
adapted from a Czechoslovakian folktale

Long ago in a small village, there lived a prosperous farmer. Instead of being generous and charitable with his riches, he guarded his wealth nearly as much as his life. He always drove a hard bargain and took advantage of his poor neighbors whenever he could.

One day, one of his neighbors, a poor shepherd, labored for three days on the rich man's farm. In return, the farmer promised him a cow. However, when the shepherd came to collect the cow, the devious farmer refused to honor the agreement.

The shepherd took the matter to the local magistrate, who listened to both sides. Since the farmer denied he owed the debt and the shepherd could not prove it, the magistrate decided on an unusual solution.

"I am going to ask you both a riddle. Whoever gives me the best answers shall have the cow. Here is my riddle: What is the swiftest thing in the world? What is the sweetest thing? What is the richest?"

Then the magistrate looked at both men and said, "Go home, and return with your answers at this same time tomorrow."

When the farmer returned home, he was in a foul mood. "What sort of magistrate is this who decides a case on the basis of some ridiculous riddle?" he complained to his wife.

"What is the riddle?" she asked.

When the farmer repeated it to her, the wife laughed. "Why, I know the answers! Our horse is the swiftest thing. No one passes us on the road. The honey from our beehives is the sweetest thing, as anyone will confirm. And could there be anything richer than our chest of gold coins we have saved up all these years?"

The farmer was ecstatic, for he was sure that the shepherd could not come up with better answers.

When the shepherd returned to his humble cottage, he felt dejected and hopeless. His daughter asked him what was wrong.

The shepherd's daughter is introduced just before the climax. Explain how she is important to the plot.

The falling action is the part of the plot that occurs after the climax. In which paragraph do you find the falling action?

What is the resolution of the story?

"I have lost the cow, dear daughter," he said. "The magistrate gave us a riddle. Whoever answers it the best gets the cow. I know I will never come up with the answers."

"Tell me the riddle, father. Perhaps I can figure it out."

Now, the shepherd knew his daughter was clever. So, he told her the riddle and listened to her answers.

The next day, at the magistrate's home, the rich farmer waited eagerly to answer the riddle. He was confident he would win. When the magistrate asked him for the answers, the farmer repeated what his wife had told him. He smiled smugly and crossed his arms, casting a contemptuous glance at the shepherd.

The magistrate turned to the shepherd. "And what do you say?" he asked.

The shepherd bowed politely and cleared his throat nervously. "The swiftest thing in the world is thought, for it can run any distance in the blink of an eye. The sweetest thing of all is sleep, for what can be sweeter to an exhausted man at the end of the day? The richest thing is the earth, for out of the earth come all the riches in the world."

The magistrate beamed with delight at the shepherd's answers. "Those are superb answers, indeed. The cow goes to the shepherd!"

The rich farmer was furious and opened his mouth to protest the decision, but the magistrate gave him such a stern look that the farmer realized it would be wiser to walk away. He turned on his heels and marched quickly out of the room.

The next day, the farmer handed over the cow to the shepherd, who led it home happily and enjoyed a celebration supper with his clever daughter.

Answer the following questions.

1. Read this sentence from the passage.

   Long ago in a small village, there lived a prosperous farmer.

   This sentence comes from the part of the plot known as the

   A. conflict.

   B. climax.

   C. rising action.

   D. exposition.

2. Which of these events happens during the rising action?

   A. The rich farmer guards his wealth.

   B. The shepherd does work for the farmer.

   C. The magistrate gives the men a riddle.

   D. The farmer gives the cow to the shepherd.

3. Which of the following BEST explains the main conflict in the passage?

   A. The shepherd must solve a riddle to get his cow.

   B. The shepherd must work for the farmer to get his cow.

   C. The magistrate must figure out who truly deserves the cow.

   D. The shepherd's daughter must solve the magistrate's riddle.

4. Which event is the climax?

   A. The farmer refuses to give the cow to the shepherd.

   B. The shepherd's daughter gives him the answers.

   C. The magistrate awards the cow to the shepherd.

   D. The shepherd celebrates with his daughter.

5. Why does the magistrate use a riddle to decide the case?

   _____

   _____

   _____

   _____

   _____

   _____

5 Character

RL.7.6, RL.7.10, W.7.9.a

Getting the Idea

A **character** is a person, animal, or other creature in a fictional text. Characters have **traits**, or qualities that define them. You can tell a character's traits by what he or she does, says, or thinks. For example, a boy who always does what he wants and doesn't care about others is selfish. A girl who makes up stories to get out of trouble is dishonest. You can also determine characters' traits by how they interact with other characters. A character's relationships with parents or friends can reveal a lot about him or her.

Most literary texts have a central character who interacts with minor, or supporting, characters. For example, in the novel *A Tree Grows in Brooklyn* by Betty Smith, the central character is a young girl named Mary Frances Nolan, or Francie, as she is called by her family and friends. Francie interacts with other characters, including her mother, Katie; her father, John; her brother, Cornelius, or "Neeley"; and other friends and family members.

Like most characters, Francie's actions are motivated by her needs and desires. **Motivation** is the reason why characters act the way they do. Growing up in impoverished circumstances, Francie dreams of a better life. So, she reads and studies in order to educate herself and make the life of her dreams a reality. Other characters have their own motivations. For example, Katie Nolan is driven by the need to provide for her children and help them succeed. So, she works hard and saves every penny. Her husband wishes to escape a life of hardship, but he does it in self-destructive ways.

A character may have more than one trait or motivation. He or she may also undergo a transformation, or change, as a result of his or her experiences and interactions with other characters. A character's transformation is an essential part of character development. Authors give their characters complex personalities and allow them to grow in order to make them interesting to readers. Motivation is also what brings characters into conflict with each other.

Point of view is the perspective of a character or narrator. Often, a story's narrator is not a character in a story. The narrator is a detached observer who describes the characters and events. Sometimes the narrator is a character in the story, as in the novel *Dragonwings* by Laurence Yep. This story is told from the point of view of a young boy named Moon Shadow. We see the events and other characters through his eyes.

Authors often create multiple points of view in their stories. In that way, readers see what happens from different characters' perspectives. When you read, contrast these points of view. Think about why characters view things differently and how their perspectives shape the story.

Thinking It Through

Read the following paragraph, and then answer the questions that follow.

My sister, Kayla, is a really talented pianist. My brother, Mark, on the other hand, has no musical ambitions. He wants to play in the NFL one day. I want to be an astronaut. "Lucas," he tells me, "aren't you scared to fly up into space?" My mother smiles when she hears that. "Lucas is fearless," she says.

This story is told from which character's point of view? How can you tell?

_____

_____

_____

_____

_____

HINT The reader sees the other characters through this character's eyes.

Coached Example

Read the passage and answer the questions.

As I walked down the hallway to English class, I made a secret wish over and over again. *Please let Mr. Lang be out today. Please let Mr. Lang be out today.* I entered the room and stopped in my tracks. A substitute teacher was sitting at Mr. Lang's desk! I couldn't believe it. She wouldn't know that Mr. Lang had warned me that if my paper wasn't in today, my grade would go down to a D. And, of course, I still hadn't finished my paper. First of all, I had misplaced the assignment sheet twice and got a late start. Then I had trouble deciding how to begin my paper, so I lost another couple of days. Finally, I started it, but it was due the next day, so what could I do? Mr. Lang gave me an extension, but I found lots of things more fun than writing my paper. I played video games with my friend. I played baseball. I watched TV. But I sure had caught a lucky break today! After I sat down, I suddenly noticed that the substitute was looking at Mr. Lang's grade book. She raised her head and called my name. My lucky streak sure was a short one.

1. Why does the narrator want Mr. Lang to be absent?

   A. He does not like Mr. Lang.

   B. He did not do his assignment.

   C. He did not study for a test.

   D. He wants to go home early.

   HINT The narrator's motivation is stated in the passage.

2. Which of the following BEST describes the narrator?

   A. determined

   B. irresponsible

   C. thoughtful

   D. impatient

   HINT A character's actions, thoughts, and words reveal his or her traits.

Lesson Practice

Use the Reading Guide to help you understand the passage.

Reading Guide

The use of the word *I* gives you a clue to the point of view from which this story is told. Is the narrator a character in the story or an outside observer?

How is Diane different from the narrator?

What is the mother's motivation for taking her children fishing?

A New Life

As soon as school was over for the year, we left Connecticut and went to live in the Midwest. "We" is our family—my mom, my sisters Paula and Diane, and me. When we left the East, we left my dad, too. My mom found a new job, located in the middle of nowhere. At least that's what I thought of our new place. My sister Diane, however, liked it a lot. But, then, she also likes frogs' legs and rabbit stew. I wouldn't eat those if my life depended on it. Paula had mixed feelings. She hadn't really liked our old neighborhood, but she would have preferred to move down south.

We didn't know anybody in our new town. We lived in a big new apartment complex. "Isn't this fabulous?" my mom said to us as we drove up to the complex the first day. "No," I said. "It's okay," said Paula. "Love it!" shouted Diane. My mom wasn't quite sure what to say after that.

One day, we met three kids we liked—two boys and a girl. One of the boys, Dave, was my age, 12. The other, Danny, was Paula's age, 10. Amy was Diane's age, 9. We all got along fine. Our mothers became friends, too. Things began to look up.

My mom had this thing about our not having a dad at home. She thought a dad would take us to hockey games or wrestling matches, I guess. Anyway, she decided that since she had to fill two roles, she should take us catfish fishing. Catfish was a local delicacy.

Not everyone was enthusiastic about the idea. Well, to make a long story short, we went fishing. We took Dave, Danny, and Amy with us to Catfish Lake. Catfish are bottom feeders. To catch one, you drop your line where you think a big catfish might be. The line has a hook with bait and a lead sinker on it, so it drops to the bottom. You reel the line in slowly to tempt your prey to grab it. It works! We caught quite a few big catfish. I began to think that fishing was not such a lame thing to do.

"Pretty nice, huh?" I said, holding up my catch.

"If you say so," Paula answered. She swatted a mosquito on her arm.

After a couple of hours, Dave grew bored with catching gross-looking whiskered catfish. He had been fishing once for salmon. He thought he was big stuff.

"Watch this," he said. He put a giant four-pronged hook on his line.

"Are you sure you should be doing that?" I asked.

"Oh, let him do it, Kyle. This could be interesting," Paula said. She grimaced and slapped her arm again. "Dumb mosquitoes!" she said angrily.

"They're just innocent creatures," Diane said.

"Oh, you mean like those fish we just caught?" Paula asked.

"Pay attention, guys," Dave said. Then, with all his might, he heaved back his pole ready to cast this giant prong into the water. He missed the water but caught my mom. The hook went right into her shoulder.

"Ow-w-w-w-w-w-w!" she screamed.

Diane jumped up and started wringing her hands. "Mom! Mom!"

Dave dropped the hook and put his hands in his pockets. I almost expected him to start whistling.

"Really, dude? This is the way you react?" I asked. I yelled at the owner of the boat we had rented to get us back to shore.

Paula sat next to our mom and held her hand.

The doctor gave our mom a tetanus shot and a few stitches. He said she was going to be just fine.

Dave apologized but said his sister had dared him to do it. But we didn't let him get away with that. Finally, he confessed. Mom never talked about going fishing after that. And over time, life in the Midwest turned out to be a pretty good deal.

What characters say and do reveals their traits. For example, what do Paula's actions tell you about her personality?

How does Dave react when his fishing hook injures the kids' mom? What word would you use to describe Dave?

How does Kyle change by the end of the story?

Answer the following questions.

1. Which sentence from the passage BEST shows that the narrator is unhappy in his new home?

   A. "We lived in a big new apartment complex."

   B. "We didn't know anybody in our new town."

   C. "My mom found a new job, located in the middle of nowhere."

   D. "As soon as school was over for the year, we left Connecticut and went to live in the Midwest."

2. How does Paula's point of view differ from Diane's?

   A. Paula wants to move down south, but Diane wants to move back east.

   B. Paula is happy about the move, but Diane has mixed feelings.

   C. Paula thinks fishing is fun, but Diane thinks it is boring.

   D. Paula views mosquitoes as pests, but Diane feels sorry for them.

3. Why does Dave switch to a four-pronged hook?

   A. He wants to show off.

   B. He wants to catch more catfish.

   C. He wants to play a joke on Kyle.

   D. He wants to throw the fish back in the lake.

4. How does the mom's experience on the fishing trip affect her?

   A. She stops bringing Dave on fishing trips.

   B. She decides never to go fishing again.

   C. She realizes she wants to move back east.

   D. She develops a love for fishing.

5. How does the narrator change by the end of the passage?

   _____

   _____

   _____

   _____

   _____

6 Theme

RL.7.2, RL.7.10, W.7.9.a

Getting the Idea

The **theme** of a literary text is its central message or lesson. You have probably read quite a few fables by Aesop and know that they typically involve animal characters that learn a lesson. In "The Hare and the Tortoise," for example, the hare learns that "slow and steady wins the race." In fables, the theme is usually directly stated in the text. In most stories, plays, and poems, you have to figure out the theme.

Themes are general statements about life and people. A written work may have a single theme or multiple themes. Common themes in literature include:

- Honesty is the best policy.
- Don't be afraid to try something new.
- Don't put off till tomorrow what you should do today.
- Don't pretend to be something you're not.
- Hard work and determination are rewarded.
- Appearances can be deceiving.
- Be loyal to your friends.

The title of a passage may be a clue to its theme. You can also determine the theme by thinking about what characters say or do and the lessons they learn. Pay attention to recurring images, events, or objects. Consider the story's setting and its important ideas. See how these elements work together to suggest a larger message. Authors often use repetition to draw attention to important ideas or themes. For example, a play in which a character helps her friends or neighbors in several scenes might have the theme "Be kind to people in need."

To identify the theme, you have to consider all the details in the passage and come up with a statement that captures the essential lesson or message of the passage. This is similar to summarizing.

A **summary** is a short restatement of a text in your own words. A summary includes the main idea or theme of a passage and only the most important and relevant details. For instance, a summary of "The Hare and the Tortoise" could be: *A hare and a tortoise have a race. The hare is overconfident and loses the race. The hare learns that being slow and steady is a better strategy than running full speed ahead.*

When you summarize, do <u>not</u> include minor details or information that is not in the original text. Also, be sure to use your own words.

Thinking It Through

Read the following paragraph, and then answer the question that follows.

Chris checked the list outside Coach Wilson's office. His heart sank when he saw that he had not made the basketball team. After that day, Chris played basketball nearly every day, working on his shooting and dribbling skills. The following year, he tried out again. This time his name was on the list.

What is the theme of this story?

_____

_____

_____

_____

 HINT Think about what Chris does after he fails to make the team.

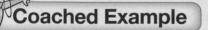

Coached Example

Read the poem and answer the questions.

excerpted from

Mr. Nobody

I know a funny little man,
As quiet as a mouse,
Who does the mischief that is done
In everybody's house!
5 There's no one who's ever seen his face,
And yet we all agree
That every plate we break was cracked
By Mr. Nobody.

'Tis he who always tears our books,
10 Who leaves the door ajar.
He pulls the buttons from our shirts,
And scatters pins afar;
That squeaking door will always squeak,
For, pray thee, don't you see,
15 We leave the oiling to be done
By Mr. Nobody.

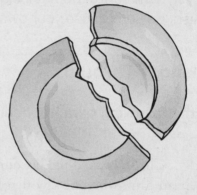

---

1. What is the theme of the poem?

   A. No one wants to take responsibility for mistakes.

   B. No one ever sees Mr. Nobody.

   C. Don't take the blame for others.

   D. Nobody is perfect.

   HINT Mr. Nobody is not a real person.

2. Which line from the poem BEST supports this theme?

   A. "As quiet as a mouse"

   B. "I know a funny little man"

   C. "There's no one who's ever seen his face"

   D. "'Tis he who always tears our books"

   HINT Test each answer choice against the correct theme.

Lesson Practice

Use the Reading Guide to help you understand the passage.

Duplicating any part of this book is prohibited by law.

Reading Guide

The theme is the central message or lesson in a passage. This passage contains two themes. One relates to King Midas himself, and the other relates to the farmer in the story Midas tells his daughter.

Notice how the princess's conversation with her father about her servant sets up the response from the king.

Why does King Midas tell his daughter the story about the farmer? What is he trying to help her to understand?

What is the farmer's mistake?

King Midas's Golden Touch
adapted from a Greek myth

Long ago, there was a Greek king named Midas. The king was a kind man who ruled his kingdom fairly and was loved by all, especially by his daughter. The king loved her as well, with all of his heart.

King Midas and his daughter often took walks in the royal garden, enjoying the beautiful flowers and birds. Sometimes the princess asked advice from her father. One day, she complained about one of the servants who waited on her.

"I do not trust her, Papa," the princess said, as she paused to admire a yellow butterfly.

"Why not? Has she done something I should know about? I shall dismiss her immediately," the king replied.

"To be fair, she has not done anything yet, but there is something about her that I do not like. It is her face. It is not the face of an honest woman."

The king stopped and sat on a bench, motioning for his daughter to sit beside him. "Let me tell you a story, child, that will help you put your situation in perspective."

The princess settled onto the bench and listened.

"There was a farmer who hired two young men to help him at harvest time. The men received free room and board. One of the men was handsome and smiled easily and always said what the farmer wanted to hear. The other was ordinary-looking and shy and only spoke when necessary. When the harvest proved less fruitful than anticipated, the farmer was forced to let one of the men go. He chose to keep the handsome man. Soon, he discovered that it was the other who had done the bulk of the work. The handsome man was lazy and useless. Do you understand the moral of this lesson?"

The daughter was thoughtful for a moment, then nodded. "I do, Papa."

The king smiled at the princess, and the two resumed their peaceful walk in the garden.

What is wrong with the king's wish? What causes Midas to realize his mistake?

In a summary of this story, you would include only the most important details of the plot. Details such as descriptions of the palace garden or moods of the characters do not belong in a summary.

Although the king was good at giving advice, he was not always good at taking it himself. He was also occasionally known to make foolish decisions. One day, King Midas did a favor for an elderly man who just happened to be a friend of the god Dionysus.

When Dionysus heard about King Midas's kindness, he rewarded the king by granting him one wish. Quickly King Midas said, "I wish for everything I touch to turn to gold."

"Your wish is granted," replied Dionysus and went on his way.

At first King Midas was delighted with his new power. When he touched the twig of an oak, it turned to gold. When he picked up a stone, it turned to gold. He fingered an apple in his garden and it, too, turned to gold.

"I am a lucky man, indeed! I shall be richer than any king who ever lived," the king said merrily as he danced around the garden.

Then the unthinkable happened. His beloved daughter ran to him, shouting, "Papa, Papa! How I missed you today."

Instantly, the king realized the drawback to his golden touch. "Stay back!" he cried. But before he could stop her, the princess took hold of his hands and kissed him, and he watched in horror as his beautiful, lively daughter turned instantly to hard, glittering gold.

Devastated, King Midas begged Dionysus to turn everything back to the way it had been.

Dionysus took pity on the king and granted his request. "If you go to the river and wash yourself," he told the king, "you will wash away your golden touch."

King Midas hurried to the river. When he jumped in the flowing waters, his gold-creating power passed into them. At home, he found that all he had touched had returned to its original state, including his daughter. He embraced her warmly and vowed never to make such a foolish mistake again.

Answer the following questions.

1. What is the theme of the story King Midas tells his daughter?

   A. Trust your instincts.

   B. Honesty is the best policy.

   C. Appearances can be deceiving.

   D. Don't hire strangers to work for you.

2. Which detail does NOT belong in a summary of the farmer story?

   A. A farmer hires two men.

   B. A farmer has to let one of the men go.

   C. The men receive free room and board.

   D. The handsome man is lazy and useless.

3. How does the author demonstrate the theme of "King Midas's Golden Touch"?

   A. by showing how happy the king is when he turns things into gold

   B. by describing the relationship between the king and his daughter

   C. by stating the theme directly in the passage

   D. by showing the harmful effects of the king's wish

4. Which of the following BEST summarizes "King Midas's Golden Touch"?

   A. A king helps an elderly man who is a friend of the god Dionysius. As a reward, Dionysius gives the king the power to turn everything into gold.

   B. A king gets his wish to turn everything he touches into gold, but when he accidentally turns his daughter into gold, he gives up his power to get his daughter back.

   C. King Midas and his daughter take walks in the garden. One day, he tells her a story about a farmer. Then, the king accidentally turns his daughter into gold.

   D. There once was a Greek king who was very popular and loved his daughter dearly. After he turns her into gold, he washes away his power in the river.

5. Write the lesson that King Midas learns at the end of the passage.

   _____

   _____

7 Figurative Language

RL.7.4, RL.7.10, RI.7.4, RI.7.10, W.7.9.a–b, L.7.5.a

Getting the Idea

Figurative language is the use of words to create an image in the reader's mind. Figurative language is creative, colorful, and often relies on comparisons. Read the chart below.

Types of Figurative Language	
simile	a direct comparison of two unlike things, using the word *like* or the word *as* *Examples:* The detective was like a bloodhound after its prey. Roy is as huggable as a teddy bear.
metaphor	a comparison of two unlike things, without using the word *like* or the word *as* *Example:* The cat's eyes were two sparkling green jewels.
imagery	language that appeals to the five senses (sight, sound, touch, taste, and smell) *Example:* David poured the thick, sweet syrup over the steaming stack of buttery pancakes.
personification	giving an animal, object, or abstract idea human qualities *Examples:* Your plants are begging for water. Time can be your enemy or your friend.

Figurative language can enhance meaning and emphasize ideas. Think about the first simile example in the chart. It's one thing to say that a detective is persistent and focused. It's quite another to compare the detective to a bloodhound, a hunting dog that has the ability to find just about anything. The simile expresses the same idea more vividly.

Although figurative language is more commonly seen in literature, it is also used in informational texts. For example, a newspaper editor may write, "The new mayor is as sharp as a butter knife." Since butter knives are actually not sharp, the editor's meaning is clear. He thinks the mayor is dim-witted. The simile also impacts the tone of the statement. **Tone** is an author's attitude toward his or her subject, in this case, the mayor. The tone of the editor's statement is sarcastic.

An **allusion** is an indirect reference to a well-known person, place, event, or object in history or in a literary work.

- *literary allusion:* "Jaime is driving me crazy. I don't know when he's going to be Dr. Jekyll or Mr. Hyde." The novel *The Strange Case of Dr. Jekyll and Mr. Hyde* explores the duality of good and evil within the human mind.

- *biblical allusion:* "After the fight, Frank stood triumphantly over Walter—like David over Goliath." In the story from the Bible, young David manages to slay the giant Goliath.

- *mythological allusion:* "The candidate's Delphic response to our question left us confused." In Greek mythology, the Oracle of Delphi was famous for her puzzling answers to questions about the future.

Thinking It Through

Read the following sentences, and then answer the question that follows.

The first thing I do when I wake up is open the window and look outside. I love how the sun greets me in the morning.

How is the sun described in sentence 2? What type of figurative language is used?

_____

_____

_____

_____

HINT   Think about the action word *greets* in the sentence. Could the sun do this?

Coached Example

Read the passage and answer the questions.

Meerkats are mammals that live in the Kalahari Desert in southern Africa. They grow to about 12 inches tall and weigh about two pounds. Despite their small size, meerkats have impressive survival skills. They can live without drinking water. They obtain the moisture they need by eating melons and other fruit as well as roots. These adaptable creatures are also immune to the venom of poisonous snakes and scorpions, so they can kill and eat them.

Meerkats live in large groups called gangs or mobs. Up to thirty meerkats make up the typical gang. Members stick to each other like glue, creating a tight family unit. They live in burrows usually dug by other animals. The burrows have multiple entrances and exits as well as tunnels that lead to various chambers. Meerkats also dig thousands of holes, called bolt holes, for quick escapes from predators. When a predator is near, a sea of meerkats pours into the nearest bolt hole to safety.

1. Read this sentence from the passage.

   When a predator is near, a sea of meerkats pours into the nearest bolt hole to safety.

   This sentence is an example of

   A. personification.

   B. metaphor.

   C. allusion.

   D. simile.

   HINT The meerkats are compared to a sea.

2. Which sentence from the passage is a simile?

   A. "Meerkats live in large groups called gangs or mobs."

   B. "Members stick to each other like glue, creating a tight family unit."

   C. "Despite their small size, meerkats have impressive survival skills."

   D. "Meerkats also dig thousands of holes, called bolt holes, for quick escapes from predators."

   HINT Look for a comparison using the word *like* or the word *as*.

Lesson Practice

Use the Reading Guide to help you understand the passage.

Reading Guide

Figurative language includes a variety of literary devices that help to create vivid images in the reader's mind.

Find the metaphor in paragraph 4. Who is Aunt Natalie being compared to?

Explain the figurative language used in paragraph 5.

A Day to Remember

When I was twelve years old, my aunt Natalie would come to our house for dinner a few Sundays each month, and after dinner, she would take me on afternoon excursions around the city. One Sunday's trip changed my life.

Aunt Natalie came over in the early afternoon and dined with our family as usual—it was pork roast and new potatoes that Sunday. Then Aunt Natalie said I should put on a pair of comfortable shoes, and she'd see me downstairs in five minutes. I went upstairs and changed out of my dress and into jeans and running shoes that my feet were especially fond of. I found Aunt Natalie in the kitchen with my mother, cleaning up after the meal.

Aunt Natalie said, "Let's go, Olivia. We've got a big day ahead of us." *Where were we going?* I wondered. But before I could speculate, my aunt grabbed my arm, and my train of thought came to an abrupt halt. We were off on our adventure.

My trips around the city with Aunt Natalie were always wonderful, even when we did nothing except wander around. Aunt Natalie had a great eye for spotting details, and she loved exploring uncharted corners of the city. She was a modern-day Columbus, except she didn't travel by ship.

Aunt Natalie was a writer, and I think our excursions were fuel for her imagination. I know they inspired mine. Though she and my mother grew up here, she said there were still places to explore. She knew she could never exhaust the city's possibilities. The city was like an open book, and she was still on chapter one.

Aunt Natalie would never divulge where we were going. I loved the mystery, and she knew it, which made the beginning of an outing a delightful diversion. When I asked where we were headed today, she answered, "The subway." That's all she would tell me, and I expected no more. At the subway station, we paid our fares and went to the downtown platform. At least I knew which direction we were heading. I stared into the dark, musty tunnel, listening for the thunderous rumble of the approaching train. It arrived in about ten minutes.

Remember, figurative language appeals to the senses: sight, sound, taste, smell, touch.

Find an example of personification in paragraph 8.

Find an example of personification at the beginning of the last paragraph. Find the simile at the end of the passage.

We got off at 14th Street, which didn't mean we were near our destination. Often Aunt Natalie would have us get off the train several stops before we had to, so we could get some exercise and explore before we got where we were going, if indeed we were going someplace. Today we were headed somewhere. She looked at her watch as we strolled west along 14th Street, and we didn't even stop at Union Square Park.

We picked up our pace as we crossed over to Sixth Avenue and dropped down to 11th Street, and then continued west to Seventh Avenue. This was pretty far west—we had already passed through the heart of Greenwich Village. Then we stopped in front of an oddly wedge-shaped building. An unusual, hand-lettered sign above the door reading "Village Vanguard" beckoned us inside. We went down some stairs, and then Aunt Natalie had a hushed conversation with a man at the door. She knew him, I could tell. She gestured back at me, and then the man waved us in.

As the door opened, I could hear the sounds of music. Inside, the room it was dim, though the Sunday sunlight peeked through the small windows here and there. Aunt Natalie led us to a table and ordered sodas. I sat transfixed for what seemed like hours as I heard the music that would change my life. On a small stage was saxophonist John Coltrane, and he played the sweetest music I had ever heard or have ever heard since. The jazz he was playing washed over me like a warm wave. Aunt Natalie turned me into a musician that day in 1961.

Answer the following questions.

1. When the narrator says her feet were "fond of" her running shoes, she is using

    A. simile.

    B. metaphor.

    C. imagery.

    D. personification.

2. The narrator alludes to Christopher Columbus in paragraph 4 to emphasize Aunt Natalie's

    A. love of the sea.

    B. Italian heritage.

    C. love of exploration.

    D. interest in history.

3. Read this sentence from the passage.

    Aunt Natalie was a writer, and I think our excursions were fuel for her imagination.

    This sentence contains

    A. a metaphor.

    B. a simile.

    C. an allusion.

    D. imagery.

4. Which phrase in paragraph 8 uses figurative language?

    A. "the heart of Greenwich Village"

    B. "a hushed conversation"

    C. "sign above the door"

    D. "pretty far west"

5. Write the sentence from paragraph 6 that uses imagery.

    _____

    _____

    _____

    _____

8 Make Inferences

RL.7.1, RL.7.10, RI.7.1, RI.7.10, W.7.9.a–b

Getting the Idea

Much of the information that you gather from your reading is explicitly stated in the text. In other words, authors tell you the information directly. This is true for both informational and literary texts. For example, read the sentence below.

The whiskers on catfish are actually barbels, or feelers.

Now, answer this question: "What are catfish whiskers called?" You know the answer because it is directly stated in the sentence: barbels.

Sometimes, however, you have to make inferences. Making an inference is a little like reading between the lines. An **inference** is an educated guess based on information and evidence in a text. Read the sentences below.

Catfish are attracted to nearly any kind of bait. Worms, chicken livers, grasshoppers, cheese, shrimp, or even a piece of ribbon will work. Some people have caught catfish with bare hooks!

Based on these sentences, you can infer that catfish are fairly easy to catch. When you make an inference, you must be able to support it with textual evidence. In this case, details about being able to catch catfish with almost any type of bait or even a bare hook support the inference that they are easy to catch. Although this idea is not directly stated by the writer, you clearly understand it.

Being able to make inferences can help you analyze the elements of literary texts. For instance, it can help you understand characters. Read the following paragraph.

Megan wiped her sweaty palms on her jeans and stared at the math problems on the exam. She chewed on her pencil eraser and stole another glance at the clock.

You can infer that Megan is nervous. There are several pieces of textual evidence to support this inference; specifically, her palms are sweaty, she is chewing on her pencil eraser, and she keeps looking at the clock. In this case, you also used your own prior experience to help you make the inference.

You can make inferences to understand events. If people are gathered in a city park to watch an elaborate fireworks display, you can infer that they are most likely celebrating the Fourth of July. Making inferences can help you identify the setting. If kids are playing in a mound of red and orange leaves, you can infer that the story takes place in autumn.

Thinking It Through

Read the following paragraph, and then answer the question that follows.

> Ari sat against a coconut tree and tried not to panic. He had been walking for hours and not encountered another human being. There was only jungle, sand, and a limitless ocean. Suddenly, Ari leaped up and ran to the water's edge, waving his arms frantically.

Why does Ari most likely run to the water's edge and start waving?

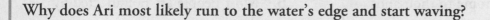

_____

_____

_____

_____

HINT   Pay attention to the details in the paragraph.

Coached Example

Read the passage and answer the questions.

Over the past 100 years, average temperatures on Earth have increased by about 1.4 degrees Fahrenheit. Many scientists believe this warming trend will continue, and they are very concerned. If it does continue, they say, Earth's climate will change, and then life as we know it will have to change. Scientists call this phenomenon global warming. When something burns, such as fuel in a car, carbon dioxide enters the air. Carbon dioxide keeps the sun's heat from escaping Earth, and then Earth gets warmer.

Global warming is the result of various factors. One of the biggest contributors to global warming is deforestation. Forests are cleared to make room for housing developments and farms. Trees are also cut down for fuel or to make products like furniture and paper. As the world population grows, so does the demand for wood. It is estimated that over 200,000 acres of rainforest are destroyed every day. Since trees remove carbon dioxide from the atmosphere, more of this gas is retained on Earth.

---

1. Which of the following information is stated directly?

   A. Developers get rich when they cut down trees.

   B. Rainforests are home to thousands of plants and animals.

   C. Carbon dioxide traps the sun's heat on Earth.

   D. People can prevent global warming by saving energy.

   HINT Use key words in each answer choice to see if those ideas are discussed in the passage. For example, does the passage say anything about saving energy?

2. What can you infer from this passage?

   A. Publishing fewer books and newspapers could reduce global warming.

   B. Most people are not affected by deforestation.

   C. Rising temperatures on Earth do not really matter.

   D. Cars have very little impact on global warming.

   HINT Eliminate answer choices that you know are incorrect. Then focus on the others. Review what the passage said about the effects of deforestation.

Lesson Practice

Use the Reading Guide to help you understand the passage.

Duplicating any part of this book is prohibited by law.

Reading Guide

What is Jason most likely going to do in the park? What clues help you to infer your answer?

What can you infer about the grandfather's mood before he talks to Jason?

Based on the information in paragraph 4, what can you infer about the Silver Screen Theater?

Remember, find textual evidence to support all of your inferences.

More Than a House of Bricks

Jason grabbed his glove and ball and hurried down the stairs and into the kitchen. It was Saturday, and his friends Stephen and Andre were waiting for him at Oakwood Park. Jason figured he had time for a quick bowl of cereal. In the kitchen, he saw his grandfather sitting at the table, absorbed in the daily newspaper.

"Hi, Grandpa," he said.

His grandfather barely nodded, not lifting his eyes from the newspaper. Jason got a box of cereal from the cupboard and sat down. As he poured milk into his bowl, Jason observed his grandfather. He seemed especially fascinated by one particular article.

Jason concentrated on the upside-down letters of the headline. Slowly, he made out the words "Final Curtain for the Silver Screen Theater." What did this mean? The Silver Screen Theater was on the other side of town. Jason had caught glimpses of the boarded-up structure a number of times when he rode past it in the family car.

His grandfather stared at the photograph of the movie theater in the article and shook his head. Finally, he looked up to see Jason.

Jason smiled. "Are you reading something interesting?"

"Bad news. The town is tearing down the Silver Screen Theater on Wagner Street."

"I know the one. It's been boarded up for years."

"Closed down fourteen years ago. You weren't born yet. I just never thought they would tear it down. The article says they're planning to build a supermarket on the site."

"Isn't that a good thing? People need places to buy groceries."

"Supermarkets come and go, but there will only be one Silver Screen Theater," his grandfather responded. "Back when I was your age, this town was a different place. No big supermarkets and department stores. This was just a small town where people knew their neighbors' names and greeted them every morning. The Silver Screen Theater was the place to be on a Saturday night. It wasn't one of these multiplex theaters that shows ten movies and charges a fortune for a box of popcorn. The Silver Screen had just one screen, but everyone in town caught a movie there once in a while."

Authors state explicit information, such as the facts about the Silver Screen Theater, directly in a passage.

Based on the grandfather's memories, how was the Silver Screen different from today's movie theaters?

What do you think Jason will say to his friends when he arrives at the park?

"Wow, I never knew that. I thought it was just an old, abandoned building."

His grandfather nodded thoughtfully. "There's more to the Silver Screen than the bricks used to build it. I can remember the flashing lights on the marquee and the line of people eager to catch the next show. Did you know that they used to show cartoons before a movie back then? And they had short films featuring songs with the words on the screen. A bouncing ball in the film landed on each word as people in the theater sang along."

"People in the theater sang along together? That's goofy!"

"It was goofy, but it was so much fun." He looked down at the photograph of the boarded-up theater, and his grin disappeared.

Jason contemplated what his grandfather had said about the old theater. A thought was developing in Jason's mind as he, too, stared at the photograph.

"Hey! I just had an idea. Remember how a group of dog owners wrote letters and organized a rally to get the town to build a dog run in Oakwood Park? My teacher says that when a building is declared a landmark, it can't be torn down. Why don't we start a letter-writing campaign to declare the Silver Screen a landmark? We'll get the town to fix it up and show movies again. We'll write to the newspaper and the mayor. We'll get people to sign a petition; we'll call the local news—"

"Whoa! You sure you're up for all this? Don't you have things to do this summer?"

Jason thought about his friends waiting in the park. He was pretty sure he could persuade them to help. "I do now."

1. The speaker's "wooden laugh" suggests that

   A. she laughs loudly.

   B. she laughs suddenly.

   C. the laugh is not genuine.

   D. the laugh is hard to hear.

2. Which line from the poem contains alliteration?

   A. "Who danger and the dead had faced"

   B. "I scanned the windows near"

   C. "My hand, with trembling care"

   D. "I never saw before"

3. What is the rhyme scheme of the first four lines?

   A. AABB

   B. ABCD

   C. ABAB

   D. ABCB

4. Which of the following BEST describes the speaker?

   A. eager

   B. secretive

   C. anxious

   D. determined

5. Write a line from the poem that contains a simile. How do you know it is a simile?

   _____

   _____

   _____

   _____

   _____

   _____

Read the passage and answer the questions that follow.

Going West

John climbed down from the covered wagon and stared out into the distance. The prairie stretched out before him like a vast sea of grass. The men had circled the wagons and released the cattle to graze. About half a dozen children chased each other through the encampment, their laughter somewhat strange in the solemn silence of the prairie.

"Sure is mighty pleasant out here tonight, isn't it, John?" his mother said.

John looked up at his mother, still sitting in the wagon. He didn't think her fingers had stopped moving since they had left Pennsylvania last year. They were either busy knitting winter sweaters, kneading dough for bread, or sewing up holes in the family's shirts or trousers. But what was truly amazing to John, beside his mother's apparent tirelessness, was her ability to do it all with a smile. John knew his mother did not want to be here.

When his father had first proposed the trip west nearly two years ago, his mother had resisted.

"No, Wilhelm. This is our home. Did we not travel far enough to get to America?" she had said.

"We did, indeed. But have you not heard the stories, Abigail? There is open land for the taking out west. All we have to do is claim it and settle it. Our own farm! And a house of our own, built with our very own hands. Can't you picture it, Abigail?"

But his mother had not wanted to picture it. The trip west would have meant traveling from Pittsburgh on the Ohio River until they reached Independence, Missouri. Then, they would have needed to purchase a wagon, oxen, flour, and other supplies for the hardest leg of the trip—the Oregon Trail. They would have to spend the winter in Missouri before hitting the trail because it was grueling enough to travel in the spring and summer. Being stuck on the trail in bitter weather surrounded by snow and ice could have deadly consequences. Plus, after enduring the punishing journey, the family would have to build a house from scratch then till and farm the land. As far as John's mother was concerned, moving west involved too much labor and too much risk. In addition, she would have to leave her mother behind because she was too frail to venture on such a strenuous journey.

Despite his mother's misgivings about the trip, his father had prevailed. They had convinced John's cousins to come along, as well as John's father's closest friend and family. They had joined a group of emigrants and pooled their money to hire two mountain men to serve as guides and hunters. Through it all, John's mother had chosen to keep her worries and longing for home to herself.

It had not been as easy for John. He liked living in the East. He wanted to go to school there and become a doctor.

"This is not fair!" he had shouted at his father, desperation overtaking his better judgment.

His father had been uncharacteristically patient with him. "You will grow to like it out west. Wait and see. We will have our own farm—"

"I do not want to be a farmer! Leave me here. I will live with grandma. She will need a man here, now that you are abandoning her!"

John had seen the color rise in his father's cheeks and anger flash in his eyes like sudden lightning. John was pushing his father to the limit but did not care.

"You know very well your uncle and aunt are staying here to look after your grandmother. She will not be alone. I have to think of our family's future, and that means making hard decisions. You call yourself a man, but you are only 12. One day you will understand. I know you want to be a doctor. It is a noble profession. But so is farming your own land, and leaving it for your children and your grandchildren. The deed is done. We are moving west, and I expect you to act like the man you say you are. We shall have no more discussion on this matter."

And that had been the end of that. Now, as John stood by the side of the wagon, looking up into the quiet strength of his mother's eyes, he was filled with admiration and love for her. She had felt very much like John did, but she had accepted her destiny with courage and optimism. If she could do so, perhaps he could, too.

John saw his father approaching with another man and a teenage boy. They stopped at the wagon and nodded a greeting at John's mother. John's father looked at her warmly and smiled.

"It is a pleasant evening tonight, Abigail. Put down those sewing needles and join the other women at the fire. I believe they are complaining about us men. I am sure you must have plenty to add to the conversation."

John's mother smiled. "Well, I must join them then, though we shall easily talk all night."

John's father held out his hand and helped her down from the wagon. She kissed John on the cheek then walked toward the fire.

"John," his father said, "Karl spotted some deer as we reached the camp. We are going hunting before it gets dark. If we are fortunate, we shall eat well for the next few days. I think you are ready to join us. What do you say?"

John grinned. "Really? I'm ready!"

"Then let's go," his father said.

John grabbed his hat and strode out of the camp beside his father, his heart swelling with pride and excitement.

6. What is the theme of the passage?

   A. Never take unnecessary risks.

   B. Some dreams are worth the sacrifice.

   C. Fathers and sons sometimes don't get along.

   D. Life is better in the West than it is in the East.

7. Why is going on the Oregon Trail such a big step for John's family?

   A. They have to travel with strangers.

   B. It is a very difficult and dangerous trail.

   C. They have to buy supplies for the trail.

   D. Part of the trail goes over the prairie.

8. Based on the passage, what can you infer about John?

   A. He will be glad his family moved west.

   B. His father will regret taking him hunting.

   C. His relationship with his mother will become strained.

   D. He will never forgive his father for moving the family west.

9. This passage is BEST described as historical fiction because it

   A. includes realistic dialogue.

   B. illustrates how family members get along.

   C. has fictional elements like setting, plot, and characters.

   D. describes events that happened during a real period in history.

Read the passage and answer the questions that follow.

excerpted and adapted from

The Oregon Trail

by Francis Parkman, Jr.

During the 1800s, pioneers emigrated west by horse, oxen, and wagon, forging through the wilderness into unexplored territory. They cleared the land, built homes, and settled vast regions of our country. One of the most famous trails west was the Oregon Trail. This overland route extended from several cities on the Missouri River to the Oregon Territory. It covered about 2,000 miles and took six to seven months to complete. Thousands of pioneers made the difficult and dangerous journey along this trail. In 1846, a man named Francis Parkman traveled through the West in search of adventure. He wrote about his experiences, including his encounters with pioneers, mountain men, and Plains Indians, in a book called The Oregon Trail. *Below is an excerpt from this historical account.*

We were now arrived at the end of our solitary journey along the St. Joseph's trail. On the evening of the 23rd of May we camped near its junction with the old trail of the Oregon emigrants. We had ridden long that afternoon, trying in vain to find wood and water, until at last we saw the sunset sky reflected from a pool encircled by bushes and a rock or two. The water lay in the bottom of a hollow, the smooth prairie gracefully rising in ocean-like swells on every side. We pitched our tents by it. Soon, however, the keen eye of Henry Chatillon had noticed some unusual object upon the faintly defined outline of the distant swell. But in the moist, hazy atmosphere of the evening, nothing could be clearly seen. As we lay around the fire after supper, a low and distant sound, strange enough amid the loneliness of the prairie, reached our ears. There were peals of laughter, and the faint voices of men and women. For eight days we had not encountered a human being, and this singular warning of their presence deeply affected us.

About dark, a sallow-faced fellow descended the hill on horseback and, splashing through the pool, rode up to the tents. He was wearing a huge cloak, and his broad felt hat was weeping about his ears with the drizzling moisture of the evening. Another followed, a stout, intelligent-looking man, who announced himself as leader of an emigrant party camped a mile ahead of us. About twenty wagons, he said, were with him; the rest of his party were on the other side of the river, waiting for a woman who was in the pains of childbirth, and quarreling meanwhile among themselves.

These were the first emigrants that we had overtaken. However, we had found many sad traces of their progress throughout the journey. Sometimes we passed the grave of one who had sickened and died on the way.

We were late in breaking up our camp the following morning. We had scarcely ridden a mile when we saw, far in advance of us, drawn against the horizon, a line of objects stretching at regular intervals along the level edge of the prairie. As we drew closer, we saw before us the emigrant caravan. Its heavy white wagons crept on in their slow procession, and a large drove of cattle following behind. Half a dozen Missourians, mounted on horseback, were shouting among themselves. They were dressed in brown homespun cloth, probably cut and adjusted by the hands of a domestic female tailor.

As we approached, they greeted us with the polished salutation: "How are ye, boys? Are ye for Oregon or California?" As we pushed rapidly past the wagons, children's faces were thrust out from the white coverings to look at us. The care-worn, thin-featured matron or girl seated in front suspended the knitting in which most of them were engaged to stare at us with wondering curiosity. By the side of each wagon stalked its owner, urging on his patient oxen, who shouldered heavily along, inch by inch, on their endless journey.

It was easy to see that fear and disagreement had taken hold of the group. Some of the men looked wistfully upon us as we rode lightly and swiftly past, and then impatiently at their own lumbering wagons and heavy-footed oxen. Others were unwilling to advance at all until the party they had left behind should have rejoined them. Many were murmuring against the leader they had chosen, and wished to unseat him; and this discontent was stirred up by some ambitious spirits, who had hopes of taking his place.

The women felt both regret for the homes they had left and fear of the deserts and the dangers before them. We soon left them far behind, and fondly hoped that we had taken a final leave. But unluckily, our companions' wagon stuck so long in a deep muddy ditch that, before it was freed, the van of the emigrant caravan appeared again, descending a ridge close at hand. Wagon after wagon plunged through the mud; and as it was nearly noon, and the place promised shade and water, we were relieved to see that they decided to encamp and would not continue to accompany us.

Soon the wagons were wheeled into a circle; the cattle were grazing over the meadow, and the men with sour, sullen faces, were looking about for wood and water. They seemed to meet with limited success. As we left the ground, I saw a tall, slouching fellow with the nasal accent of "down east," contemplating the contents of his tin cup, which he had just filled with water.

10. Why do the narrator and his companions MOST LIKELY not want to travel with the emigrant group they encounter on the prairie?

   A. They do not enjoy listening to the group's laughter.

   B. They do not want the group to slow them down.

   C. They will have a hard time keeping up with the group.

   D. They are not sure they want to continue on the journey.

11. Read this sentence from the passage.

   The water lay in the bottom of a hollow, the smooth prairie gracefully rising in ocean-like swells on every side.

   This sentence is an example of

   A. personification.

   B. metaphor.

   C. allusion.

   D. imagery.

Use "Going West" and "The Oregon Trail" to answer questions 12–13.

12. Both "Going West" and "The Oregon Trail" show that

    A. small children were not allowed on the Oregon Trail.

    B. women and men shared hunting duties on the journey west.

    C. women were responsible for making and mending clothes.

    D. the members of emigrant groups found it easy to get along.

13. How does "Going West" illustrate information found in "The Oregon Trail"?

    _____

    _____

    _____

    _____

    _____

    _____

    _____

    _____

CHAPTER

2 Reading Informational Text

2 Diagnostic Assessment for Lessons 9–15

Read the passage and answer the questions that follow.

The Journey North

The Underground Railroad was a secret network that helped slaves escape to freedom to the North and Canada. Its name derived from the railway terms used in the system. The routes to freedom were called "lines." Safe places to stop were called "stations." The leaders who guided slaves along the routes were known as "conductors." The slaves they led to freedom were called "packages." The slaves did not actually travel underground, but because they had to move in secret, usually under cover of darkness, the name was appropriate. The network may have started as far back as the late 1700s. However, the term "Underground Railroad" became publicly known in 1842, when it appeared in print in a publication.

A slave took tremendous risks when he or she decided to make a run for freedom. But for many, it was worth every danger and hardship they encountered. The life of a slave was harsh, at times brutal. Most slaves lived in wooden shacks with dirt floors. Their "beds" were made of grass, straw, or old rags. Sometimes twelve or more slaves were crammed into one house. Families were often separated, and members sold away by their owners. Children could be separated from their parents, and husbands from their wives. Children as young as 8 years old could be made to work in the fields. In most states, slaves were forbidden from learning how to read and write. Those who did learn studied in secret and at great risk.

Slaves were killed or severely punished for disobedience, assaulting a white person, or anything else that displeased their owners. Punishments included whippings, severe beatings, and other atrocities. Frederick Douglass, who escaped to freedom and became a famed abolitionist, was overwhelmed with emotion when he realized he was free. As he put it, "I felt like one who had escaped a den of hungry lions." He could not have expressed it any better. It is hardly surprising that slaves would endure the physical and psychological hardships of the Underground Railroad for a chance at freedom.

The first step for slaves was to escape from their owners. Often, the slaves were on their own at this point. They had to come up with their own escape plan and use their own resources. Sometimes a conductor would pose as a slave, enter the plantation, and lead the slaves northward. The journey was long and nerve-wracking. The slaves traveled by night for hundreds of miles, covering between ten and twenty miles before they stopped to rest and eat at stations along the way. They usually had little to eat or drink, but they survived on what they could get. The stations were typically barns, houses, and places that were out of the way of peering eyes. Being spotted could end their flight to freedom. Slave owners, unwilling to lose what they considered valuable property, did all they could to get their slaves back.

Plantation owners often put advertisements in newspapers to alert others to be on the lookout for their runaway slaves. The ads included a physical description and where the slave was headed or would most likely be found. The reward for turning in a runaway slave could be substantial. Some owners were willing to pay $1,000 or more. It was worth it to them, considering the lifetime of free labor they could get from a slave.

Such large sums provided real incentive for people to turn in runaways. Some men became professional slave catchers, hunting runaways for profit. Slaves knew anyone who realized they were runaways posed a potential danger. Any black person dressed in tattered clothes would attract suspicion. Individuals and groups raised money to provide new, clean clothes for the runaways. This allowed slaves to board trains or boats when necessary. It was still a risk, but at least they had a chance of blending in.

The second Fugitive Slave Act of 1850 made it legal to forcibly return runaway slaves to their owners. Furthermore, anyone caught helping a fugitive slave faced severe punishment. Despite the dangers, many whites and free blacks participated in the Underground Railroad. Harriet Tubman was one of the most famous conductors; over ten years, she led approximately 300 slaves to freedom. She herself escaped to freedom in 1849.

Quakers, a religious group that had renounced slavery in 1688, offered their homes as stations on the Underground Railroad. They gave the slaves a place to hide, food and clothing, and even transported them in covered wagons or boats. Quakers and other whites who participated often received pressure from their families and friends to cease helping runaways. Some of them felt that the slaves should be returned to the South. Others agreed that slaves should be free in principle, but they thought it was too much of a risk to help them. One Quaker named Levi Coffin helped more than 3,000 slaves escape to freedom. The house in which Coffin sheltered so many runaways is now a National Historical Landmark in Indiana.

Thousands of slaves fled plantations every year, but the majority never made it to freedom. Some returned of their own will—exhausted, starving, and unable to withstand the pressure of being wanted fugitives. Others were caught and brought back in chains. Nonetheless, many succeeded. Although no one knows the exact number, it is estimated that several thousand slaves gained their freedom on the Underground Railroad each year. In 1865, the Thirteenth Amendment to the Constitution outlawed slavery in the United States.

Timeline about Slavery

1834 Slavery banned in Canada

1850 Second Fugitive Slave Act passed

1861 Civil War begins

1865 13th Amendment outlaws slavery

1830 — 1840 — 1850 — 1860 — 1870

1849 Harriet Tubman escapes to freedom

1860 Lincoln elected president

1863 Emancipation Proclamation issued

1. What is the main idea of paragraph 3?

   A. Slaves suffered greatly at the hands of their owners.

   B. The Underground Railroad gave slaves the chance to escape.

   C. Frederick Douglass escaped to freedom.

   D. Slaves were expected to obey their owners.

2. Which sentence from the passage is an opinion?

   A. "Children as young as 8 years old could be made to work in the fields."

   B. "The first step for slaves was to escape from their owners."

   C. "He could not have expressed it any better."

   D. "Some owners were willing to pay $1,000 or more."

3. Which event in the timeline BEST illustrates the risks Harriet Tubman took as a conductor on the Underground Railroad?

   A. Slavery is banned in Canada.

   B. The second Fugitive Slave Act is passed.

   C. The Civil War begins.

   D. The Thirteenth Amendment outlaws slavery.

4. What would make the BEST new title for this passage?

   A. "A Helping Hand"

   B. "The Road to Freedom"

   C. "The Life of an American Slave"

   D. "Thank you, Harriet Tubman"

Read the passage and answer the questions that follow.

During the 1800s, thousands of slaves escaped to freedom in the North through the Underground Railroad, a secret network of routes and stations. Along the way, many kind people risked their lives to help the runaways. For over 30 years, a Quaker named Levi Coffin participated in the network. He helped over 3,000 slaves make it safely to the North. In the following excerpt, Coffin describes what it was like to be part of the Underground Railroad.

excerpted and adapted from

Reminiscences of Levi Coffin
by Levi Coffin

In the winter of 1826–27, fugitives began to come to our house. As it became more widely known on different routes that the slaves fleeing from bondage would find a welcome and shelter at our house, and be forwarded safely on their journey, the number increased. Friends in the neighborhood had formerly stood aloof from the work, fearful of the penalty of the law. Now they were encouraged to engage in it when they saw the fearless manner in which I acted, and the success I had. They would contribute to clothe the fugitives, and would aid in forwarding them on their way. However, they were timid about sheltering them under their roof; so that part of the work went to us. Some seemed really glad to see the work go on, if somebody else would do it. Others doubted the appropriateness of it, and tried to discourage me, and prevent me from running such risks. They showed great concern for my safety and financial interests, telling me that such a course of action would injure my business and perhaps ruin me. They said I ought to consider the welfare of my family and warned that my life was in danger, as there were many threats made against me by the slave-hunters and those who sympathized with them.

At one time there came to see me a good old Friend, who was apparently very deeply concerned for my welfare. He said he was as much opposed to slavery as I was, but thought it very wrong to hide fugitive slaves. No one there knew of what crimes they were guilty. They might have killed their masters, or committed some other atrocious deed. Then those who sheltered them, and aided them in their escape from justice, would indirectly be accomplices. He mentioned other objections which he wished me to consider, and then talked for some time, trying to convince me of the errors of my ways. I heard him patiently until he had relieved his mind of the burden upon it. Then I asked if he thought the Good Samaritan stopped to inquire whether the man who fell among thieves was guilty of any crime before he attempted to help him. I asked him if he were to see a stranger who had fallen into the ditch, would he not help him out until satisfied that he had committed no atrocious deed?

Many of my pro-slavery customers left me for a time, so my sales were diminished, and for a while my business prospects were discouraging. However, my faith was not shaken, nor my efforts for the slaves lessened. New customers soon came in to fill the places of those who had left me.

I had to keep a team and a wagon always at command, to carry the fugitive slaves on their journey. Sometimes, when we had large companies, one or two other teams and wagons were required. These journeys had to be made at night, often through deep mud and bad roads, and along by-ways that were seldom traveled. We had to take every precaution, as the hunters were often on the track, and sometimes ahead of the slaves.

Three principal lines from the South converged at my house: one from Cincinnati, one from Madison, and one from Jeffersonville, Indiana. The roads were always in running order, the connections were good, the conductors active and zealous, and there was no lack of passengers. Seldom a week passed without our receiving passengers by this mysterious road. We found it necessary to be always prepared to receive such company and properly care for them. We never knew what night or what hour of the night they might arrive. A gentle rap at the door was the signal for the arrival of a train of the Underground Railroad, for the locomotive did not whistle, nor make any unnecessary noise.

I have often been awakened by this signal, and sprang out of bed in the dark and opened the door. Outside in the cold or rain, there would be a two-horse wagon loaded with fugitives. Many of them might often be women and children. I would invite them, in a low tone, to come in, and they would follow me into the darkened house without a word, for we knew not who might be watching and listening. When they were all safely inside and the door fastened, I would cover the windows, strike a light, and build a good fire. The care of so many brought much work and anxiety on our part, but we assumed the burden of our own will and bore it cheerfully. It was never too cold or stormy, or too late at night for my wife to rise from sleep, and provide food and comfortable lodging for the fugitives.

Sometimes when the fugitives were very poor, we kept them several days until they could be provided with comfortable clothes. Sometimes fugitives have come to our house in rags, foot-sore and toil-worn, and almost wild, having been out for several months traveling at night, hiding in canebrakes or thickets during the day. Often they had become lost and could make little headway at night, sometimes almost perishing for want of food, and afraid of every white person they saw, even after they came into a free State, knowing that slaves were often captured and taken back after crossing the Ohio River.

5. In paragraph 2, Levi Coffin bases his argument against his friend on

    A. the fear of making the wrong choice.

    B. logical arguments against slavery.

    C. the rewards of doing the right thing.

    D. the duty of helping others in need.

6. Which of the following BEST identifies Coffin's text as a primary source?

    A. He writes about events that really happened.

    B. He includes specific historical information.

    C. He lived through the events he is describing.

    D. He provides detailed descriptions.

7. The main text structure used in paragraph 1 of "Reminiscences of Levi Coffin" is

    A. procedure.

    B. sequence.

    C. cause and effect.

    D. comparison and contrast.

8. Which sentence BEST summarizes the excerpt from "Reminiscences of Levi Coffin"?

    A. Helping runaway slaves was difficult and dangerous but worth it.

    B. Not everyone agreed that helping fugitive slaves was a good idea.

    C. Slaves underwent great hardship to seek freedom in the North.

    D. The Underground Railroad was a well-organized network.

Use "The Journey North" and "Reminiscences of Levi Coffin" to answer questions 9–10.

9. Which key details in "Reminiscences of Levi Coffin" support information in "The Journey North"?

_____

_____

_____

_____

_____

_____

_____

_____

10. Explain a central difference between the two passages.

_____

_____

_____

_____

_____

_____

_____

_____

9 Main Idea and Supporting Details

RI.7.2, RI.7.3, RI.7.10, RH.7.2, RH.7.10, RST.7.1, RST.7.5, RST.7.10, W.7.9.a–b, WHST.7.9

Getting the Idea

Nonfiction is writing that conveys information using facts and other details. This type of writing tells about actual people, events, or other real-life subjects. Nonfiction, or informational, texts usually include a **main idea**, or a central message. Often, the main idea is explicitly stated in the text, but sometimes you may need to figure it out.

A main idea is more than a topic. It makes a statement about a topic. For example, the topic of a newspaper article is public libraries. The main idea is: *Public libraries help increase literacy*. The author must develop this main idea with details. **Supporting details** are the facts, reasons, examples, and other details that back up the main idea. For example, the author may develop the main idea with details such as the following:

- **fact:** Currently, there are nine branch libraries in our county.
- **reason:** Free books give people more opportunity to read.
- **example:** Students in Bedford County increased their reading and writing test scores after they began using public libraries.
- **statistics:** Reading scores rose by 8 percent and writing scores rose by 5 percent as a result of increased library use.
- **quotation:** Famous author Li Chang says, "I wouldn't be a writer today if I hadn't used the library as a child."

A text may have more than one central idea. For instance, another main idea in the article could be: *Public library hours should be extended*.

Authors structure their texts to emphasize key points and clarify information. A science article about a complex topic like the human circulatory system could be divided into sections on the heart, blood, and blood vessels to make it easier for readers to understand. All of the sections contribute to the main idea of the article. An author writing an article about an upcoming mayoral election might structure the text to compare the major candidates, so that readers make the best choice.

Details interact in a text to form a unified whole. For instance, an article may include the points of views of several individuals in order to analyze a topic more fully. A book about World War I would describe key events in the war and explain how they relate to each other, showing their causes and effects. An article about an activist could show how her ideas influenced others and led to social change.

To summarize a text, focus on the main idea and key supporting details. Do not include your opinions or other information that is not in the text.

Thinking It Through

Read the following excerpt from John F. Kennedy's inaugural address, and then answer the question that follows.

Let every nation know, whether it wishes us well or ill, that we shall pay any price, bear any burden, meet any hardship, support any friend, oppose any foe, in order to assure the survival and the success of liberty.

In one sentence, write the main idea of this excerpt.

_____

_____

_____

 Leave out the details and focus on the main message.

Coached Example

Read the passage and answer the questions.

Every year Americans celebrate Labor Day on the first Monday in September. Labor Day has come to symbolize the end of summer. Many people are unaware of the origins and true meaning of the holiday. Labor Day was created by the labor movement to recognize the achievements and importance of American workers.

It is uncertain who exactly came up with the idea for the holiday, but the Central Labor Union adopted the proposal for the holiday and organized a demonstration and a picnic. The first Labor Day was celebrated in New York City on September 5, 1882. It fell on a Tuesday. In 1884, the holiday was permanently moved to the first Monday of the month. As labor organizations grew, other cities began to celebrate the holiday. Still, Labor Day was not an official government holiday. This evolved as states passed legislation to make it official. On June 28, 1894, by act of Congress, Labor Day became a national holiday.

---

1. What is a main idea of the passage?

   A. The first Labor Day fell on a Tuesday.

   B. People see Labor Day as the end of summer.

   C. Labor Day was created to celebrate American workers.

   D. Over time, labor organizations grew bigger and more powerful.

   HINT Choose the idea that is most important, not just a detail.

2. Which sentence BEST summarizes paragraph 2?

   A. The Central Labor Union organized the first Labor Day.

   B. Labor Day was not celebrated on Monday until 1884.

   C. No one knows who first had the idea to create the holiday.

   D. First celebrated in 1882, Labor Day became a national holiday in 1894.

   HINT The correct answer captures the main idea of the paragraph as a whole.

Lesson Practice

Use the Reading Guide to help you understand the passage.

Reading Guide

Why does the author divide the passage into sections? How do the headings help you understand the passage?

Where in paragraph 1 is the main idea of the passage stated?

Often, the main idea of a paragraph is stated in the first sentence of the paragraph. How do the supporting details in paragraph 4 support the main idea of the paragraph?

Animals in Motion

All animals compete with other living things for their basics of survival. Animals have body structures that help them survive in their own environments and find the things they need. Some structures help animals move around their environment.

How Invertebrates Move

Invertebrates do not have a spinal column, or backbone. The oceans contain many different invertebrates. Jellyfish are mostly free swimmers. They use their hollow body shape to pump themselves through the water, much like an umbrella opening and closing.

Mollusks such as snails and clams use a muscular foot to slowly drag themselves along. Squid and octopi use a form of water jet propulsion to shoot through the water. Echinoderms such as sea stars use their tube feet with suction cups to slowly crawl from place to place. The tube feet are powered with the pumping of ocean water.

Worms move in many different ways depending upon their habitat. Bristle worms, which live in the ocean, have structures that are not only their means of locomotion, but also serve as gills for respiration. Earthworms use contractions of their muscles to move through soil. In addition, earthworms have structures called setae. Setae are short, bristly hairs that anchor one end of the worm in the soil while the worm's muscles extend the body, moving the worm forward.

The best movers in the invertebrate class are the arthropods. Arthropods have jointed appendages. Appendages are structures that are attached to, and grow outward from, the main body. Lobsters, spiders, mites, and insects all have jointed appendages. Jointed appendages are a huge advancement for these creatures because they allow for fast movement.

How Vertebrates Move

Like invertebrates, vertebrates also show amazing diversity in body structures for locomotion. However, vertebrates have a backbone and can move in more complex ways than invertebrates can. This is because of the internal skeletons that all vertebrates have.

How do the supporting details in paragraph 9 support the main idea that birds have different structures to help them fly?

To summarize this passage, remember to focus on the main ideas and most important supporting details.

What would be another good title for the passage?

For example, fish have a slime layer and a streamlined shape, which reduce friction as they swim. Fish use specialized fins for fast, precise swimming.

Amphibians live in water and swim early in life but then develop muscular legs for hopping and running on land. Frogs and salamanders are examples of amphibians. While it might seem difficult for reptiles to move about on land with their heavy, dry scales, many are very fast. Some common reptiles are snakes, alligators, and crocodiles. Reptiles and other animals use their tails for balance.

Most, but not all, birds fly. Some birds can run very fast, and others can swim quickly. Some birds can do all three. For example, ducks can fly, walk, and swim. Their walk is more of a waddle, but they can get along on the ground. Ducks have webbed feet, and this structure is perfect for swimming. When a duck pushes its feet back, the web spreads; this creates more surface for ducks to thrust through the water. Then, when the duck draws its feet forward and brings its toes together, the web folds up, reducing the resistance to the water.

Birds have various structures that enable them to fly. Their wings are designed with feathers to provide lift. They have strong, hard-working hearts to get enough oxygen to their muscles. They also have hollow bones, which make them light and able to take flight. Some birds have wings, but they cannot fly. Penguins, for example, are flightless birds. They walk on land, using their tail for balance. Sometimes they slide over the snow on their bellies. Like ducks, penguins can swim. They have strong wings shaped like flippers, which allow them to swim up to 30 miles an hour.

The most varied types of locomotion are seen in mammals, such as humans, dogs, horses, and monkeys. Mammals can run, walk, fly, swim, swing arm over arm through the trees, gallop, jump, skip, and walk on two legs—all due to specialized arrangements of their appendages.

Answer the following questions.

1. Which of the following states a main idea of the passage?

   A. Amphibians live in water and on land.

   B. Animals use different methods to get around.

   C. Earthworms contract their muscles to move.

   D. Penguins have wings shaped like flippers.

2. Which supporting detail BEST shows that ducks are built for motion in the water?

   A. Ducks waddle when they walk.

   B. Ducks can swim, fly, and walk.

   C. Ducks have webbed feet.

   D. Ducks are vertebrates.

3. What is the relationship between birds' bones and their ability to fly?

   A. The hollow bones make the birds light.

   B. The strong bones help birds flap their wings.

   C. The bones help bring oxygen to birds' muscles.

   D. The bones are small enough to fit inside the wings.

4. What is the main idea of paragraph 5?

   A. Appendages are structures that grow outward from an animal's body.

   B. Examples of arthropods with appendages are lobsters, spiders, and insects.

   C. Animals with jointed appendages have a big advantage when they move around.

   D. Due to their jointed appendages, arthropods move the best among invertebrates.

5. Explain how a penguin's body structures help it to move. Give two examples.

   _____

   _____

   _____

   _____

10 Argument and Author's Point of View

RI.7.2, RI.7.5, RI.7.6, RI.7.8, RI.7.10, RH.7.6, RH.7.10, RST.7.10, W.7.9a–b, WHST.7.9

Getting the Idea

An **argument** is an attempt to convince others to think or act in a certain way. It is an opinion that must be supported with facts and evidence. An argument expresses an author's **point of view**, or perspective. It usually begins with a **claim**, a statement of the author's point of view that the author must prove. For example, here is an excerpt from a letter that a student at Green Valley Middle School wrote to the school newspaper.

> Students should not be forced to take foreign language classes. The only language people need to know to get along in life is English. Some kids may find it fun to learn French, Spanish, or Italian, but it's just a waste of time. Instead of learning languages we will never use, we should be learning more valuable skills, like how to use computers.

The author's claim is stated in the first sentence: *Students should not be forced to take foreign language classes*. But how well does the author support this claim? An argument must be sound. In other words, its reasoning must be logical. The student says that English is the only language one needs to know. He ignores the value of being able to communicate with others in a multilingual world, and the advantage of being bilingual for many careers. He says "we will never use" foreign languages, but since millions of English-speakers also use other languages, his statement is not valid. The student's **purpose** is to persuade readers that students should not have to take foreign language classes. But because his reasoning is flawed, he will leave many readers unconvinced.

Sometimes authors present others' points of view in an argument. This is often the case with complex issues. For example, an author may write an argument about health insurance in the United States. She knows that politicians, health professionals, the insurance industry, and the average person have widely different points of view on this issue. She addresses these points of view but is careful to distinguish her position from others'. For example, she presents a point of view she disagrees with, but she refutes it, or argues against it, to show why it is flawed. Pointing out the weaknesses in opposing viewpoints makes an argument stronger.

An argument must also provide relevant and sufficient evidence to support its claims. Suppose the middle school student's evidence is that his grandfather never spoke anything but English. This is not convincing support. His grandfather's personal experience does not apply to the experiences of the student's readers. One man's experience is also not enough to show that the student's claims have any merit.

Thinking It Through

Read the following paragraph, and then answer the question that follows.

Today, many people skip breakfast. For example, dieters skip breakfast to save calories. However, studies show that eating a healthy breakfast helps you lose weight by boosting your metabolism and helping you burn more calories.

In one sentence, explain the author's point of view regarding breakfast.

_____

_____

_____

 The author's point of view is how he or she feels about the subject.

Coached Example

Read the passage and answer the questions.

Last month, a player on the school football team was badly hurt during a game. Luckily, he is going to be alright. Unfortunately, some parents and school officials want our school to eliminate the football program. This is a terrible idea! Sure, football has its risks, but so does getting into a car, and the same parents who complain about football put their kids in a car almost every day. Car accidents cause a lot more injuries than we'll ever see in football. People should also remember that football is more than a game. It's a way for thousands of high school students who cannot afford college to earn athletic scholarships. I happen to be on the team. My parents do not have a lot of money. I hope to help them out by earning a scholarship one day. The risks of playing football are minimal, but the potential benefits are great.

1. Which of the following states a central claim made by the author?

   A. "The risks of playing football are minimal, but the potential benefits are great."

   B. "Last month, a player on the school football team was badly hurt during a game."

   C. "I hope to help them out by earning a scholarship one day."

   D. "Luckily, he is going to be alright."

   HINT Choose the sentence that expresses an opinion that the author must prove.

2. Which of the following states the MOST convincing and relevant evidence to support the author's point of view?

   A. "Luckily, he is going to be alright."

   B. "It's a way for thousands of high school students who cannot afford college to earn athletic scholarships."

   C. "My parents do not have a lot of money."

   D. "Car accidents cause a lot more injuries than we'll ever see in football."

   HINT Eliminate answers that rely on personal experiences or bring in unrelated ideas.

Lesson Practice

Use the Reading Guide to help you understand the passage.

Reading Guide

What is the author's point of view? Which words in paragraph 1 convey her point of view?

Find an opinion in the passage that you agree or disagree with, and explain why.

Notice how the author describes the activities of fishermen. How does her choice of words influence the reader's understanding of the information?

Animals Deserve Better

Animals are commonly used in sports and for our entertainment. Hunting and fishing for sport are so popular that television shows are made about these activities. And most people don't think twice about going to see animals in a circus. The fact is, however, that using animals in these ways is an abuse of our power over these innocent creatures.

Hunting and fishing are called "blood sports" for good reason. Animals are killed for the sake of someone's good time. Hunters display the heads and antlers of animals on their walls like trophies, as if killing a helpless animal were an accomplishment to be proud of. Professional fishermen catch fish then throw them back into the water. Is it really necessary to pierce any animal with a hook simply to prove how good you are at catching it? It's one thing to hunt and fish for food. Although some people oppose this as well, animals do provide people with sustenance. Many cultures throughout time survived nearly entirely by fishing and hunting. However, there is no legitimate reason to do it for sport.

Horses are also abused for our sporting pleasure. They are forced to run in races, often subjected to whipping to make them run faster. Occasionally, a horse will break a leg during the race and have to be euthanized. To make things worse, once these horses are past their prime, they are often abandoned or sold to slaughter houses.

Perhaps the cruelest sport of all is bullfighting. It is a popular sport in a number of countries, including Spain and Mexico. In bullfighting, the *matador*, or bullfighter, essentially stabs a bull to death in an arena. The bulls are taunted and stabbed with spears until they collapse from their injuries. All the while, thousands of spectators encourage the matador with cheers and applause. Supporters of bullfighting argue that the sport is an important cultural tradition. They cite the courage and skills of the *matadors*. If it is such a valued tradition, why is there so much opposition to bullfighting within the societies that practice it? As far as courage is concerned, a bullfight is hardly a fair fight. It is designed to the bullfighter's advantage. Bullfighters are rarely seriously hurt or killed, but the bull dies every time.

An argument must be supported with sound reasoning. How well does this author support her opinions?

In which paragraphs does the author present opposing points of view? How does she argue against them?

How does the last paragraph provide a logical conclusion to the argument?

Finally, there is the circus. Most of us have gone to the circus at least once in our lives. Circuses are fun. We enjoy the clowns, the tightrope walkers, and the trapeze artists. The circus does indeed appeal to children of all ages. Unfortunately, animal acts are a major part of the circus. While some acts may seem harmless, such as poodles walking on two legs, others illustrate humans' thoughtless cruelty to animals.

Although circus trainers may deny it, some of them use whips and sticks to get animals to perform tricks. Wild animals, in particular, suffer greatly. Lions, tigers, and elephants are meant to be in the wild, roaming free in their natural environment. Instead, they are kept in cages that are often too small. They are forced to ride bicycles, stand on their heads, or jump through hoops of fire. There are countless cases of animal abuse in the circus.

Despite testimony and even video evidence of this abuse, some people defend the use of animals in circuses. They claim that abuse is the exception, not the rule. They say that many animals enjoy performing and develop loving relationships with their trainers. Even if we accept that the majority of circus owners and workers love animals and do not mean them any harm, the facts cannot be denied. Animals are commonly mistreated in circuses. They suffer needlessly for our entertainment.

Just because we *can* use animals for sport and entertainment does not mean we *should*. Their lives are worth more than our desire to make money or experience a few thrills or laughs.

Answer the following questions.

1. What is the author's point of view regarding hunting and fishing?

   A. Only select cultures have a legitimate right to hunt and fish.

   B. They should not be done under any circumstances.

   C. They are acceptable as a sport, but not for entertainment.

   D. They are acceptable if done for food, but never for sport.

2. The author's purpose for writing this passage is to

   A. provide a brief history of animal abuse through the ages.

   B. compare how different countries use animals for sport and entertainment.

   C. convince readers to stop buying tickets to sporting events and circuses.

   D. persuade readers that animals should not be used for sport or entertainment.

3. Which new detail would BEST make the argument more convincing?

   A. statistics proving that many horses get hurt in sports

   B. a quote from a child who enjoys going to the circus

   C. examples of cultures that traditionally hunt for food

   D. a list of television programs about sport fishing

4. Which of the following states the author's opinion about circuses?

   A. Animals form loving bonds with their trainers.

   B. It is cruel to force animals to perform in circuses.

   C. Many animals enjoy performing in the circus.

   D. Most circus owners and workers like hurting animals.

5. How does the author respond to the arguments of supporters of bullfighting?

   _____

   _____

   _____

   _____

   _____

11 Primary and Secondary Sources

RH.7.1, RH.7.2, RH.7.9, RH.7.10, RST.7.1, RST.7.2, RST.7.10

Getting the Idea

A **source** is something that provides information, such as a printed text, and electronic text, or a video. A **primary source** is material created by an eyewitness or a participant in an event. A **secondary source** is material created by someone who studied an event, but was not present for it. This kind of source discusses information originally presented elsewhere. It may interpret or evaluate a primary source.

The chart below lists common examples of primary and secondary sources.

Primary Sources	Secondary Sources
autobiographies, diaries, letters, journals, speeches, interviews, photographs, news film footage, research data, original documents (e.g., the Declaration of Independence, wills, transcripts), and creative works (e.g., novels, stories, music, art, drama.)	biographies, encyclopedias, dictionaries, textbooks (e.g., history, science, social studies), newspaper and magazine articles (if written immediately after the event, may be considered primary sources), book or movie reviews, and literary criticism

When you read a primary and a secondary source on the same topic, you have the benefit of a first-hand account as well as an evaluation of, or other commentary on, this account. For instance, the letters and journal of Christopher Columbus are primary sources. Columbus is the author. So, reading them allows you to learn first-hand what Columbus saw and did and how he felt about his experiences. In a biography of Columbus, another author would interpret the explorer's actions and analyze the historical significance. The biography would put into perspective what you learned from the primary sources. When doing research, seek out both primary and secondary sources to enrich your understanding of your topic.

As with any text, you may sometimes need to determine the central ideas of a primary or secondary source. Think about Dr. Martin Luther King Jr.'s "I Have a Dream" speech. What is a central idea of this primary source? The hope that someday people will be judged by the content of their character and not by the color of their skin.

You may also have to summarize a source. A summary is a short restatement of a text in your own words. For example, you're writing a research paper about a government program created during the Great Depression. To establish the context, you want to begin with a brief overview of the causes of the Great Depression. First, look in the library and on the Internet to find primary and secondary sources that contain this information. Then, summarize the key events that led to the Great Depression. Be sure the summary is accurate and distinct from your own ideas and opinions.

You might need to determine the conclusions of source. Authors will usually state these at the end of their texts. For example, you might read a science article about space exploration that ends with the statement below.

> Space exploration has led to the development of technologies and products used in everyday life, including satellite dishes, cell phones, GPS, and various medical instruments.

A summary of the author's conclusions could be: *Space exploration has resulted in many useful products and technologies*.

When you analyze primary or secondary sources, be sure to cite specific evidence from the texts to back up your conclusions. Remember to name the author of the primary source and put her or his exact words in quotes. Finally, list all of your sources in a bibliography at the end of your paper.

Thinking It Through

Read the following paragraph, and then answer the question that follows.

In 1543, physician Andreas Vesalius published *De humani corporis fabrica,* or *On the Fabric of the Human Body*. In the book, Vesalius brought anatomy, the study of bodily structures, to a new level. The book contained detailed descriptions of all parts of the human body, carefully drawn illustrations, and directions for performing dissections. This may not seem like much of an accomplishment today, when similar information is available in medical textbooks or encyclopedias. However, in Vesalius's time, such anatomical studies were revolutionary. Before Vesalius's study of human anatomy, scholars and physicians relied greatly on the work of Galen, a physician and philosopher from ancient Greece. His studies informed medicine for centuries. Many scholars would not even dream of questioning Galen's scientific conclusions. But Vesalius realized that Galen's ideas about anatomy were flawed. Galen had based his findings on his experiments on animals and applied his discoveries to human anatomy. Vesalius corrected many errors in traditional thought about body structure. He emphasized the importance of studying the human body in order to truly learn about human anatomy.

Write a brief summary of this source.

_____

_____

_____

_____

_____

_____

 Determine the main idea and most important details expressed in the paragraph, and then put them in your own words.

Coached Example

Read the passages and answer the questions.

excerpted from

General Dwight D. Eisenhower's
Order of the Day (D-Day Message)

Soldiers, Sailors, and Airmen of the Allied Expeditionary Force!

You are about to embark upon the Great Crusade, toward which we have striven these many months. The eyes of the world are upon you. The hopes and prayers of liberty-loving people everywhere march with you. In company with our brave Allies and brothers-in-arms on other Fronts, you will bring about the destruction of the German war machine, the elimination of Nazi tyranny over the oppressed peoples of Europe, and security for ourselves in a free world.

Your task will not be an easy one. Your enemy is well trained, well equipped and battle hardened. He will fight savagely. But this is the year 1944! Much has happened since the Nazi triumphs of 1940–41. The United Nations have inflicted upon the Germans great defeats, in open battle, man-to-man. Our air offensive has seriously reduced their strength in the air and their capacity to wage war on the ground. Our Home Fronts have given us an overwhelming superiority in weapons and munitions of war, and placed at our disposal great reserves of trained fighting men. The tide has turned! The free men of the world are marching together to Victory! I have full confidence in your courage, devotion to duty and skill in battle. We will accept nothing less than full Victory!

D-Day

On June 6, 1944, nearly 175,000 troops from the United States, Canada, and Great Britain landed in Normandy, a region of northwest France on the English Channel. Called "Operation Overlord," the attack played a pivotal role in World War II. Its objective was to win a beachhead in France. A beachhead is a position on an enemy shoreline that is captured by troops in advance of an invading force. If the troops could take Normandy, then they could open a second area of attack against the German armies. The beachhead would also serve as a springboard to free France and Belgium, which were under German occupation. Achieving this could eventually lead to the conquest of Nazi Germany. The attack was fierce and thousands of lives were lost, but by nightfall, the Allied forces had succeeded. The historic day is commonly known as D-Day. One of its most famous documents is General Dwight D. Eisenhower's Order of the Day, which was distributed to the troops the day before the attack. In it, Eisenhower rallied the troops, inspiring them to victory.

1. How can you tell the first passage is a primary source?

   A. It makes references to historical events.

   B. It emphasizes statements with exclamation points.

   C. It includes dates and other specific information.

   D. It is an original document from a period in history.

 A primary source is created closest to the time and events it discusses.

2. What does the primary source provide that the secondary source does NOT?

   A. historical context

   B. strong emotion

   C. details and facts

   D. objective viewpoint

HINT Think about the purpose of the primary source. Compare the content with that of the secondary source.

3. Explain how the secondary source helps you understand the primary source.

_____

_____

_____

_____

_____

_____

_____

HINT Think about what you learn from the secondary source.

Lesson Practice

Use the Reading Guides to help you understand the passages.

Reading Guide

Think about what makes this passage a primary or secondary source.

What is a central idea in the passage?

What conclusions does the author reach?

Civil War Letters

The American Civil War was fought from 1861–65. Although the battles were intense, there were often long breaks between the fighting. Sitting around the camps with little to do was tedious. One of the ways that soldiers alleviated the boredom was to write letters. Receiving letters in return was a great joy to them.

From the many soldiers' letters that survived the war, it is evident how much letters from home meant to the soldiers. Soldiers pleaded with their families, friends, and sweethearts to write back quickly. The luckiest soldiers received not only letters, but packages filled with items they might have trouble obtaining, such as cakes, candies, and soap.

Soldiers got the paper, pen, ink, and envelopes they needed from sutlers. A sutler was a vendor who followed a military unit from place to place, selling food and other supplies to the soldiers. The paper and envelopes were often imprinted with patriotic scenes or political statements. Some stationery printers created special envelopes for specific units. For example, one printer made envelopes for the 99th Pennsylvania Infantry that listed all of the battles it had participated in during 1864.

In their desire to keep their families and friends up to date, soldiers sometimes revealed too much information. They wrote about their unit's exact location or military plans. This posed a potential security risk, since these letters could fall into enemy hands. It was not until World War I that army officials began to censor soldiers' letters to prevent the soldiers from giving away military secrets.

Most soldiers had little or no formal education, and their letters often reflect that. There were errors in grammar and style—errors that the soldiers themselves have acknowledged. But it was the spirit of the letters and their content that mattered to the soldiers' loved ones.

How does this letter help you understand the soldier's experience?

What qualities of the passage tell you if it is a primary or secondary source?

Find details in this letter that support ideas stated in "Civil War Letters."

Confederate soldier John Sweet wrote this letter to his parents in November 1863 while he was serving in the 9th Tennessee Infantry. His infantry was battling Union troops in Chattanooga, Tennessee.

A Letter Home

We have just returned from a trip into East Tenn where we got big amounts of everything to eat and everything we eat is so good to me as I had been starved out so long on some bread & beef, all that we got while we were here besieging Chattanooga. Up there we got sweet and Irish potatoes, chickens, molasses, wheat bread and everything that was good for a poor soldier. Oh, how I do wish that I could be at home now, for it is getting late in the evening and I have had nothing to eat since breakfast and no telling when we will get rations for our rations are out, since we left our ration wagons behind in coming here to this place, for I know you have all had a good & plentiful dinner. I know you will say poor John, but this is only a chapter in military service which we often read, but I am content and will be more so when we get rations. The independence of the bounty is what I want and I am willing to suffer for something to eat many, many days if it will only send me to my dear parents, a full and independent boy.

The enemy still holds their position in Chattanooga and our lines drawn up close around the place. We are now on the top of Lookout Mountain overlooking the town. We have a fine view of our entire line and also of theirs. It is said that we can see into five different states from our position….You must excuse this exceedingly bad letter as I have written in great haste. My love to you and all. Write when you can and a long letter as I am very anxious to hear from you.

John H. Sweet

Answer the following questions.

1. According to "Civil War Letters," one of the reasons that soldiers wrote letters was to

   A. pass the time.

   B. avoid fighting in battles.

   C. develop their writing skills.

   D. leak secrets to the enemy.

2. Which sentence BEST summarizes paragraph 3 of "Civil War Letters"?

   A. Sutlers were vendors who followed military units, selling them supplies.

   B. Printers created special stationery that marked the accomplishments of specific units.

   C. Soldiers obtained writing supplies from sutlers, including customized stationery.

   D. The 99th Pennsylvania Infantry used envelopes that listed their battles in 1864.

3. Which excerpt from "A Letter Home" BEST illustrates the sacrifices soldiers made during the war?

   A. ". . . this is only a chapter in military service which we often read . . ."

   B. "We have a fine view of our entire line and also of theirs."

   C. ". . . I have had nothing to eat since breakfast and no telling when we will get rations . . ."

   D. "… it will only send me to my dear parents, a full and independent boy."

4. Which idea from "Civil War Letters" is illustrated by the first sentence of John Sweet's letter?

   A. Receiving mail from home was a source of great happiness to soldiers.

   B. Soldiers sometimes used stationery imprinted with patriotic scenes.

   C. Soldiers received packages from home containing food and other items.

   D. Some soldiers' writing reflected their lack of formal education in those days.

5. Explain how John Sweet's letter supports the author's point about security risks in "Civil War Letters."

   _____

   _____

   _____

   _____

   _____

12 Compare and Contrast

RI.7.3, RI.7.5, RI.7.6, RI.7.9, RI.7.10, RH.7.5, RH.7.9, RH.7.10, RST.7.9, RST.7.10, W.7.9.a–b, WHST.7.9

Getting the Idea

Sometimes you have to analyze how individual texts relate to each other. When you **compare** texts, you examine their similarities. When you **contrast** texts, you analyze their differences. This is true whether you are gathering primary sources, such as an autobiography written by an astronaut, or secondary sources, such as a book about the U.S. space program. Read the paragraphs below.

In 1803, the United States acquired a territory of almost 900,000 square miles from France. The transaction, known as the Louisiana Purchase, nearly doubled the area of the United States. The territory extended from the Mississippi River west to the Rocky Mountains. The U.S. paid France 15,000,000 dollars for the land.

The Louisiana Purchase was the greatest real estate deal in American history. The United States gained a vast area of land, nearly doubling its size. This became extremely important as the population grew. There was more land for agriculture, mining, and commerce, and pioneers were able to travel west and make new lives for themselves on the frontier.

What do you notice when you compare and contrast these paragraphs? The first paragraph provides more details about the purchase (the territory's location and size, the sale price). The second paragraph focuses on the effects of the purchase. It also expresses opinions, whereas the first paragraph is objective and does not offer the author's point of view.

The two paragraphs on the Louisiana Purchase demonstrate that authors shape the content of their texts, even when they are writing about historical or scientific facts. Even when the basic topic of two texts is the same, authors can develop it in very different ways.

Authors with strong points of view may emphasize evidence that supports their attitudes toward a topic. In addition, they may ignore evidence that contradicts their points of view or purpose. For example, two authors write about Thomas Jefferson. For one author, this American president was a hero who played a crucial role in our country's early history. In her article, she focuses on Jefferson's achievements, highlighting the positives. The other author, who has a more mixed view of Jefferson's character and legacy, includes information that illustrates Jefferson's flaws—details that the other author leaves out.

Authors interpret the facts differently, which raises the question: Is anything in our history books absolutely true? Of course it is. But when historians look back on the past, they do it through a subjective lens. They all have unique experiences, beliefs, prejudices, and agendas. Sometimes they lack key pieces of information. These factors may color their perspective and how they interpret and present the facts.

Sometimes, an author may present information on one topic while using comparison and contrast. For example, an author may contrast what agriculture was like before and after the Louisiana Purchase.

As a student, you make comparisons, too. For example, you might compare information you gained from doing a science experiment with what you learned on the same topic from a science textbook.

Thinking It Through

Read the following paragraphs, and then answer the question that follows.

Beginning around 1760, England experienced technological, economic, social, and cultural changes that came to be known as the Industrial Revolution. Prior to 1760, England was chiefly an agrarian society. This meant its economy depended largely on agriculture. In addition, most products, including clothing and shoes, were manufactured by hand, often at home or in small shops. The Industrial Revolution changed this. Machines were invented that mechanized labor. For example, the power loom and the spinning jenny made spinning wool and cotton faster and easier. Thus, production increased.

Before the Industrial Revolution, people used wood for fuel, and water and wind to power machines. The Industrial Revolution introduced the use of new energy sources, such as coal, the steam engine, and electricity. The factory system spread, creating more jobs and the need for specialized skills. Farming changed, too, as new machines and methods enabled farmers to produce more food for a growing nonagricultural population. From about 1830, the Industrial Revolution spread to other countries, including the United States. It would have a permanent impact on the world.

Write three key changes brought about by the Industrial Revolution.

_____

_____

_____

_____

_____

HINT The author contrasts life before and after the Industrial Revolution.

Coached Example

Read the passages and answer the questions.

An Important Discovery

Before the invention of the compass, sailors and explorers would often get lost. All they had to work with were crude maps; natural landmarks, such as cliffs; and celestial bodies, like the sun and stars. While these provided some direction, they were limited and far from foolproof. Then, people discovered that lodestone, a magnetic mineral, aligned itself to point north and south. This occurs because Earth has a magnetic field with two poles in the north and south. As early as the 12th century, Chinese, western European, and Arab navigators began using lodestone to determine their position and direction. Early compasses were made of a piece of wood or cork set to float in a bowl of water. Eventually, the needle itself was made of lodestone. Over time, cards marked with directions were added to compasses to make them easier to read. The development of the compass had a major impact on navigation and exploration of new worlds.

GPS: Global Positioning System

GPS is a navigation and location system that uses satellites, computers, and receivers. Originally developed for the United States military, it is operated by the United States Air Force. How does it work? A constellation of twenty-four satellites in outer space, inclined to 55º to the equator, transmit signals around the world twenty-four hours a day. The satellites are monitored and controlled at stations throughout the world. The system provides precise information for people on Earth on their position, velocity, and time. It can determine the longitude and latitude of a receiver on Earth. Today, GPS systems are used by people everywhere, including hikers, sailors, pilots, and drivers, to determine where they are and how to arrive at their destination. Officers on ships, for example, use GPS to know their location in the open seas, how fast they are traveling, and to determine the best route. GPS is not affected by weather and can be used by anyone who has the equipment to receive the signals from the satellites. For many people, it has become an essential navigational tool.

1. The authors' main purpose in both passages is to

   A. describe the challenges that navigators on land and sea overcome.

   B. persuade readers that GPS systems are more effective than compasses.

   C. inform readers about devices that help people find destinations.

   D. inform readers about recent advances in technology.

   HINT The correct answer must apply to both passages.

2. A key difference between the two passages is that

   A. only "GPS: Global Positioning System" is about navigation.

   B. "An Important Discovery" has more historical context than "GPS: Global Positioning System."

   C. "An Important Discovery" has more technical information than "GPS: Global Positioning System."

   D. only "An Important Discovery" includes a before-and-after comparison.

   HINT Check each answer choice against both passages.

3. How would having GPS technology have helped early navigators?

   _____

   _____

   _____

   _____

   _____

   _____

   _____

   HINT Use information from both passages to answer the question.

Lesson Practice

Use the Reading Guides to help you understand the passages.

Reading Guide

The title can reveal a passage's main purpose and focus.

Words like *similar*, *like*, *likewise*, and *same* signal a comparison.

Compare and contrast texts by analyzing how they are alike or different.

A Brief History of the Automobile

The automobile was a hugely significant invention. Yet, there is conflicting information about who invented it.

Most people would say Henry Ford. However, he was not the first person to invent the automobile. There are records of early autos as far back as the late 1700s, but some details are sketchy. One of the earliest American automobiles was invented in New York City in 1866 by Richard Dudgeon. His automobile was powered by a steam engine. It was not like the cars we think of today, of course. It was called "the Dudgeon steam wagon." It was a self-propelled vehicle and looked like a small locomotive, similar to the kind you see pulling railroad cars.

Dudgeon was a machinist, and his motivation for creating an automobile was his love of animals. At the time, most people used horses and horse-drawn carriages for transportation. Sometimes the horses were mistreated or abused. Dudgeon wanted to end what he called "the fearful horse murder and numerous other ills inseparable from their use." So, Dudgeon built a steam wagon to provide an alternative to horse power. His vehicle burned coal for power and reached speeds up to 30 miles an hour. It had a boiler, a firebox, a smokestack, and wheels made of wood and iron.

Some historians credit German Karl Benz with creating the first true automobile in 1885. His vehicle had an internal combustion engine and was powered by gasoline. Likewise, in 1908, Henry Ford introduced the Model T. Affordable and reliable, it soon became the most popular car in America. Within ten years, half the cars in this country were Model Ts.

The invention of the automobile cannot be credited to just one person. The combined efforts of innovative thinkers contributed to one of the greatest inventions in history.

What's So Great About Cars?

Based on the titles, what differences can you expect between the passages?

Words like *different*, *on the other hand*, *but*, *unlike*, and *however* signal contrast.

Reread the first paragraph of each passage. What clues do they give you about the content of the passage?

A long time ago, there were no cars on the road. People walked, rode bicycles or horses, and traveled in horse-drawn carriages. Today we live in a much different world. We are a nation of motorists. For many people, the car is a sign of progress and human ingenuity. Some of us, on the other hand, wish that the automobile had never been invented.

Let's talk about the first obvious problem caused by cars: pollution. In the United States alone, cars emit over 300 million tons of carbon into the atmosphere every year. This constitutes about one third of this country's total production of carbon dioxide—a chief contributor to global warming. This could have catastrophic results, including an increase in floods, droughts, and storms, and a reduction in the amount of fresh water available.

Our dependence on cars has naturally led to a dependence on oil, since gasoline is derived from crude petroleum, and we use it to fuel our cars. Unfortunately, we buy much of our oil from foreign countries, which has had negative economic and political consequences. In addition, off-shore drilling for oil has resulted in many accidental oil spills, including the disastrous oil spill in 2010, which had a devastating impact on the environment, wildlife, and the people of the Gulf Coast region.

The truth is, automobiles are multi-ton battering rams. In the United States alone, tens of thousands of people die every year in car crashes. Car accidents are the leading cause of death for teenagers in our country. Automobile-related deaths are a personal and national tragedy.

Centuries ago, people began conceiving the idea of a self-propelled vehicle. It seemed like a good idea at the time, but history has proven that cars have major drawbacks. As a society, we need to reconsider our dependence on automobiles.

Answer the following questions.

1. In "A Brief History of the Automobile," the author compares Dudgeon's automobile to

   A. a Model T.

   B. a locomotive.

   C. an airplane.

   D. a horse-drawn carriage.

2. Why does the author of "What's So Great About Cars?" compare automobiles to "multi-ton battering rams"?

   A. to point out that battering rams are dangerous

   B. to emphasize the deadly force of cars

   C. to suggest that cars can break doors

   D. to show that heavier cars use more fuel

3. Which is true of BOTH passages?

   A. They discuss the impact of global warming.

   B. They remind readers that riding in cars has certain risks.

   C. They emphasize the skill and imagination it took to invent cars.

   D. They point out how people traveled before cars were invented.

4. Which is NOT a key difference between the two passages?

   A. One includes facts and details, while the other does not.

   B. One focuses on "positives," while the other focuses on "negatives."

   C. One is written to inform, while the other is written to persuade.

   D. One discusses environmental issues, while the other does not.

5. List three benefits of automobiles that the author of the second passage ignores.

   _____

   _____

   _____

   _____

   _____

   _____

13 Text Structures

RI.7.5, RI.7.10, RH.7.3, RH.7.5, RH.7.10, RST.7.3, RST.7.5, RST.7.6, RST.7.10, W.7.9.a–b, WHST.7.9

Getting the Idea

The **text structure** of a passage is its pattern of organization. Authors choose the structure that best suits the content and purpose of their texts.

A text arranged according to **sequence** presents ideas in the order in which they occur. This is a common pattern in biographies, where events occur in chronological order. Look for key words that indicate sequence, including *first*, *next*, *last*, *then*, *finally*, *before*, and *after*. The dates in a text also help you to follow the sequence, and to see how much time has elapsed between events. Read this example.

> Ella Fitzgerald was born in Newport News, Virginia, in 1917. After Ella's father died, her mother took her to live in Yonkers, New York. She soon developed an interest in singing. In 1934, she performed at the Apollo Theater.

Comparison-and-contrast texts analyze the similarities and differences between two or more things. Notice how the key words *both*, *however*, and *differences* are used in this example.

> Squids and octopuses are both cephalopods, a type of marine mollusk. However, there are differences between them. An octopus has eight arms, but a squid has ten arms, two of which are tentacles. Squids can also grow to be much larger than octopuses.

Cause-and-effect texts analyze the **causes**, or reasons why things happen, and the **effects**, or the results of a cause. Key words and phrases like *because*, *as a result*, *therefore*, *due to*, and *consequently* signal cause and effect. Read this example.

> For centuries, people from other countries have migrated to the United States. Some migrate here because they want to escape political or religious persecution. Some come here for other reasons, such as new work opportunities and a better life. Immigrants have had a great impact on American culture, including food, music, and language.

A **procedure** explains how to do something in a series of steps. For example, science experiments require that you follow a specific procedure. The following are the first three steps in an experiment to compare how mold grows on three different types of cheese.

1. Cut three pieces of Swiss, American, and cheddar cheese and apply a mold solution to each one.
2. Seal each piece in a plastic bag and label each bag.
3. Wait 24 hours.

A text organized according to **process** explains how a series of actions or functions bring about a result. For example, an author would use this pattern to explain how the president is elected or how the digestive system works. A procedure involves steps that someone must take. A process does not necessarily require action; it may happen naturally.

Authors sometimes divide their texts into sections. This helps readers follow complex ideas. Each section contributes to the text as a whole.

Thinking It Through

Read the following paragraph, and then answer the question that follows.

One of the best-known effects of heat is the change that it causes in the size of a substance. Heat causes all liquids to occupy more space, or to expand. For example, water heated in a tube will expand and force its way up the tube. As the water cools, it will contract and recede back into the tube.

Why does the water force its way up the tube?

_____

_____

_____

_____

 Look for the key words *cause* and *effect* to help you understand the process being described.

Coached Example

Read the passage and answer the questions.

For this experiment, you will need: water, sand, teaspoon, filter paper, paper towels, jar with lid, salt, funnel, jar without lid, shallow aluminum pan

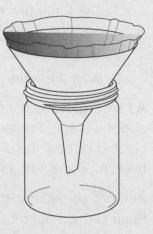

1. Pour 1/4 cup of water into a small jar that has a lid.

2. Add 1 teaspoon of salt to the water. Put the lid on the jar and swirl the contents to mix them well. Observe the mixture.

3. Add 1 teaspoon of sand to the mixture. Put the lid on the jar and swirl the mixture again. Observe the mixture. Record your observations.

4. Allow the mixture to stand and observe it again after 5, 10, and 15 minutes. Record your observations.

5. Fold a piece of filter paper in fourths and place it into a funnel. Place the funnel into the second jar.

6. Swirl the mixture well. Quickly remove the lid and pour the mixture into the filter paper. After the liquid has passed through the paper, observe the liquid and the contents of the filter paper.

7. Set the filter paper and its contents aside on a paper towel.

8. Pour the liquid into a shallow pan and let it sit out overnight.

9. The next day, observe the contents of the pan and the filter paper.

---

1. Which part of the procedure must be performed several times?

   A. observing your results

   B. adding a teaspoon of sand

   C. pouring the liquid into a pan

   D. folding a piece of filter paper

   HINT Read the steps of the procedure carefully.

2. Which step of the procedure must be done first?

   A. Allow the mixture to stand.

   B. Set the filter paper aside.

   C. Add a teaspoon of salt.

   D. Place the funnel into a jar.

   HINT The numbered steps will help you find the correct answer.

Lesson Practice

Use the Reading Guide to help you understand the passage.

Reading Guide

The passage tells a true story from history. Which text structure would be most appropriate for this kind of passage?

Look for patterns of organization in the passage. Key words like *after, at that time, finally,* and *eventually* help you track the information.

Identify a text structure used in paragraph 3.

Which word in paragraph 4 signals a sequence?

Rosa Parks and the Bus Law

On December 1, 1955, Rosa Parks was riding a bus in Montgomery, Alabama, when she was ordered by the bus driver to give up her seat to a white man who had just boarded. Rosa Parks refused. A city ordinance at the time made this action illegal. The bus driver stopped the bus and had her arrested.

At that time, there were a number of laws, called Jim Crow laws, that denied African Americans the rights enjoyed by white people. Public places such as restaurants, schools, and movie theaters were segregated. African Americans had trouble voting in elections and were mistreated in other ways. Rosa Parks knew that obeying unfair laws would only lead to more mistreatment. By refusing to give up her seat, she took a stand against Jim Crow laws.

She was born Rosa Louise McCauley in Alabama in l913. Her mother believed that one should "take advantage of the opportunities, no matter how few they were." She instilled this belief in her children. When Rosa was eleven, she began attending the Montgomery Industrial School for Girls. The philosophy of the school was self-worth, so Rosa learned from a young age to value herself in a society that often treated African Americans as if they had no worth.

As a girl, Rosa knew what it was like to live in fear. She was painfully aware that African Americans were subjected to lynching and house burnings. On some nights, she lay awake, wondering if men were coming to burn down her house. After she was arrested, Rosa said that growing up in fear had helped her get through a situation that might have terrified others.

Rosa married Raymond Parks in 1932. Her husband belonged to the local chapter of the National Association for the Advancement of Colored People (NAACP). Mrs. Parks joined as well. Together, they worked for many years trying to improve the lives of African Americans in the South. Their successes were few, but Mrs. Parks never gave up trying because, as she explained, it was important "to let it be known that we did not wish to continue being second-class citizens."

In paragraph 6, the phrase *chain of events* suggests that causes and effects will be discussed. What happened leading up to the formation of the Montgomery Improvement Association? Who formed the Montgomery Improvement Association, and why?

Remember, causes are the reasons; effects are the results.

Find a cause and several specific effects described in paragraph 8.

How does the comparison with U.S. presidents add to your understanding of Rosa Parks's achievement?

Rosa Parks's arrest started a chain of events that for many historians signaled the beginning of the civil rights movement. After learning of the incident, a group of African Americans, including a young pastor named Dr. Martin Luther King Jr., formed the Montgomery Improvement Association. They called for a boycott of the bus company, which was owned by the city. African Americans answered the call. They walked, carpooled, and rode bikes, refusing to ride the buses until the law was changed. The boycott lasted 382 days, despite pressure, threats, and violence against the boycotters. African Americans had boycotted before for different reasons, but never for such an extended period of time.

Mrs. Parks's arrest enabled lawyers to challenge the city ordinance. They took the case all the way to the U.S. Supreme Court. Finally, on November 13, 1956, the court ruled—declaring segregation on buses unconstitutional.

Rosa Parks sparked a local revolution that spread across much of the country. African Americans realized how much they could accomplish if they worked together. Dr. King gained a following as a result of his organization of the boycott, and he soon had a national platform from which to continue his struggle for equality and justice. Many whites also joined the cause; some even sacrificed their lives. Eventually, federal laws were instituted to guarantee equal rights to all people. African Americans could eat in the same restaurants, go to the same schools, and vote in the same elections as other Americans.

Rosa Parks passed away on October 24, 2005. Her casket was placed in the United States Capitol for two days to allow the nation to pay its respects. She is the only woman and second African American in U.S. history to lie in state at the capitol. It is an honor usually reserved for U.S. presidents, but one that this quiet woman from Alabama richly deserved.

Answer the following questions.

1. What was the effect of Jim Crow laws?

   A. African Americans gained new rights.

   B. African Americans were treated unfairly.

   C. Whites had their rights taken away.

   D. Lawyers were banned from arguing cases.

2. Rosa Parks joined the NAACP

   A. after she got married.

   B. after she was arrested.

   C. just before she passed away.

   D. before she graduated high school.

3. A key difference between the Montgomery bus boycott and previous boycotts by African Americans is that

   A. previous boycotts received more support from African Americans.

   B. the Montgomery bus boycott did not have the intended effect.

   C. the Montgomery bus boycott ended rather quickly.

   D. previous boycotts had not lasted as long.

4. Lawyers challenged the city ordinance

   A. when it first became a law.

   B. after Rosa Parks passed away.

   C. after the bus boycott ended.

   D. after Rosa Parks was arrested.

5. What were the effects of the bus boycott in Montgomery, Alabama?

   _____

   _____

   _____

   _____

   _____

   _____

   _____

14 Graphics

RI.7.7, RI.7.10, RH.7.7, RH.7.10, RST.7.7, RST.7.10

Getting the Idea

Graphics are visual representations of information and ideas. Graphics show information instead of explaining it with words. They allow readers to "see" information and understand complex ideas more easily.

A **timeline** is a graphic representation of events in chronological order. For example, a timeline may list inventions and the dates, in order, when they were invented.

A **map** is a graphic representation of regions on Earth and their geographical features. Maps can show many other things, too; for example, the network of roads in a city, the population density in a state, or the locations of airports in a country.

A **chart** is a graphic organizer that presents information arranged into columns and rows in a box. The chart below shows the names of three early explorers of North America, and where and when they explored.

Explorer	Places Visited	Year of Exploration
John Cabot	Canada	1497
Jacques Cartier	St. Lawrence River	1534
Henry Hudson	Hudson River and New York harbor	1609

A **diagram** is an illustration with labels that describes something or shows how it works, usually pointing out its individual parts. The diagram below shows Earth's biosphere, the zone where all life forms are found. It includes the land, water, and part of the atmosphere.

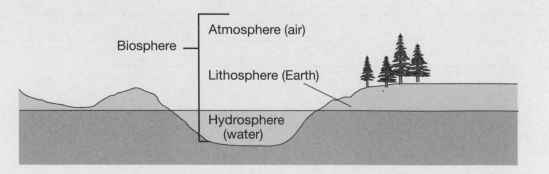

A **graph** shows relationships between sets of data, such as a bar graph or line graph. The line graph below shows how the temperature in a town changed from November to May. To find the average temperature for any given month, follow the line that extends up from that month and stop at the black dot. Then, trace your finger along the horizontal line to the left to find the temperature.

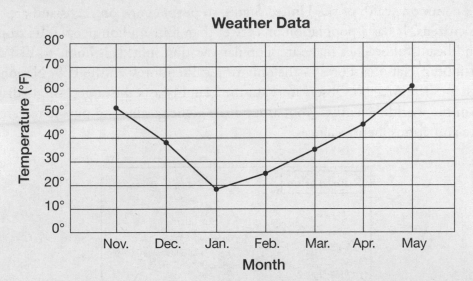

Another way that authors represent ideas visually is through **videos**, or electronic recordings. For example, documentaries about wild animals are videos.

Thinking It Through

Look at the following chart, and then answer the question that follows.

Country	Capital	Official Language
Greece	Athens	Greek
Algeria	Algiers	Arabic
Sweden	Stockholm	Swedish
Tunisia	Tunis	Arabic

In which two countries is Arabic the official language?

_____

_____

HINT   Find "Arabic" in the "Official Language" column, then follow the rows back to the "Country" column.

Coached Example

Read the passage. Study the map and answer the questions.

Puerto Rico is a small island located between the Atlantic Ocean and the Caribbean Sea. It is a commonwealth of the United States, so people born on the island are American citizens. It has a population of a fewer than four million people. Its tropical climate and beautiful beaches make it a popular vacation spot. It is home to El Yunque, or the Caribbean National Forest—the only tropical rainforest in the U.S. National Forest System. The Arecibo Observatory on the island boasts the largest single-dish radio telescope in the world. Scientists from around the globe go there to pursue research in astronomy and atmospheric sciences.

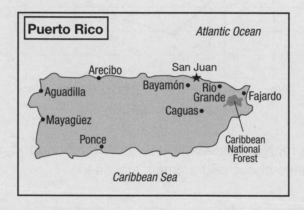

1. According to the map, the Arecibo Observatory would be nearest to which part of the island?

   A. northeast

   B. southeast

   C. northwest

   D. southwest

   HINT Look for Arecibo on the map, then check its location against each answer choice.

2. According to the map, which two cities or towns are closest to each other?

   A. Mayagüez and Caguas

   B. San Juan and Rio Grande

   C. Ponce and Bayamón

   D. Fajardo and San Juan

   HINT Find each set of locations, then compare the differences in distance.

Lesson Practice

Use the Reading Guide to help you understand the passage.

Reading Guide

Articles about the human body are often accompanied by graphics. Refer to the graphic on the next page as you read.

Notice the text structure used in paragraphs 3 and 4. Key words such as *when*, *then*, and *once* help you understand the steps in the process.

The Circulatory System

The human circulatory system involves three kinds of circulation: pulmonary, coronary, and systemic. Pulmonary circulation involves the lungs; coronary circulation involves the heart; systemic circulation applies to the rest of the system.

Two key components in the circulatory system are veins and capillaries. These tubes, or vessels, run throughout your body. Veins carry deoxygenated blood *to* the heart. However, pulmonary veins carry oxygenated blood from the lungs to the heart. Arteries carry oxygenated blood *from* the heart to the cells, tissues, and organs of the body. One exception is the pulmonary artery. This large artery carries deoxygenated blood from the heart to the lungs.

Pulmonary circulation is the movement of the blood from the heart, to the lungs, then back to the heart. When the veins bring the blood back to the heart, they enter the right atrium, one of the chambers of the heart. The blood enters the heart through two large veins called *vena cavae*. The right atrium fills up with the blood and then contracts, pushing the blood into the right ventricle, another chamber in the heart. The right ventricle also fills and contracts. Then, it pushes the blood into the pulmonary artery that leads to the lungs.

Once the blood is in the lung capillaries, there is an exchange of oxygen and carbon dioxide. The oxygen-rich blood then goes through the left ventricle of the heart, which contracts, pushing the blood into the aorta. The aorta is the single largest blood vessel in your body. It carries the oxygenated blood to various parts of the body.

Coronary circulation is the movement of blood within the heart. Systemic circulation nourishes the tissues throughout your body, except the heart and lungs, which, as you just learned, have their own systems. During systemic circulation, the blood passes through the kidneys. The kidneys filter much of the waste from the blood. The blood also passes through the small intestine and the liver.

In this graphic, veins are identified on the left side of the image, and arteries are identified on the right. Follow the lines on the graphic to see what each label describes.

How does the graphic help you understand the vessels of the circulatory system?

Explain why a graphic of the heart would also serve a useful purpose with this passage.

The circulatory system is a vital part of the body. The graphic below show some features of this system.

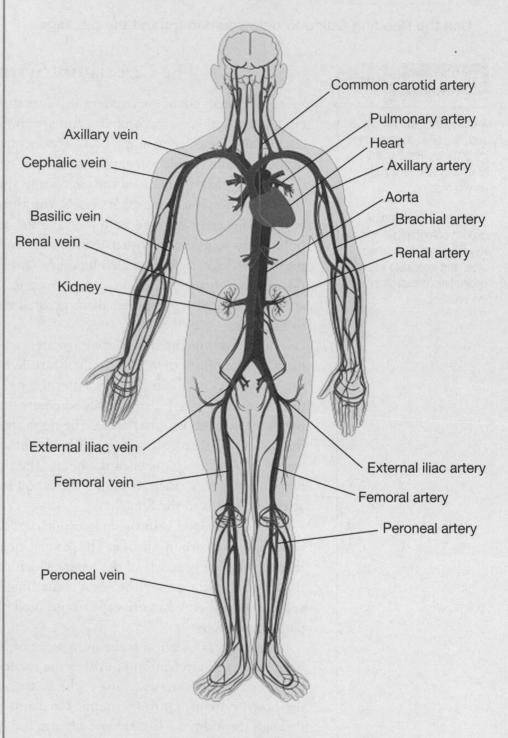

Axillary vein

Cephalic vein

Basilic vein

Renal vein

Kidney

Common carotid artery

Pulmonary artery

Heart

Axillary artery

Aorta

Brachial artery

Renal artery

External iliac vein

Femoral vein

Peroneal vein

External iliac artery

Femoral artery

Peroneal artery

Answer the following questions.

1. The graphic that accompanies the passage is called a

   A. model.

   B. graph.

   C. diagram.

   D. photograph.

2. Which of the following is an artery in the leg?

   A. common carotid artery

   B. axillary artery

   C. peroneal artery

   D. brachial artery

3. The brachial artery is located in the

   A. shoulder.

   B. heart.

   C. chest.

   D. arm.

4. Based on the passage, which vein would be involved in kidney function?

   A. axillary vein

   B. renal vein

   C. cephalic vein

   D. femoral vein

5. What kind of graphic would be BEST to show the sequence of dates when discoveries about the circulatory system were made? Why?

   _____

   _____

   _____

   _____

   _____

15 Fact and Opinion

RI.7.10, RH.7.8, RH.7.10, RST.7.8, RST.7.10, WHST.7.9

Getting the Idea

Understanding a text often requires evaluating authors' statements. This kind of analysis can help you determine if the content is valid and reliable. When you read, consider carefully what authors say and how they say it. Distinguish between facts, opinions, and reasoned judgments.

A **fact** is a statement that can be verified, independently and objectively. The statements below are facts.

- Hawaii became the 50th U.S. state on August 21, 1959.
- An asteroid is a celestial body that orbits the sun.
- The Sahara is the largest desert in the world.

An **opinion** is a personal belief that cannot be proven true and with which others may disagree. Do not confuse an opinion with a fact, even when an author tries to present it as such. In an argument, for example, an author will make many strongly worded statements. He or she is trying to persuade you to think or act in a certain way. Even if you agree, you need to remember that these personal viewpoints are opinions. You need to evaluate them based on the facts the author uses to support them. The statements below are opinions.

- Nobody could possibly be entertained by that silly movie.
- William Shakespeare was the best playwright of all time.
- Soccer will never be as popular in America as football is.

A **reasoned judgment** is a statement based on an issue for which there is more than one standard of judgment. A standard is a law or rule with which a group of people agree. However, people have different standards. This is why a reasoned judgment can be a source of disagreement. Distinguishing between an opinion and a reasoned judgment can be tricky. Keep in mind that a reasoned judgment is usually weighed more carefully. A person makes a reasoned judgment after carefully considering the pros and cons of the issue. A scientist makes a reasoned judgment based on the findings of his or her research. The statements on the following page are examples of reasoned judgments.

- Everyone should exercise regularly and eat healthy foods.
- State funding for libraries should be maintained.
- The government should provide health care for all citizens.

These statements express a point of view, so they are not facts. However, the statements are logical and reasonable. They are reasoned judgments based on standards with which many people would agree.

Thinking It Through

Read the following excerpt from the Declaration of Independence, and then answer the question that follows.

We hold these truths to be self-evident, that all men are created equal, that they are endowed by their Creator with certain unalienable Rights, that among these are Life, Liberty and the pursuit of Happiness.

This excerpt is BEST described as what type of statement?

_____

_____

_____

 Is the sentence a fact that can be proven true? Is it an opinion, or someone's personal belief? Or is it a reasoned judgment based on serious study and observation of an issue. As you consider your answer, keep in mind that the sentence is part of the Declaration of Independence.

Read the passage and answer the questions.

excerpted and adapted from

The Voyage of the Beagle
by Charles Darwin

The *guanaco*, or wild llama, is the characteristic four-legged animal of the plains of Patagonia. It is an elegant animal. It has a long, slender neck and fine legs. It is very common throughout the temperate parts of the South American continent, as far south as the islands near Cape Horn. It generally lives in small herds from half a dozen to thirty in each. They are generally wild and extremely cautious. But they are very easily domesticated, and I have seen some thus kept in northern Patagonia near a house. They are in this state very bold, and readily attack a man by striking him from behind with both knees. The wild *guanaco*, however, do not know how to defend themselves. Even a single dog will secure one of these large animals, till the huntsman can come up. In many of their habits, they are like sheep in a flock.

---

1. Which sentence is an opinion?

   A. "It is an elegant animal."

   B. "The wild *guanacos*, however, do not know how to defend themselves."

   C. "It generally lives in small herds from half a dozen to thirty in each."

   D. "The *guanaco*, or wild llama, is the characteristic four-legged animal of the plains of Patagonia."

   HINT An opinion expresses a personal belief.

2. Read this sentence from the passage.

   In many of their habits, they are like sheep in a flock.

   This sentence is

   A. a fact.

   B. an opinion.

   C. a fact and an opinion.

   D. a reasoned judgment.

   HINT Review the definition of each type of statement.

Lesson Practice

Use the Reading Guide to help you understand the passage.

Reading Guide

A fact is a statement that can be verified in a book or other authoritative source.

Does paragraph 2 of the letter contain mostly opinions or facts?

An opinion is a statement with which some people may disagree.

Find a sentence in paragraph 4 that expresses the author's opinion.

This letter, written in 1621, describes the pilgrims' life in New England soon after the Mayflower *landed.*

A Pilgrim's Life

excerpted and adapted from a letter by Edward Winslow

Although I received no letter from you on the ship that just arrived, I am keeping my promise, which was to write to you truly and faithfully of all things.

You shall understand that in the short time our small group has been here, we have built seven houses for dwelling and four for the use of the plantation, and have made preparation for others. Last spring we planted some twenty acres of Indian corn, and sowed some six acres of barley and peas. According to the methods of the Indians, we fertilized our ground with herrings, or rather shads, which we have in great abundance. Our corn did prove well, and we had a good increase of Indian corn. Our peas were not worth gathering, for they were sown too late. They came up very well and blossomed, but the sun parched them in the blossom.

After the harvest, four men went hunting for fowl, so that we might rejoice together after we had gathered the fruit of our labors. They killed as much fowl to serve the group almost a week. At that time, many of the Indians joined us, among them their greatest king, Massasoit, with some ninety men. For three days we entertained and feasted. The Indians went out and killed five deer, which they brought to the plantation and gave to our governor, the captain, and others. And although our food has not always been so plentiful as it was this time, yet by the goodness of God we are far from want.

We have found the Indians very faithful in their vow of peace with us, very loving and ready to please us. We often go to them, and they come to us. Some of us have traveled fifty miles by land in the country with them…. We walk as peaceably and safely in the wood as on the highways in England. We entertain them familiarly in our houses, and they are as friendly, offering their venison to us….

Look for reasoned judgments in the letter.

Though the author's instructions in the last paragraph are based on his personal experience, the information is likely to be accepted as true.

We have fish and fowl in great abundance. Fresh cod in the summer is but coarse meat to us. Our bay is full of lobsters all summer, and provides a variety of other fish as well. In September we can take a hogshead of eels in a night, with small labor, and can dig them out of their beds all winter. There are no oysters nearby, but we can have them brought by the Indians when we wish. All spring, the earth sends forth naturally very good salad herbs. Here are grapes, white and red, and very sweet and strong also; strawberries, gooseberries, raspberries, etc.; plums of three sorts—white, black, and red.

Now, because I expect you are coming to join us with other of our friends, whose company we much desire, I thought it wise to advertise a few things you need to know. Be careful to have a very good bread-room [the area on a ship where bags of biscuits were stored] for your biscuits. Do not have your meat dry-salted; none can do it better than the sailors. Trust not too much on us for corn at this time, for by reason of the last group that arrived, who depended wholly upon us, we shall have little enough till harvest…. Build your cabins as open as you can, and bring a good store of clothes and bedding with you. Bring juice of lemons, and take it fasting; it is of good use. If you bring anything for comfort in the country, butter or salad oil, or both, is very good. Bring paper and linseed oil for your windows, with cotton yarn for your lamps.

Your loving friend,
E. W.

Answer the following questions.

1. Which sentence from the passage is an opinion?

   A. "For three days we entertained and feasted."

   B. "Our bay is full of lobsters all summer, and provides a variety of other fish as well."

   C. "There are no oysters nearby, but we can have them brought by the Indians when we wish."

   D. "Be careful to have a very good bread-room for your biscuits."

2. Read this sentence from the passage.

   Some of us have traveled fifty miles by land in the country with them.

   This sentence is

   A. a reasoned judgment.

   B. a fact and an opinion.

   C. an opinion.

   D. a fact.

3. Which sentence from the passage is a fact?

   A. "Build your cabins as open as you can, and bring good store of clothes and bedding with you."

   B. "Last spring we planted some twenty acres of Indian corn, and sowed some six acres of barley and peas."

   C. "Do not have your meat dry-salted; none can do it better than the sailors."

   D. "If you bring anything for comfort in the country, butter or salad oil, or both, is very good."

4. Read this sentence from the passage.

   We walk as peaceably and safely in the wood as on the highways in England.

   This sentence is an opinion because

   A. it can be proven.

   B. it is a personal belief.

   C. no one will agree with it.

   D. it is logical and reasonable.

5. Choose a sentence from the passage. Then explain why it is a fact, an opinion, or a reasoned judgment.

   _____

   _____

   _____

   _____

   _____

2 Cumulative Assessment for Lessons 9–15

Read the passage and answer the questions that follow.

The Science of Plants

Most people enjoy being around plants. Some people grow their own garden while others simply buy plants at the store. Few of us stop to think about the fascinating science of plants. Did you know that the plants you look at and pass by each day are multicellular organisms? Plants have specialized cells, which perform functions such as transporting materials, supporting the plant, and storing food. What are the different parts of a plant, and how do the plant's parts do these important jobs?

Types of Plants

Plants can be divided into two categories based on how they transport materials. Small plants, such as mosses, transport food and water through simple diffusion. Larger plants have a more complex system. Specialized plant cells have vascular tissue that forms tube-like structures. These tubes transport water and food throughout the plant. These are called vascular plants. Flowering plants and trees are vascular plants. Many of the plants you see every day, such as trees, shrubs, and flowers, are vascular plants.

All vascular plants have three main parts: roots, stems, and leaves. The vascular tissue forms a continuous set of tubes from the root, through the stem, and into the leaves. These tubes make up the "veins" that you can see in green stems and in leaves. There are two kinds of vascular tissue. One is called xylem, which carries water upward through the plant, from the roots to the leaves. The other is phloem, which carries food made in the leaves to the rest of the plant, including the root where the food is stored.

Roots

Roots are structures that branch out into the soil. They absorb water and nutrients from the soil. Roots also anchor the plant in the soil to hold the plant in place. A plant's roots often store food for the plant as well. There are two types of roots. Taproots are long, thick single roots that grow into the soil. A carrot is an example of a taproot. Trees have taproots, which anchor them very well, helping a tree stay upright, even during a storm with strong winds. The taproot of a tree has branches which can grow out from the taproot much like the branches of the tree grow out from the trunk. Trees that grow in a dry environment have very long taproots to reach water deep under the ground.

Fibrous roots are root systems that have many long, thin fiber-like roots that spread out over a large area. There is no main root. Instead, all the roots are about the same thickness. Grasses have fibrous roots. Plants with fibrous root systems make good ground cover and hold soil in place so that it does not wash away when it rains.

Stems

Water and nutrients move up from the roots into the stem of a plant. Most of the tissue in a stem is vascular tissue. The stem connects a plant's roots to its leaves. Stems also provide support for a plant, keeping it upright. You have probably noticed that some stems are green and flexible, while other stems are brown and rigid. Tomatoes and wildflowers have green stems called herbaceous stems. Trees and shrubs have strong stems called woody stems. The cell walls of the xylem of a woody stem are hard and strong.

Leaves

Leaves are the structures in which plants make food. Leaves grow out from the stem. Leaves are wide and thin to capture the sun's energy. Inside the plant's leaves, this energy is used to convert water and carbon dioxide into food in a process called photosynthesis. Leaves are green because they contain a chemical called chlorophyll, which is needed for photosynthesis. Chlorophyll is able to change the energy from sunlight into chemical energy, which is stored as food. The food made in leaves is needed for the entire plant. This food is then transported from the leaves to the roots through the stem.

How Photosynthesis Works

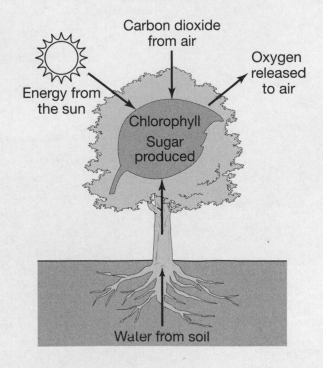

Flowers

In addition to the three main parts, most vascular plants produce flowers. The flower is the structure responsible for sexual reproduction in plants. Flowers produce eggs, the female sex cell, and pollen, the male sex cell. When pollen is transferred from one flower to another, it fertilizes the egg. The fertilized egg develops into a seed. The flower develops into a fruit, a structure that encloses and protects the seed.

A Delicate Balance

Maintaining the correct amount of water inside the plant is very important. If too much water evaporates from the plant, the cells begin to shrink. Think of how soft a balloon gets as it loses air. As the plant cells lose water, they become soft, and the whole plant droops. This is called wilting. A plant could die if it loses too much water. To keep this from happening, the guard cells that surround the stoma (an opening on the underside of a leaf) close the opening if the plant starts to wilt. This decreases the water loss from the plant. It also slows down gas exchange. When the plant receives more water, the guard cells open the stoma, and the plant is able to exchange gases again.

1. The diagram illustrates that sugar is produced in a tree's

   A. trunk.

   B. leaves.

   C. roots.

   D. soil.

2. According to the passage, which structure of a plant prevents soil from being washed away?

   A. leaves

   B. phloem

   C. roots

   D. flowers

3. Which sentence from the passage is an opinion?

   A. "Most people enjoy being around plants."

   B. "This decreases the water loss from the plant."

   C. "All vascular plants have three main parts: roots, stems, and leaves."

   D. "The flower develops into a fruit, a structure that encloses and protects the seed."

4. Which detail from the passage BEST shows that trees are adaptable?

   A. Trees need sun and water.

   B. Trees are vascular plants.

   C. Tree leaves grow out from stems.

   D. Trees in dry areas have longer roots.

Read the passage and answer the questions that follow.

In 1835, Thomas Bridgeman published The Young Gardener's Assistant, *the first gardening manual in the United States. His book included a catalogue of flower and vegetable seeds and advice on how to grow them.*

excerpted and adapted from

The Young Gardener's Assistant
by Thomas Bridgeman

Before I begin the Catalogue, it may be necessary for me to direct the reader's attention to some important matters. They are essential to the good management of a Kitchen garden.

The mode of laying out the ground is a matter of taste, and may be left to the gardener himself. The form is a thing of small importance in the production of useful vegetables. The ground can be laid out in beds of four or ten feet wide, provided it is well worked and the garden is kept neat and free from weeds. Those who have not a garden already formed, should, however, fix on a level spot where the soil is deep. Since we do not always have a choice, I would recommend the reader to make the most of what he has.

It may be necessary to state further that, though shade is useful when raising Celery, Cabbage, and other small plants, slips, etc., in the summer, all standard trees should be excluded from a garden for the following reasons. First, they absorb so much moisture from the ground that little is left for the nourishment of any plant nearby. Second, when in full leaf, they shade a large space and block the free circulation of the air, which is so essential to the well-being of all plants. Third, the droppings from trees are particularly harmful to whatever vegetation they fall upon.

Before starting the work of a garden, the gardener should provide himself with a blank book. In this he should first lay out a plan of his garden, allowing a place for all the different kinds of vegetables he intends to grow. As he proceeds with the planting, if he were to keep an account of everything he does in his garden, he would soon obtain some knowledge of the art.

It is important to have a supply of good old manure and other composts, ready to incorporate with the earth; also a portion of ashes, soot, tobacco dust, and lime, for the purpose of sowing over seed beds in dry weather. This will help to destroy insects, which sometimes cut off the young plants as fast as they come up.

The next important matter is to have the ground in suitable condition to receive the seed. I wish it to be understood that I believe in early sowing and planting, even at the risk of losing a little seed, provided the ground be fit to receive it. A light sandy soil will be helped if worked when moist, as such treatment will have a tendency to make it more compact. On the contrary, if a clay soil is worked when too wet, it kneads like dough, and binds together when drought follows. This not only prevents the seed from rising, but injures the plants in their subsequent growth. The soil slowly becomes resistant to the moderate rains, dews, air, and sun, all of which are necessary in the growth of vegetation.

Some gardeners, as well as some writers, recommend certain fixed days for sowing and planting particular kinds of seed. I think it necessary to guard my readers from being misled. The failure of crops may be often attributed to the observance of certain days for sowing. If some kinds of seed are sown when the ground is wet and cold, they will become chilled in the ground and seldom vegetate. If they are sown in very dry weather, the germinative parts of the seed may become injured by the burning rays of the sun, or the young plants may get devoured by insects. To prevent these difficulties, I have generally allowed a week or ten days for the sowing of seed, intending the medium as the proper time for the vicinity of New York. With this clearly borne in mind, the reader who observes the difference in the degrees of heat and cold in the different parts of the country will know how to apply these instructions accordingly.

Much depends on the manures used on particular kinds of soil. There is a great art to improving sandy and clay soils. For sandy soils, give them such dressings of clay and manure as will help to bind them and make them more compact, so they can hold more moisture. For clay soils, apply coats of horse dung, ashes, sand, and other composts that may help to separate the particles and open the pores of the clay, so it begins to resemble a loam.

Earth of a consistency that will hold water the longest, without becoming hard when dry, is of all others, the best adapted for raising most plants in the greatest perfection.

5. According to "The Young Gardener's Assistant," a key step in planting a garden is

    A. buying more land.

    B. hiring an assistant.

    C. preparing the soil.

    D. planting more trees.

6. Thomas Bridgeman believes that gardeners

    A. should grow more vegetables than flowers.

    B. will have better results if they don't try too hard.

    C. will benefit from writing down what they do in the garden.

    D. should have fixed days for planting all types of plants.

7. What would make the BEST new title for "The Young Gardener's Assistant"?

    A. "My Life as a Gardener"

    B. "Grow a Better Garden"

    C. "All About Plants"

    D. "Working with Soil"

8. Which of the following BEST identifies "The Young Gardener's Assistant" as a primary source?

    A. It describes the author's personal experiences.

    B. It includes specific information about plants.

    C. It is about a common hobby.

    D. It was published in 1835.

Use "The Science of Plants" and "The Young Gardener's Assistant" to answer questions 9–10.

9. How is the purpose of "The Science of Plants" different from the purpose of "The Young Gardener's Assistant"?

_____

_____

_____

_____

_____

_____

_____

_____

10. How does reading both passages enhance a reader's knowledge of plants?

_____

_____

_____

_____

_____

_____

_____

_____

CHAPTER

3 Writing

3 Diagnostic Assessment for Lessons 16–20

This passage contains mistakes. Read the passage and answer the questions that follow.

The Cow on the Roof

adapted from a Welsh folktale

(1) Long ago, there lived a man named Steffan who constantly grumbled about his wife's inadequacies. (2) As far as he was concerned. (3) Gwenda did not keep the house tidy enough. (4) She could not prepare a proper meal. (5) She did not wash his shirts to his liking. (6) On and on, he complained until his wife could bear it no longer.

(7) "Enough, Steffan!" she said angrily. (8) "You think you can do my chores better? (9) So be it. (10) I will go out and work in the vegetable garden. (11) You stay home and take care of the baby, feed the pig, put the cow out to graze, sweep the floor, and make the porridge for our supper." (12) Then, she left the house in a huff.

(13) Steffan was all too happy to have the opportunity to prove his claims to his wife. (14) His happiness was brief. (15) A moment later, the baby woke up and begins to cry loudly and persistently. (16) This only made the baby cry louder. (17) Steffan jumped up and began to rock the cradle and sing to the infant. (18) Then, the pig ran inside and began to squeal. (19) Steffan remembered he was supposed to feed it. (20) He ran to get some buttermilk to make food for it, but he spilled the buttermilk on the floor. (21) Between the crying and the squealing, it was more than Steffan could take.

(22) "All right, you two! (23) Give a man a chance! (24) Out, pig! (25) I will make your meal soon enough."

(26) Steffan pushed the pig out of the house and wiped the sweat from his brow. (27) The baby sniffled then fell asleep. (28) Steffan knew that he had to start cooking the porridge, but first he wanted to turn the cow out to graze. (29) The field where the cow normally grazed was some distance from the house. (30) If Steffan led it there, he would not return in time to make the porridge. (31) Then, Steffan remembered that some fine grass was growing on the roof of the house. (32) Due to a rise at the back of the house, the roof there almost reached the ground. (33) So, Steffan tied a rope around the cow's neck and body, led it up to the roof, and dropped the other end of the rope down the chimney. (34) Then, he went inside to cook the porridge. (35) In order to have both hands free, Steffan tied the end of the rope to his ankle. (36) As the cow grazed, it moved too close to the edge of the roof and fell over, pulling Steffan up the chimney feet first.

(37) Just then, Gwenda returned home. (38) She screamed when from the roof she saw the cow dangling. (39) She ran inside, finding her husband hanging upside down in the chimney. (40) Steffan never complained to his wife again.

1. Which sentences in paragraph 1 should be combined to correct the sentence fragment?

   A. sentences 2 and 3

   B. sentences 3 and 4

   C. sentences 4 and 5

   D. sentences 5 and 6

2. Which revision would BEST improve the organization of paragraph 3?

   A. Delete sentence 14.

   B. Move sentence 17 before sentence 16.

   C. Move sentence 18 before sentence 17.

   D. Delete sentence 19.

3. What is the correct way to write sentence 15?

   A. A moment later, the baby woke up and is beginning to cry loudly and persistently.

   B. A moment later, the baby woke up and begins to cries loudly and persistently.

   C. A moment later, the baby woke up and began to cry loudly and persistently.

   D. A moment later, the baby wakes up and began to cry loudly and persistently.

4. Which is the BEST paraphrase of sentence 28?

   A. Steffan realized he had to begin to cook the porridge, but he wanted to put the cow out to graze first.

   B. Steffan was aware that the porridge needed cooking first but only if he had put the cow out to graze.

   C. Steffan understood that it was important to get the porridge cooking before he put the cow out for grazing.

   D. Steffan began to cook the porridge then remembered that he needed to put the cow out to graze.

5. What is the BEST way to revise sentence 38?

- **A.** She screamed when she saw, dangling from the roof, the cow.

- **B.** She screamed from the roof when she saw the cow dangling.

- **C.** She screamed when she saw from the roof the cow dangling.

- **D.** She screamed when she saw the cow dangling from the roof.

6. Which is the BEST resource to find more folktales from Wales?

- **A.** an encyclopedia entry on folktales

- **B.** a magazine article on Welsh culture

- **C.** a Web site for tourists at www.traveltowales.com

- **D.** a book called *Folktales from Around the World*

Narrative Prompt

Write about a character who experiences an event in life that starts off poorly but turns out to be something good. Maybe the character had an injury and learned an important lesson from the experience. Perhaps the character lost a friend or a possession but gained something more valuable. Maybe the character got a birthday gift he or she hated at first but learned to love. Tell the story of that event and describe how a negative experience was transformed into a positive one. Be sure your narrative includes character dialogue, a plot, and a setting. Use descriptive details and transitions.

Use the checklist below to help you do your best writing.

Does your story

❏ have a point of view?

❏ have a setting, plot, and characters?

❏ develop the setting, plot, and characters with well-chosen details?

❏ connect its different sections with effective methods?

❏ use word choice to develop a mood?

❏ have a satisfying ending?

❏ have good spelling, capitalization, and punctuation?

❏ follow the rules for good grammar?

Write your response on the page provided. You may use your own paper if you need more space.

16 Write an Argument

W.7.1.a–e, W.7.4, W.7.5, W.7.9.b, W.7.10, WHST.7.1.a–e, WHST.7.4, WHST.7.5, WHST.7.10

Getting the Idea

An **argument** is an attempt to convince others to think or act in a certain way. Its main **purpose** is to persuade its audience, or readers. When you write an argument, you need to support your statements, organize your ideas, and present them clearly.

The first paragraph of your argument is the **introduction**. This is where you state your **claim**. The claim is the central idea that you want to persuade your readers to agree with. It expresses your point of view. For example, you might write an argument with this claim:

> Professional athletes need a salary cap to put an end to their excessively high salaries.

Next, write at least three or four **supporting paragraphs** to develop your claim; the paragraphs should include facts, examples, and other relevant details. Each paragraph should have its own **topic sentence**. You could create an **outline** to plan the main ideas of your argument. Look at the sample outline below.

I. Introduction (claim)

    A. The high salaries of professional athletes result in higher ticket prices.

    B. Athletes' exorbitant salaries send the wrong message to young people.

    C. Playing sports is not a job that justifies such high salaries.

II. Conclusion

The **conclusion** is the last paragraph in the composition. It summarizes the main ideas of the argument. Include a concluding statement, such as: *Professional athletes should be paid a reasonable salary*.

Use logical reasoning, or common sense, when you argue. Provide evidence, such as examples and data, to back up your claims. For the salary cap argument, include the names of actual athletes and specific details about their multimillion-dollar contracts. Be sure that your evidence is accurate. Any errors will cause your readers to doubt the validity of your argument. Use details that are relevant to the topic and your purpose. For example, do not mention the high price of hot dogs at a game unless you can directly connect it to athletes' high salaries.

Acknowledge opposing claims and refute them. For example, suppose you include the following opposing claim in your argument: *Athletes claim that team owners make so much money that their salaries represent a fair share of the owners' profits*. If you don't refute it, you are essentially arguing against yourself. So, you should include a refutation, such as the following: *There is nothing fair about the profit that either owners or players make at the fans' expense*.

Create cohesion, or link ideas, in your argument. Transitional words and phrases such as *for example, in contrast, furthermore, thus, in addition,* and *however* will clarify the relationships among your ideas.

Sometimes you may need **sources** to find information for your argument. Choose sources that are accurate and credible, such as government Web sites, educational Web sites, encyclopedias, and reputable newspapers.

Your writing style should be formal. Use standard English; do not be too casual or use slang. Remember that your audience for school compositions is your teacher and sometimes your fellow students.

Sometimes you will write an argument based on a science or history topic. Use the same principles you would use to write any argument.

Coached Example

Read the topic sentences below. Then write a supporting paragraph for each one, developing it with reasons and evidence. You can choose to take the <u>opposite</u> point of view for either topic.

1. Students should not be required to learn history in school.

_____

_____

_____

_____

_____

_____

_____

 You can use specific history topic(s) as examples.

2. The United States should provide financial aid to struggling countries.

_____

_____

_____

_____

_____

_____

_____

 Consider how providing aid affects the United States and/or struggling countries.

Lesson Practice

Use the Writing Guide to help you understand the passage.

Writing Guide

Which sentence in the introduction is the author's central claim?

Which transitional words or phrases does the author use to connect ideas?

Notice the specific reasons the author includes to support his claim.

Should We Save Endangered Species?

Natural extinction of animals has been going on ever since life began on this planet. So, why should we care about plants and animals that are now on the endangered species list? Some scientists believe that humans will cause ten times the normal number of animals to become extinct over the next 100 years. The main reason for this is habitat destruction. These plants and animals need to be saved from extinction.

One reason we should protect them is because of the benefits of natural diversity. No living thing truly lives alone. All are connected. When one thing is removed from its ecosystem, many other plants and animals are affected. When one species leaves, others may soon follow.

Furthermore, these species are vital to the medical field. Every species has unique genetic DNA. Some of this material can be used in medicines. For example, some plants have been found to have anti-cancer agents. Only a tiny fraction of the more than 250,000 known plant species has been tested for possible medical uses. Think of all the diseases we might be able to cure with more testing. If a plant species disappears, we will never know which disease we might have been able to cure.

Write the conclusion to this argument and include a concluding statement.

_____

_____

_____

_____

_____

_____

_____

Plan Your Writing

Read the writing prompt, and plan your response below.

Imagine that your school receives a federal grant of one million dollars to spend in whatever way school officials deem best. How would the money best be used to improve the school? Write a persuasive essay that describes specific problems at the school, and explain how the money would help solve them. Be sure to organize your essay and support your argument with reasons and evidence.

I. **Introduction/Claim:** _____

_____

_____

    A. **Topic Sentence 1:** _____

_____

_____

    B. **Topic Sentence 2:** _____

_____

_____

    C. **Topic Sentence 3:** _____

_____

_____

    D. **Topic Sentence 4:** _____

_____

_____

II. **Conclusion:** _____

_____

Write Your Response

Write your response in the space provided. You may use your own paper if you need more space.

17 Write an Informative Text

W.7.2.a–e, W.7.4, W.7.5, W.7.9.b, W.7.10, WHST.7.2.a–f, WHST.7.5, WHST.7.10

Getting the Idea

An **informative text** informs the reader or explains something. Textbooks, research reports, how-to manuals, and newspapers are examples of informative texts. When you write an informative text, you need to choose its text structure. The **text structure** is the organizational pattern of a text.

Choose the text structure that is best suited to the **purpose** of your writing. For example, a cause-and-effect structure would be best for a text that examines why the French Revolution happened and how it changed French society. A comparison-and-contrast structure would best explain how a hurricane and a tornado are alike or different. Use a classification structure to inform readers about different categories of plants. Choose a sequential structure to explain how to record on a DVD player.

An informative composition should have an **introduction**, **supporting paragraphs**, and a **conclusion**. The introduction will introduce the main topic and preview the key ideas. The supporting paragraphs will develop the topic, using relevant details, such as:

- **facts:** statements that can be verified, such as the dates of historic events or the chemical composition of minerals

- **details:** descriptive information that expands upon the main idea

- **quotations:** the exact words of someone other than the writer; Thomas Paine said, "It is error only, and not truth, that shrinks from inquiry."

- **examples:** things that represent a group or type; for example, crabs, shrimp, and lobsters are types of crustaceans.

Your composition may include headings. A **heading** is a title over a section of text. It is usually in boldface print. Authors use headings to organize smaller sections within a text. An informative text often includes graphics, like charts and diagrams, to illustrate concepts.

Use **transitions** to clarify relationships between ideas and improve the flow of your writing. Transitional words and phrases include *therefore, in addition, for example, in contrast, furthermore,* and *as a result*.

Word choice is important in a composition. Choose your words carefully and use precise language. Avoid vague words like *bad* and *things*. For example, don't say: "Picasso was a good painter." Replace *good* with *talented, accomplished,* or *skillful*. Use vocabulary that is specific to the field of your topic. Your science report, for example, would include scientific terms and any necessary definitions.

Use a formal writing style for your compositions. Do not use language that is too conversational or includes slang. Standard English is appropriate for your audience, which is typically your teacher or fellow students. The graphic organizer below shows how a text on the French Revolution might be organized.

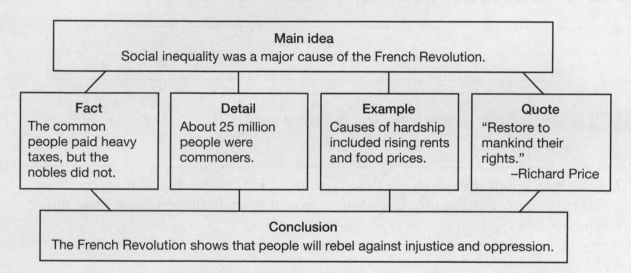

Coached Example

Read the topics below. Then use what you learned about informative texts to develop the topics.

1. Write an informative paragraph about the duties of the United States president.

_____

_____

_____

_____

_____

_____

_____

 Use facts and/or examples to show what the president does.

2. Write an informative paragraph about a person in U.S. history you admire. Tell about his or her accomplishments. Use whatever facts or other details you know about this person's life.

_____

_____

_____

_____

_____

_____

_____

 For example: you could write about a political leader, an athlete, an astronaut, a scientist, an inventor.

Lesson Practice

Use the Writing Guide to help you understand the passage.

Duplicating any part of this book is prohibited by law.

Writing Guide

Which processes are described in the passage?

What comparisons does the author make to explain the concepts?

Definitions of unfamiliar terms help the reader to understand science texts. Which words or terms are defined in the passage?

Understanding Plate Tectonics

The lithosphere is the part of Earth made up of the crust and the solid upper part of the mantle. The lithosphere itself is divided into giant moving chunks of rock called tectonic plates. Each plate is similar to a piece of a puzzle. Below the solid upper part of the mantle is a region that acts like a thick liquid. This region is called the asthenosphere. Tectonic plates float on top of the asthenosphere.

Why don't the solid plates sink into the partially molten, or melted, layer below them? Actually, they do sink a little, but not all the way. The reason they don't sink completely is that the asthenosphere exerts an upward force called a buoyant force that supports the plates. Buoyant force is the upward force a liquid exerts on an object placed in the liquid. This is the same force that allows ice cubes to float in water.

Earth's tectonic plates move slowly and constantly. How do they move? Think again about ice cubes floating in water. If you stir the water gently, the ice cubes move, carried on the current you made when you stirred the water. The currents that carry Earth's plates are not made by stirring. Heat from Earth's interior causes these currents.

Explain how the author uses cause and effect and comparison/contrast in the passage.

_____

_____

_____

_____

_____

_____

Plan Your Writing

Read the writing prompt, and plan your response below.

Have you ever wondered what your city or town was like a century ago? Do some research to find out some details about your town in the early twentieth century. How big was it? How many people lived there? What did the main street look like? Who was the mayor? What kinds of stores and other businesses were there? How about the number of schools and the kinds of transportation? Fill in the graphic organizer with facts and other information to convey a picture of your town long ago.

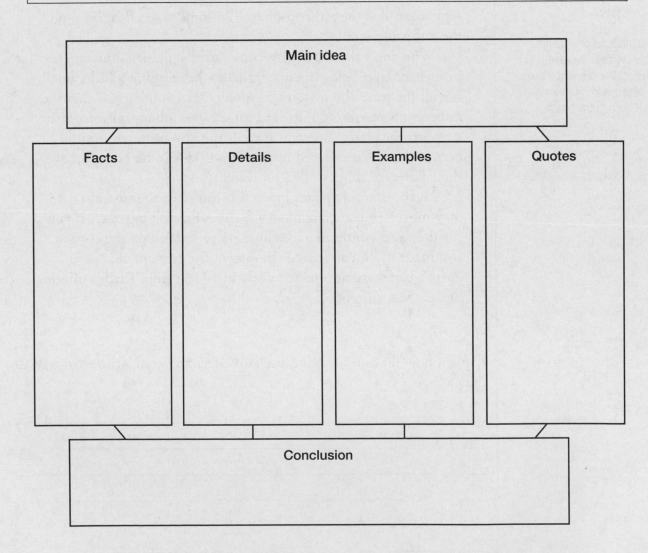

Write Your Response

Write your response in the space provided. You may use your own paper if you need more space.

_____

_____

_____

_____

_____

_____

_____

_____

_____

_____

_____

_____

_____

_____

_____

_____

_____

_____

_____

_____

_____

_____

_____

_____

_____

_____

_____

_____

_____

18 Write a Narrative

W.7.3a–e, W.7.4, W.7.5, W.7.10, WHST.7.4, WHST.7.5, WHST.7.10

Getting the Idea

A **narrative** is writing that tells a story. Fictional stories and books are narratives. A narrative can tell a true story, also, such as your retelling of events at a family picnic. Historical accounts that tell the story of a famous person's life or step-by-step descriptions of scientific investigations are also narratives.

Incorporate the following elements into your narrative:

- **plot:** the sequence of events in a narrative
- **characters:** the people, animals, or other creatures in a narrative
- **conflict:** a problem that a character must solve
- **setting:** where and when a narrative takes place
- **dialogue:** the words spoken by characters to each other

Your narrative will also need a **point of view**, or the perspective from which the narrative is told. For example, you would use a first-person narrator to describe events that happened to you. For a fictional narrative, your narrator could be first-person or third-person. Choose the point of view that is best suited to your narrative.

Establish the context of the narrative. The **context** is the background or circumstances in which events occur. For example, your narrative begins with a boy who stands on the edge of a skating rink, too afraid to join his friends. You explain his fear by establishing the context: a year ago, the boy fractured his ankle after a bad fall.

Organize events so that they flow naturally and logically from one to the next. It would not make sense if a character crying over a terrible toothache in one scene were eating pretzels a few minutes later.

Narratives often have shifts in time frame and setting, and your reader will be confused if you do not clarify these shifts. Use **transitions** to show the **sequence**, or order of events, as well as shifts in time and place. Here are some examples: *The following day; Later that evening; Meanwhile, at Jenny's apartment; After Michael finished the test.*

Pacing is the rate of speed in which events are described. If you are writing about a character who stops to enjoy the scenic view from a mountaintop, slow down the pace of the narrative. Describe what the character sees in detail to convey a sense of leisurely enjoyment.

Use precise words and sensory language to create a picture in the reader's mind. **Sensory language** appeals to the five senses: sight, hearing, taste, touch, and smell. Describe the colors of a sunset, the scent of grass after the rain, or the musical sound of a character's laugh.

Write a satisfying conclusion that follows from, and reflects, the events. It does not have to be a happy ending, but it should provide a resolution to any conflict, wrap up loose details, and provide a sense of closure.

Use a **flowchart** to plan your story. This graphic tool will help you map out the sequence of events.

Introduction/ Context	Event	Event	Event	Conclusion/ Ending
Kay loses her diary.	She accuses her brother of taking it.	She sees her dog digging a hole.	She finds her diary in the hole.	Kay apologizes to her brother.

Coached Example

Read the sentences below. Each sentence is the first line to a paragraph in a story. Complete each paragraph, using what you learned about writing narratives.

1. Rochelle's heart pounded as the roller coaster began its slow climb.

_____

_____

_____

_____

_____

_____

 HINT Describe Rochelle's experience on the roller coaster.

2. Tyler tore off the birthday wrapping and opened the box.

_____

_____

_____

_____

_____

_____

HINT Describe what is in the box. Is Tyler pleased or disappointed? Tell why he feels the way he does.

Lesson Practice

Use the Writing Guide to help you understand the passage.

Writing Guide

What is the setting of the story? How does the writer describe the setting?

What is the conflict in the story?

Find examples of sensory language. What specific words does the writer use?

The Vase

Mei Ling sat cross-legged on the hardwood floor of her aunt's living room, staring hopelessly at the vase—or what was left of it. Her aunt's prized vase, which she had bought at an auction ten years ago, lay in jagged pieces on the floor.

The porcelain vase had been exquisitely crafted. It was ivory white with tiny multicolored butterflies lingering over a garden of red roses. Mei Ling had often stopped to admire it, heeding her aunt's warnings not to touch it. This morning, however, Mei Ling had felt the urge to pick up the vase and feel its cool smoothness in her hands. When the telephone had suddenly rung, Mei Ling had been startled. The vase had slipped out of her fingers and dropped to the floor.

In the first moment of panic, Mei Ling had considered running out of her aunt's house and pretending she knew nothing about the vase. But her aunt had left her there for a few minutes while she ran a quick errand. She would know only Mei Ling could have broken the vase.

Suddenly, Mei Ling heard the jingle of keys at the door. She heard the door open and close and the click of her aunt's high heels on the floor.

"Mei Ling, I'm home!" her aunt called.

Write the next paragraph in the story. Make sure it follows logically from the previous events.

_____

_____

_____

_____

_____

_____

_____

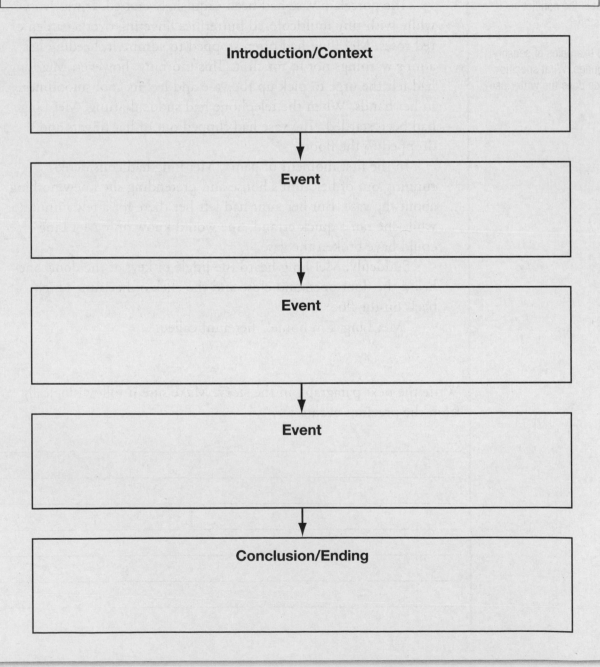

Plan Your Writing

Read the writing prompt, and plan your response below.

Imagine you wake up with a special ability you never had before. Maybe you can fly, see through walls, or hear what people are thinking. Write a story about how you spend your day using your new ability. How does it affect your life? How does it affect your family or friends? Does the new ability turn out to be a blessing or a curse? You are the main character in this story. Be sure to include other characters, a plot, and a setting. Use descriptive details and transitions.

Introduction/Context

↓

Event

↓

Event

↓

Event

↓

Conclusion/Ending

Write Your Response

Write your response in the space provided. You may use your own paper if you need more space.

_____

_____

_____

_____

_____

_____

_____

_____

_____

_____

_____

_____

_____

_____

_____

_____

_____

_____

_____

_____

_____

_____

_____

_____

_____

_____

_____

_____

_____

_____

_____

_____

19 Revising, Editing, and Publishing

W.7.5, W.7.6, WHST.7.5, WHST.7.6, WHST.7.10

Getting the Idea

No piece of writing is perfect the first time. Even professional writers make extensive changes to their drafts. To **revise** is to check the organization of your paper and making any needed changes. To **edit** is to correct errors in grammar, punctuation, spelling, and **sentence structure** (how words are arranged in a sentence).

Revising and editing make your writing suitable for publishing. To **publish** means to produce writing for others to read. You could write an editorial to be published in the school newspaper. A description of your science project and its findings could be published on the school's Web site.

Below are common errors to look for when you revise and edit.

Poor Organization

Check that every sentence in a paragraph relates to the topic sentence of that paragraph. If a sentence does not belong, move it to a different paragraph or delete it. For example, a sentence about the taste buds does not belong in a paragraph about bone structure. Also, make sure your ideas are presented in logical order. If you are explaining the sequence of a scientific procedure, make sure you present the steps in the right order.

Mistakes in Subject-Verb Agreement

Subject-verb agreement is using the right verb for the subject. Both the subject and the verb must be singular or both must be plural. Read these examples.

> *Incorrect:* <u>Cows</u> <u>belongs</u> to the family *Bovidae*.
> *Revised:* <u>Cows</u> <u>belong</u> to the family *Bovidae*.

> *Incorrect:* <u>Every</u> student <u>need</u> to read this book.
> *Revised:* <u>Every</u> student <u>needs</u> to read this book.

Errors in Sentence Structure

Read every sentence to make sure it is grammatically correct and makes its meaning clear. Check for the following common errors.

- A **sentence fragment** is a sentence that is missing either a subject or a verb.

  Incorrect: <u>When the wind blows strongly</u>. Our windows rattle.
  Revised: When the wind blows <u>strongly, our</u> windows rattle.

- A **run-on sentence** is made up of two or more independent clauses joined without the proper punctuation.

  Incorrect: Most beetles eat animals or <u>plants, some</u> eat decaying matter.
  Revised: Most beetles eat animals or <u>plants; some</u> eat decaying matter.

- Watch for awkward sentences, too.

  Incorrect: The purpose of radio was invented to entertain listeners.
  Revised: Radio was invented to entertain listeners.

Inconsistent Tenses

Tense is the form of a verb used to indicate time in a sentence, such as past, present, or future. Edit any sentences with shifts in tense.

  Incorrect: Lee <u>played</u> on the team last year and <u>scores</u> in every game.
  Revised: Lee <u>played</u> on the team last year and <u>scored</u> in every game.

Thinking It Through

Read the following sentences, and then answer the question that follows.

After Terrell finish his homework. He plays video games with his brother.

Edit the sentences and write the corrected sentence below.

_____

_____

_____

 Are these both complete sentences? If not, how can they be fixed? Are the tenses consistent?

Coached Example

Read the passage and answer the questions.

(1) Anastazy scooped shovelfuls of sand and poured them into his bucket. (2) He was determined to make a sandcastle even if his brother, Patryk, refuses to help. (3) Suddenly, Anastazy hit something with his shovel in the sand. (4) He dug deeper until he saw the edge of a golden object reflecting the summer sun. (5) Excitedly, Anastazy rapidly scooped out more sand. (6) Had he stumbled upon a buried treasure, the secret stash of a pirate ship? (7) A shadow suddenly loomed over Anastazy, and he realized Patryk was standing over him.

(8) "Ready to go in the water?" Patryk asked.

(9) "I'm busy," Anastazy answered. (10) "Go away."

(11) But his brother had grown curious and bent down to peer into the hole. (12) "It's nothing!" Anastazy shouted, trying to shield the object from Patryk's view. (13) But it was too late. (14) An excited gleam leapt into Patryk's eyes.

(15) "What is *that*?" he exclaimed.

(16) Anastazy sighed and held out an extra shovel. (17) "Just help me dig, will you?"

---

1. What revision should be made to correct sentence 2?

   A. Change *refuses* to *will refuse*.

   B. Change *was determined* to *determines*.

   C. Change *refuses* to *refused*.

   D. Change *was determined* to *was determining*.

    Check that the subject and verb agree and that the tense is consistent.

2. What is the BEST way to revise sentence 3?

   A. Suddenly, Anastazy hit something in the sand with his shovel.

   B. Suddenly, Anastazy hit in the sand something with his shovel.

   C. Suddenly, Anastazy hit with his shovel something in the sand.

   D. Suddenly, Anastazy in the sand hit something with his shovel.

    One way to detect an awkward sentence is to read it aloud.

Lesson Practice

This passage contains mistakes. Use the Reading Guide to help you find the mistakes.

Reading Guide

The purpose of this passage is to convey historical information. The audience is students and other interested readers. Therefore, notice that the tone is academic and formal.

Which sentence in paragraph 1 has an error in tense?

Which sentence in paragraph 3 is inappropriate for a formal composition?

Which sentences in paragraph 3 contain errors in subject-verb agreement? How should they be corrected?

Queen Elizabeth I

Queen Elizabeth I ruled England from 1558 until 1603. Her reign was not an easy one. At the time, English society was marked by political and religious unrest. Many people made the queen the target of their anger and discontent. Nonetheless, she overcomes these challenges with her characteristic strong will.

Elizabeth's parents were King Henry VIII and Anne Boleyn. Her father had gone to great lengths to marry her mother. Already married to Catherine of Aragon. The king had fallen in love with Anne. In order to marry her, he needed to have his marriage to Catherine annulled by the Catholic Church. In January 1533, he married Anne Boleyn, and she was crowned Queen of England. However, the Pope would not grant him an annulment. Henry was deeply in love with Anne and desperately wanted a male heir, which Catherine had not been able to provide. So, Henry broke with the Catholic Church and established the independent Church of England.

Although astronomers and philosophers assured Henry that Anne would bear him a son, the baby turned out to be a girl. I'm guessing they felt pretty stupid. Elizabeth was born on September 7, 1533. The king were bitterly disappointed. He still did not have a son to inherit the throne. Most people thought women was too weak to rule. History—and Elizabeth—would prove them wrong.

As a child, Elizabeth was highly intelligent. She was well educated and learned to speak multiple languages, including Latin, Franch, and Spanish. Her father, who had remarried after Anne's death, had finally produced a male heir. Edward VI, Elizabeth's half-brother in 1547, ascended the throne when Henry died.

In the sixteenth century, political intrigue was quite common. During the next eleven years, many individuals and organized groups struggled to retain or acquire power. Edward died young, and both his sisters Mary and Elizabeth were possible successors. But Henry VII's family line was long and complicated. In the end, Mary asserted her right to the throne and won. She was proclaimed queen in July 1553.

Find the run-on sentence in paragraph 7. What is the best way to revise the sentence?

Find the sentence in paragraph 8 that does not relate directly to the topic and should be deleted.

Look at the verbs in paragraph 9. Correct the error in the paragraph.

Queen Mary's reign was far from peaceful. She was the Catholic ruler of a country that many wished would return to Protestantism. Elizabeth was Protestant, and this was one key reason that Mary considered her a threat. Elizabeth became a political pawn, and her life was always in danger. Still, when Mary died in 1558, Elizabeth ascended the throne.

During Elizabeth's reign, her enemies plotted to remove her from power. There were numerous assassination attempts. Elizabeth also faced challenges to the throne from France and Spain. Spain had become very powerful the tension between the English and the Spanish had increased to open hostility. Elizabeth encouraged English pirates to attack and plunder Spanish ships as they returned with treasures from the New World. The king of Spain, Philip II, was furious. He prepared a massive fleet of ships to attack England. His goal was to dethrone Elizabeth and make his daughter, Isabella, queen of England.

In May 1588, the Spanish fleet sailed for England. It consisted of more than 100 ships. The English, who rumors of the invasion had heard, were prepared. They watched from cliffs along the shore, waiting for the first sign of ships. As soon as they spotted them, they lit beacons to alert the country that the Spanish were on their way. It reminds one of Paul Revere, who famously announced that the British were coming. A fierce battle ensued. Elizabeth mounted a horse and traveled to the coast to "live or die" with her people. Then, she made a powerful speech, in which she declared, "I know I have the body of a weak and feeble woman, but I have the stomach of a king, and a king of England, too."

Despite being greatly outnumbered, the English won the battle. There was great celebration throughout the country. Elizabeth gains a huge and loyal following. She earned her place as one of England's greatest rulers.

Answer the following questions.

1. Which sentence from the passage is a fragment?

   A. "Her reign was not an easy one."

   B. "Already married to Catherine of Aragon."

   C. "Elizabeth was born on September 7, 1533."

   D. "Queen Mary's reign was far from peaceful."

2. Read this sentence from paragraph 2.

   In January 1533, he married Anne Boleyn, and she was crowned Queen of England.

   The paragraph would BEST be revised if this sentence was

   A. moved to the beginning of the paragraph.

   B. moved to the end of the paragraph.

   C. moved to a different paragraph.

   D. deleted from the paragraph.

3. Which sentence has a verb that does NOT agree with the subject?

   A. "In the sixteenth century, political intrigue was the order of the day."

   B. "During Elizabeth's reign, her enemies plotted to remove her from power."

   C. "There were numerous assassination attempts."

   D. "The king were bitterly disappointed."

4. Read this sentence from paragraph 8.

   The English, who rumors of the invasion had heard, were prepared.

   What is the BEST way to revise this sentence?

   A. The English were prepared for rumors of the invasion.

   B. The English prepared for the invasion, having heard rumors.

   C. Having heard an invasion was rumored, the English were prepared.

   D. The English, who had heard rumors of the invasion, were prepared.

5. Read this sentence from the passage.

   Edward VI, Elizabeth's half-brother in 1547, ascended the throne when Henry died.

   Rewrite the sentence correctly on the lines below.

   _____

   _____

   _____

20 Using Resources

RI.7.1, RST.7.9, W.7.7, W.7.8, W.7.9.a–b, WHST.7.7, WHST.7.8, WHST.7.10

Getting the Idea

A **resource** is a text, audio recording, or video used to gather information. You use resources to conduct **research**, a scholarly or scientific investigation of a topic. For example, when you read a history book to learn the causes of World War I, you are conducting research. There are various types of sources you can use to write a research paper.

Print sources include books, newspapers, magazines, academic journals, encyclopedias, dictionaries, almanacs, and atlases. **Digital sources** include **Web sites**, online newspapers, **CD-ROMs**, **databases**, **audios**, and **videos**, such as films.

Most research papers begin with a question. For example: *What was the Battle of Waterloo?* Your research will help you generate more focused questions: *Where and when did the battle occur? Which countries took part? What happened to Napoleon as a result of the battle?* Asking questions will help you narrow and develop your topic.

Sometimes you need to use search terms, or key words, to locate information on a topic. For example, you do Internet research on Napoleon's role in the Battle of Waterloo. The search term "Napoleon" or "Waterloo" is too broad. Type in "Napoleon Battle Waterloo."

Choose sources that are credible and trustworthy. Textbooks and Web sites ending with *.gov*, *.edu*, and *.org* usually provide reliable information. Confirm the accuracy of your sources by checking more than one source. Use sources that are relevant, or most directly connected, to your topic.

When you use ideas from a source, **paraphrase** the ideas, or put them in your own words. Suppose a source says: *Amnesia is sometimes triggered by emotional pain*. You can paraphrase it to say: *Emotional suffering can cause amnesia*. Use quotation marks to **quote** the exact words from your sources: *According to May Rizzo, "Amnesia is sometimes triggered by emotional pain."* Failure to use quotation marks or give credit to your sources is called **plagiarism**. Provide **citations**, which are specific references to the sources where you obtained the information.

Also include a bibliography. A **bibliography** is an organized list of all your sources. In general, entries include the author's name, title, city and year of publication, and publisher. Below are sample entries for a book, a newspaper article, and a CD-ROM:

> García, Luz. *Understanding Magnets*. Chicago: Blue Garnet, 2008.

> Jensen, Greg. "The City Fights Back." *The Waterville Daily*. 13 July 2010: A4.

> "Botulism." *Medical Terminology*. New York: Link Press, 2006. CD-ROM.

Some disciplines, like history and science, have different formats for bibliographies and citing sources. Check with your teacher to be sure you use the correct format.

Thinking It Through

Read the following paragraph, and then answer the question that follows.

> Barnacles are shellfish with what some might consider a lazy lifestyle. They do not hunt for food in the sea. They attach themselves to rocks, ships, and other sea creatures and wait for food to swim or float by.
>
> —*Lester O'Brien*

Quote a sentence from the paragraph.

_____

_____

_____

 Lead into the quote with the author's name, and use quotation marks.

Read the passage and answer the questions.

When Martha Jane Cannary was thirteen years old, her family joined a wagon train traveling from Missouri to Montana. To her, the dangerous journey was an adventure. At stream crossings, she sometimes got on her pony and swam back and forth while the heavy wagons were slowly pulled across. Sometimes, the rushing water swept her downstream, but she always survived. She also learned to shoot, and she helped the men hunt for food.

After both of her parents died, Martha Jane was left to look after her five younger brothers and sisters. She was only a teenager. She worked at all kinds of jobs, from washing dishes and cooking to driving a team of oxen. Then she became a scout for the United States Army during conflicts with Native Americans. She told wild, exaggerated tales about her adventures. She became very popular when she began performing in Buffalo Bill's Wild West Show. Her lifestyle and her own tall tales about her life earned her the nickname Calamity Jane.

1. Which would be the BEST resource to find more information on Calamity Jane?

   A. an encyclopedia entry called "Early Pioneers"

   B. a map showing Jane's route to Montana

   C. a history Web site on famous American women

   D. the autobiography of Calamity Jane

    Choose the source that is most relevant to the topic.

2. Which resource is a type of video?

   A. a textbook entry about wagon trains

   B. a newspaper article about Calamity Jane

   C. a voice recording of a descendant of Calamity Jane

   D. a documentary about Buffalo Bill's Wild West Show

   HINT A video is a digital resource.

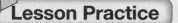

Lesson Practice

Use the Reading Guide to help you understand the passage.

<table>
<tr><td>

Reading Guide

Imagine this passage is a source for a report that you are writing. How would you paraphrase the first sentence of the passage?

Write two questions you have after reading paragraph 1.

</td><td>

excerpted from

Clues to the Past

by Annie Demetriou

Fossils are the preserved remains, traces, or imprints of ancient organisms that can be found within layers of rock. Most fossils are found in sedimentary rocks. Fossils can form when layers of sediment build up over a dead organism. Over time, these layers turn to rock. As the sediment turns to rock, parts of the organism that are buried in the sediment are preserved within the rock. A fossil may also be the preserved teeth, bones, or other hard parts of an organism. It may even be an imprint of a soft part, such as a feather, left in a rock.

Fossils provide a great deal of evidence for geologists to use. The position of fossils within rock layers helps scientists construct the geologic time scale. When layered rock is not disturbed, the lowest rock layers are the oldest. The fossils in the lowest rock layers are also the oldest. In undisturbed sedimentary rock layers, older layers of rock lie beneath younger rock layers. That's because older sediments must be laid down before younger ones pile up on top of them.

As you move from the bottom of a rock formation to the top, the rock gets younger. Therefore, fossils at the top are from organisms that lived in more recent times. Movements in the layers that make up Earth's surface can disturb rock layers by folding or turning them. Sometimes a layer can be missing from one area of rock bed. This creates a gap in the rock record; it could represent thousands or even millions of years of missing time. Understanding how rock beds have been disturbed and how the disturbance affects the sequence of rock layers is the key to determining the relative ages of the rocks.

Scientists use rocks and fossils to try to determine when events in Earth's history took place. When studying rocks and fossils, scientists use techniques to determine their absolute or relative ages.

</td></tr>
</table>

Which resource would you use to find the definition of the word *radioactive* in paragraph 5? Which resource would you use to find out more information about radioactive dating?

Which search term would you use to find information on the Internet about the fossils of extinct species?

In which resources could you look to find out more about what geologists do?

Absolute age tells the actual age of a rock or fossil. For example, a rock or fossil might be 120 million years old. Scientists determine absolute age using a technique called radioactive dating. Radioactive dating is a means of measuring the age of a material by comparing the amount of a radioactive form of a pure substance such as carbon with the amount of its decay product.

Absolute age is the most precise measurement of how long ago a fossil formed. However, it cannot always be determined. When accurate absolute dating is not possible, scientists determine a fossil's relative age. Relative age describes the age of an object or event in relation to another object or event. Relative-age information helps scientists determine which events occurred earlier or later than others without giving a specific date. Geologists use the positioning of rock layers to determine relative age.

Suppose two similar rocks in different locations contain the same kinds of fossils. The fossils may suggest that the rocks were laid down in a similar place and time. When the absolute age of a fossil can be determined, the fossil can then be used to identify the approximate age of the rock layer in which it was found. Once this rock layer is dated, the relative age of a layer above or below can be determined as well.

Fossils provide evidence that a great variety of species existed in the past. Most of these species are now extinct. A species is considered extinct when there are no more individuals of that species living and reproducing. Extinction is often the result of a change in the environment. When the environment changes, sometimes members of a species do not have adaptations that enable them to survive the change. In that case, the individuals do not survive, and the species becomes extinct.

The fossil record shows how species have changed over time. It can also show how different species relate to one another. For example, the shared traits of birds and a particular group of dinosaurs called theropods suggest that the two groups shared a common ancestor long ago.

Answer the following questions.

1. Which type of source is this passage MOST LIKELY from?

   A. a newspaper

   B. a science journal

   C. a Web site about extinct species of the world

   D. Annie Demetriou's autobiography

2. Read this sentence from the passage.

   Fossils provide evidence that a great variety of species existed in the past.

   Which is the BEST paraphrase of this sentence?

   A. Fossils prove that many types of species lived long ago.

   B. Fossils suggest that a great variety of species existed in the past.

   C. Fossils "provide evidence" that many species existed long ago.

   D. Fossils are proof that many types of humans lived a long time ago.

3. Which question would be MOST relevant to do further investigation on the topic of the passage?

   A. What are the differences between geology and geography?

   B. Which museums are famous for their fossil exhibits?

   C. What clues do fossils provide about climate changes?

   D. Which species today are at risk of extinction?

4. What is the correct way to list this source in your bibliography?

   A. Annie Demetriou. *Clues to the Past*. Chicago: Northern UP, 2005.

   B. Demetriou, Annie. *Clues to the Past*. Chicago: Northern UP, 2005.

   C. *Clues to the Past* by Annie Demetriou. Chicago: Northern UP, 2005.

   D. Demetriou, Annie. *Clues to the Past*. Chicago; Northern UP; 2005.

5. Paraphrase this sentence from the passage.

   Suppose two similar rocks in different locations contain the same kinds of fossils.

   _____

   _____

   _____

   _____

This passage contains mistakes. Read the passage and answer the questions that follow.

excerpted from

The Amazing Gorilla

by George Miller

(1) Gorillas are beautiful and fascinating animals. (2) They are the largest of the great apes, a group that includes chimpanzees and orangutans. (3) At birth, they weigh only about four to five pounds. (4) However, by the time they are 13 years old, they are quite large. (5) Females range from 150 to 200 pounds males can weigh from 300 to 500 pounds. (6) Gorillas in captivity are sometimes heavier.

(7) Gorillas have striking features. (8) Their skin and hair are black, but mature males develop gray or silver hairs. (9) Accordingly, these apes are known as "silverbacks." (10) Gorillas' brow ridges are prominent, giving their eyes a sunken appearance. (11) As vegetarians, they mostly eat plants. (12) They have strong chests and protruding abdomens. (13) Their legs are short and stocky, and their arms are long and powerful. (14) Although gorillas can walk standing up, they prefer to walk on their hands and legs.

(15) Their size and features give them an imposing, even frightening, appearance. (16) However, gorillas are surprisingly gentle. (17) In fact, they had been downright shy. (18) Nonetheless, they will attack if they feel their family is threatened. (19) Defending the family typically falls upon the silverback who leads the troop. (20) First, he tries to scare off the intruder, which may be a rival gorilla or a human. (21) He beats his chest, roars, bares his teeth, and charges. (22) This is often enough to send the intruder on a speedy retreat. (23) If the tactic does not work, the troop leader will attack.

(24) The native habitat of gorillas is the forests of equatorial Africa. (25) The lush trees and vegetation are perfectly suited for these plant-eating animals. (26) The favorite foods of gorillas include all kinds of fruit, seeds, leaves, and vines. (27) They have a hearty appetite, too. (28) Adult male gorillas can eat up to 40 pounds of food every day! (29) Gorillas move from place to place in search of food. (30) They do not sleep in the same place twice. (31) Once gorillas arrives at their new feasting ground, they spend most of the day eating until it is time to go to sleep.

(32) Gorillas are highly intelligent creatures. (33) In the early 1970s, a scientific study transformed a female gorilla named Koko into an international star. (34) Remarkably, researchers were able to teach Koko how to use sign language and understand spoken English. (35) Koko, who is still alive, has a vocabulary of more than 1,000 signs. (36) Additionally, she understands about 2,000 words of spoken English.

(37) Sadly, these gentle, beautiful creatures are in danger of becoming extinct. (38) They are hunted for their meat, and their habitat is being destroyed. (39) They are classified as an endangered species. (40) Unless more is done to protect gorillas, one day they may be gone forever.

---

1. What is the BEST way to revise sentence 5?

   A. Females range from 150 to 200 pounds, males can weigh from 300 to 500 pounds.

   B. Females range from 150 to 200 pounds; males can weigh from 300 to 500 pounds.

   C. Females range from 150 to 200 pounds. Males from 300 to 500 pounds.

   D. Females range from 150 to 200 pounds and males 300 to 500 pounds.

2. Which revision would BEST improve the organization of paragraph 2?

   A. Move sentence 7 to the end of the paragraph.

   B. Move sentence 7 after sentence 11.

   C. Move sentence 9 before sentence 8.

   D. Move sentence 11 to paragraph 4.

3. What is the correct way to write sentence 17?

   A. In fact, they can be downright shy.

   B. In fact, they are being downright shy.

   C. In fact, they were downright shy.

   D. In fact, they were being downright shy.

4. Which is the correct way to quote sentence 30?

   A. According to the author, gorillas do not sleep "in the same place twice."

   B. "According to the author, gorillas do not sleep in the same place twice."

   C. According to the author, gorillas "do not sleep in the same place twice."

   D. According to the author, "gorillas do not sleep in the same place twice."

5. Which sentence shows the correct subject-verb agreement?

   A. Once gorillas arrives at their new feasting ground, they spent most of the day eating until it is time to go to sleep.

   B. Once gorillas arrive at their new feasting ground, they spends most of the day eating until it is time to go to sleep.

   C. Once gorillas arrives at their new feasting ground, they spends most of the day eating until it is time to go to sleep.

   D. Once gorillas arrive at their new feasting ground, they spend most of the day eating until it is time to go to sleep.

6. What is the correct way to list this source in a bibliography?

   A. Miller, George, *The Amazing Gorilla*. Boston: Levin Books: 2009.

   B. *The Amazing Gorilla* by George Miller. Boston: Levin Books, 2009.

   C. Miller, George. *The Amazing Gorilla*. Boston: Levin Books, 2009.

   D. George Miller. *The Amazing Gorilla*. Boston: Levin Books, 2009.

Informative Prompt

Choose an animal that you find interesting. It could be a familiar animal, like a raccoon, or something more exotic, like a howler monkey. What are the physical features of the animal? Where is its habitat? What adaptations does the animal have that enable it to survive in its environment? What does it eat? How does it protect itself against predators? Write an informational piece about this animal. Be sure to include facts, details, and examples to back up the main ideas in your essay.

Use the checklist below to help you do your best writing.

Does your essay

❏ have a clear and focused subject?

❏ organize its information into logical categories?

❏ develop its topic with well-chosen facts, details, or other evidence?

❏ join ideas clearly with words, phrases, and sentence structures?

❏ use a style and vocabulary appropriate for the audience and purpose?

❏ build to a solid conclusion?

❏ have good spelling, capitalization, and punctuation?

❏ follow the rules for good grammar?

Write your response on the page provided. You may use your own paper if you need more space.

CHAPTER 4 — Language

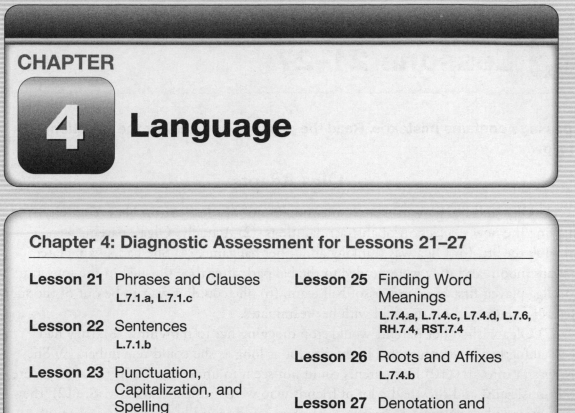

Chapter 4: Diagnostic Assessment for Lessons 21–27

Chapter 4: Cumulative Assessment for Lessons 21–27

4 Diagnostic Assessment for Lessons 21–27

This passage contains mistakes. Read the passage and answer the questions that follow.

Olga Adapts

(1) Olga and her parents were in the museum of Modern art, in New York city, enjoying the new Collection of abstract paintings. (2) Actually, Olga's parents were enjoying the art. (3) Olga was thinking about her ballgame. (4) She had a game later that afternoon, and they were headed to the ballpark after they finished in the museum. (5) Olga played first base on her softball team. (6) She couldn't wait to be out of the stale lifeless museum and on the field with her teammates.

(7) Olga wished her parents would stop dragging her to museums. (8) They had been taking her to art museums in the city for as long as she could remember. (9) She just wasn't into art. (10) Her parents could not seem to understand this. (11) They were both musicians, and they had a lot of friends who were musicians and artists. (12) They were interested in culture of all sorts. (13) They could spend hours in one section of the museum. (14) To Olga, it felt like an eternity. (15) What was so interesting about artwork? (16) Olga thought some of the paintings looked like they had been painted by a blindfolded monkey. (17) They didn't make any sense.

(18) Olga took out the sports magazine she carried around with her on museum days. (19) She sat down and flipped the pages on the bench. (20) A while back, she had asked her parents if she could sit and read while they explored the museum. (21) Although they had been reluctant at first, they had come to see Olga's reading as a compromise. (22) At least she was reading in a museum, and every now and then she might look up and appreciate a work of art. (23) They were not ready to give up hope yet.

(24) "Interesting article?" her father asked, sitting down next to her. (25) Her mother was across the room, transfixed by a huge metal sculpture.

(26) "It's okay," Olga replied.

(27) Her father smiled and said, "I'm glad your here, even if you'd rather be somewhere else. (28) One day you'll come to appreciate art like we do." (29) Olga was doubtful that would ever happen due to the fact that she hated it so much now. (30) However, she did not want to disappoint her father. (31) She had to at least try to be open-minded.

(32) Olga closed her magazine and took her father's arm. (33) There were worse things she could be doing than spending time with her parents in a museum. (34) "Let's go see what Mom is looking at," Olga said. (35) Then, she and her father strolled over to the metal sculpture.

1. Which of the following shows correct capitalization of sentence 1?

   A. Olga and her parents were in the museum of Modern Art, in new York City, enjoying the new collection of abstract paintings.

   B. Olga and her parents were in the Museum Of Modern Art, in New York City, enjoying the new collection of Abstract Paintings.

   C. Olga and her parents were in the Museum of Modern Art, in New York City, enjoying the new collection of abstract paintings.

   D. Olga and her parents were in the Museum of modern Art, in New York city, enjoying the new Collection of abstract paintings.

2. Read this sentence from the passage.

   She couldn't wait to be out of the stale lifeless museum and on the field with her teammates.

   How can this sentence be corrected?

   A. Add a comma between *stale* and *lifeless*.

   B. Add a semicolon after *lifeless*.

   C. Add a comma after *museum*.

   D. Add a dash after *field*.

3. Which of the following is a simple sentence?

    A. She had a game later that afternoon, and they were headed to the ballpark after they finished in the museum.

    B. They had been taking her to art museums in the city for as long as she could remember.

    C. They were both musicians, and they had a lot of friends who were musicians and artists.

    D. Although they had been reluctant at first, they had come to see Olga's reading as a compromise.

4. Which sentence corrects the misplaced modifier in sentence 19?

    A. She sat on the bench and flipped the pages down.

    B. She sat down on the pages and flipped the bench.

    C. She sat down on the bench and flipped the pages.

    D. She sat down and flipped the bench on the pages.

5. Read this sentence from the passage.

> **Her father smiled and said, "I'm glad your here, even if you'd rather be somewhere else."**

Which word is misspelled?

    A. smiled

    B. your

    C. rather

    D. somewhere

6. Which revision BEST makes sentence 29 more concise?

    A. Olga was doubtful that would ever happen due to the simple fact that she hated it so much now.

    B. Olga was doubtful that would ever happen because of the fact that she hated it so much now.

    C. Olga was doubtful that would ever happen in light of hating it so much now.

    D. Olga was doubtful that would ever happen because she hated it so much now.

Read the passage and answer the questions that follow.

Mollusks: Fascinating Creatures of the Sea

Mollusks are intriguing creatures with qualities that make them valuable to people throughout the world. There are about 100,000 species of animals without backbones that belong to the zoological group known as the Mollusca. Mollusks include scallops, clams, snails, octopus, squids, and the chambered nautilus.

Mollusks come in two main varieties: bivalves and univalves. Bivalves are enclosed in two shells that are joined by a hinge on one side. Oysters and clams are bivalves. Univalves have a shell that is a single piece, usually coiled. Some marine univalves, such as the snail, can seal themselves inside with an <u>operculum</u>, a hard, rounded flap that covers the open end of the shell. Their shells may come in different shapes, but mollusks are very similar on the inside. Every mollusk has a breathing siphon, a foot, a small heart and brain, and a mantle that secretes a shell-building substance. Many mollusks have teeth; and while some are blind, most mollusks have eyes.

The mollusk can lay millions of eggs, producing countless numbers of baby mollusks. Sometimes the eggs are released into the sea. Some eggs are protected in nests, while others are encased in capsules and strung like beads. When they hatch, most baby mollusks swim freely. Their bodies are so small and <u>diaphanous</u> that they are almost impossible to see. As they build their shell and increase their weight, they sink to the bottom of the sea.

Like other animals, the mollusk moves about. It pushes along on the ocean floor on its foot. Sometimes it gets around by swimming. It spends its entire life in its shell. The shell protects the mollusk, which can retreat into it when frightened. The mollusk also protects itself by concealing itself in mud and attaching itself to a rock. Predators find it hard to spot the mollusk.

Mollusks are of great importance to humans. First of all, they are a food source. Scallops, clams, and octopus are commonly found on restaurant menus, and oysters and some varieties of snails are considered a delicacy. Secondly, certain mollusks produce a gem treasured throughout the world: the pearl. Both oysters and mussels produce pearls, although oysters get most of the recognition.

What causes oysters to create pearls? Believe it or not, a pearl is basically a reaction to physical discomfort. Oysters have very tender bodies. They protect their delicate bodies by coating the inside of their shells with a smooth, crystalline substance called nacre, or mother-of-pearl. Sometimes an irritant, such as a grain of sand, gets inside the oyster's shell. It's similar to having a grain of sand in your eye. It can be quite uncomfortable and even painful. An oyster cannot wash the foreign object out of its body as you might wash it out of your eye. So, the oyster coats it with layer upon layer of nacre to create a smooth barrier between the object and its body. Eventually, the layers form a bead around the object. This bead is the beautiful gem we call a pearl.

Pearls have always been extremely popular, but since not all oysters make pearls, it was hard to keep up with the demand. In the late 1800s, the Japanese developed a way to get oysters to produce pearls. Instead of waiting for sand or other particles to naturally find their way inside oysters, they manually inserted these objects into oysters. A pearl created with human help is called a cultured pearl.

Mollusks are prized for what they have on the outside, as well. Many people enjoy collecting seashells, which are the empty shells of sea creatures, in particular, mollusks. For some, it is a passionate <u>hobby</u>. Mollusks can produce <u>magnificent</u> shells. The shells of mollusks in <u>tropical</u> zones can be especially colorful and beautiful. The process of creating these shells is remarkable. Practically from the day it is born, the mollusk builds its shell, slowly and with care. Every shell is customized, precisely designed for the shape of the particular mollusk. Certain mollusks take two to five years to build their shells. The shells of other mollusks keep growing all of their lives.

Some people study mollusks and seashells for the pure love of science. They identify these creatures by their Latin name and examine their structure with an <u>appreciation</u> of their flawless design. For true seashell lovers, however, seashells are much more than that. They are works of art—a gift from nature for land dwellers everywhere. Mollusks are truly fascinating creatures—whether they are used as a source of food, gems, seashells, or simply left alone.

7. Which word related to <u>hobby</u> has a negative connotation?

   A. fad

   B. pastime

   C. activity

   D. amusement

8. Read this sentence from the passage.

   Their bodies are so small and <u>diaphanous</u> that they are almost impossible to see.

   What does <u>diaphanous</u> MOST LIKELY mean?

   A. thick

   B. heavy

   C. peculiar

   D. transparent

9. In the word <u>magnificent</u>, the root means

   A. many.

   B. both.

   C. one.

   D. great.

10. Which of these words has the same suffix as <u>tropical</u>?

    A. decal

    B. trophy

    C. comical

    D. radical

11. What is the meaning of the word <u>operculum</u>?

    _____

    _____

    _____

    _____

12. Write another word with a positive connotation that could be used in place of <u>appreciation</u> in the last paragraph.

    _____

    _____

21 Phrases and Clauses

L.7.1.a, L.7.1.c

Getting the Idea

Understanding the parts of a sentence can help you write better sentences. A **subject** is the word that performs the action in a sentence. The **predicate** is the part of a sentence that contains the verb. A **verb** is a word that shows action or describes a state of being.

A **phrase** is a group of words that contains a subject or a predicate, but not both. The following words form a phrase: *the house on the hill*. The phrase has a subject, *house*, but no verb.

A **clause** is a group of words that contains a subject and a predicate.

> Mahendra swims in the pool twice a week.

Mahendra is the subject; *swims* is the verb; the complete predicate is the verb and the words that follow it.

An **independent clause** can stand alone as a complete sentence. It expresses a complete thought.

> Nikolai watched the fireworks light up the sky.

A **dependent clause** cannot stand alone as a complete sentence.

> Although the movie received good reviews.

The word *movie* is the subject and the predicate is *received good reviews*. However, this sentence does not express a complete thought. It begins with *although*, which is a subordinating conjunction. A **subordinating conjunction** is a word or phrase that introduces a dependent clause. Other subordinating conjunctions include: *when*, *because*, *if*, *after*, *until*, *unless*, *as soon as*, and *before*. A sentence is not complete unless the dependent clause is joined to an independent clause.

> Although the movie received good reviews, Jim thought it was boring.

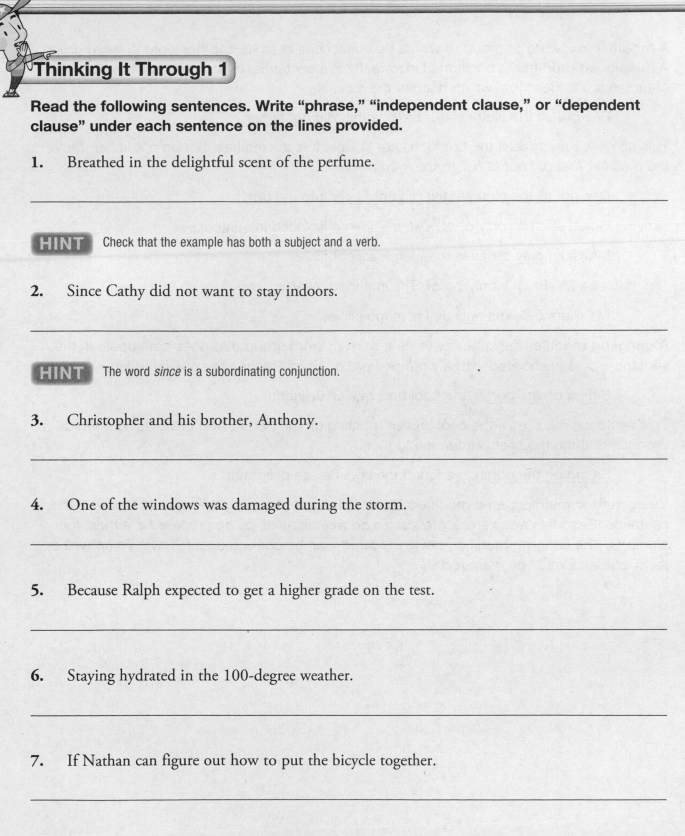

Thinking It Through 1

Read the following sentences. Write "phrase," "independent clause," or "dependent clause" under each sentence on the lines provided.

1. Breathed in the delightful scent of the perfume.

_____

HINT Check that the example has both a subject and a verb.

2. Since Cathy did not want to stay indoors.

_____

HINT The word *since* is a subordinating conjunction.

3. Christopher and his brother, Anthony.

_____

4. One of the windows was damaged during the storm.

_____

5. Because Ralph expected to get a higher grade on the test.

_____

6. Staying hydrated in the 100-degree weather.

_____

7. If Nathan can figure out how to put the bicycle together.

_____

8. You can go ice skating with Isabel today.

_____

A **modifier** is a word or group of words that describes or limits another word or word group. A **misplaced modifier** is positioned incorrectly in a sentence. It describes a word that it is not intended to describe, which distorts the meaning.

> Dee put all the clothes into the box <u>that did not fit her</u>.

This sentence reads as if the box does not fit Dee. It is the clothes that do not fit her. Move the modifier *that did not fit her* to the right place.

> Dee put all the clothes <u>that did not fit her</u> into the box.

Limiting words such as *only* or *almost* are often misplaced in sentences.

> Mr. Blum <u>only</u> believes that Jeff is responsible.

This can't be Mr. Blum's only belief. The intended meaning is:

> Mr. Blum believes <u>only</u> Jeff is responsible.

A **dangling modifier** describes or limits a word or word group that does not appear in the sentence, or is associated with a word or word group other than the one intended.

> <u>Sitting on the porch</u>, the cool breeze was delightful.

This sentence reads as if the cool breeze is sitting on the porch. Add the missing noun or pronoun that the modifier is intended to modify.

> <u>Sitting on the porch</u>, <u>we</u> found the cool breeze delightful.

You can fix some misplaced modifiers by rephrasing or changing the order of words in the sentence. Read this awkward sentence: *To do well on tests, being prepared is a must for students*. The dangling modifier, *being prepared*, can be corrected as follows: *To do well on tests, students must be prepared*.

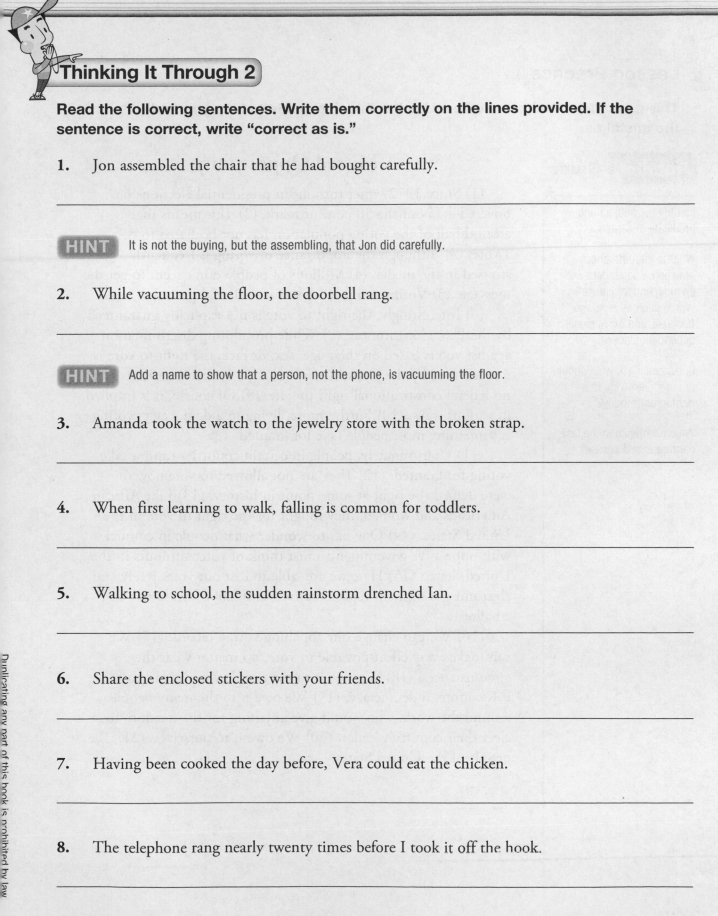

Thinking It Through 2

Read the following sentences. Write them correctly on the lines provided. If the sentence is correct, write "correct as is."

1. Jon assembled the chair that he had bought carefully.

_____

HINT It is not the buying, but the assembling, that Jon did carefully.

2. While vacuuming the floor, the doorbell rang.

_____

HINT Add a name to show that a person, not the phone, is vacuuming the floor.

3. Amanda took the watch to the jewelry store with the broken strap.

_____

4. When first learning to walk, falling is common for toddlers.

_____

5. Walking to school, the sudden rainstorm drenched Ian.

_____

6. Share the enclosed stickers with your friends.

_____

7. Having been cooked the day before, Vera could eat the chicken.

_____

8. The telephone rang nearly twenty times before I took it off the hook.

_____

Lesson Practice

This passage contains mistakes. Use the Reading Guide to help you find the mistakes.

Identify the subject and predicate in sentence 1.

What is the difference between a dependent and an independent clause? Words such as *although*, *because*, and *since* signal dependent clauses.

In sentence 10, what should the modifier *living in a democracy* modify?

Which sentence in the last paragraph is a phrase?

A Missed Opportunity

(1) Since 1972, voter turnout in presidential elections has hovered at about the 50 percent mark. (2) This means that around half of the voting population has not bothered to cast a vote. (3) Although the importance of voting is frequently stressed in the media. (4) Millions of people don't seem to get the message. (5) Voting is a privilege no one should pass up.

(6) Interestingly, the right to vote is not explicitly guaranteed by the U.S. Constitution. (7) While prohibiting discrimination against voters based on their age, sex, or race, the right to vote is not affirmed by the Constitution. (8) This means Americans have no federal constitutional right to vote. (9) Of course, it is implied in various ways. (10) Furthermore, living in a democracy, voting is something most people take for granted.

(11) Unfortunately, people in certain countries cannot take voting for granted. (12) They are not allowed to vote now or were denied the right at some point in history. (13) Like African Americans and women, they fought for the right to vote in the United States. (14) One has to wonder what people in countries with oppressive governments must think of voter turnouts in the United States. (15) Here we are, able to cast our votes freely and elect our government representatives, and half of us do not cast a ballot.

(16) We can change our appalling voting record. (17) We can make every effort possible to vote, no matter what the circumstances. (18) We owe it to the people who fought to make this country a democracy. (19) We owe it to the many people around the world who would give anything for the freedom to elect their country's leader. (20) We owe it to ourselves. (21) The people of the United States.

Answer the following questions.

1. Which sentence from paragraph 1 is a dependent clause?

   A. sentence 1

   B. sentence 2

   C. sentence 3

   D. sentence 4

2. Which is the correct way to write sentence 7?

   A. While prohibiting discrimination against voters based on their age, sex, or race, voting is not a right affirmed by the Constitution.

   B. While the Constitution prohibits discrimination against voters based on their age, sex, or race, its right to vote is not affirmed by the Constitution.

   C. While prohibiting discrimination against voters based on their age, sex, or race, we do not have the right to vote affirmed by the Constitution.

   D. While prohibiting discrimination against voters based on their age, sex, or race, the Constitution does not affirm the right to vote.

3. Which sentence corrects the dangling modifier in sentence 10?

   A. Living in a democracy, furthermore, voting is something most people take for granted.

   B. Furthermore, living in a democracy, most people take voting for granted.

   C. Furthermore, living in a democracy, something most people take for granted is voting.

   D. Living in a democracy, voting is something most people take for granted, furthermore.

4. Which sentence corrects the misplaced modifier in sentence 13?

   A. Like the United States, African Americans and women fought for the right to vote.

   B. Like African Americans and women, they fought for the right in the United States to vote.

   C. Like African Americans and women, they fought in the United States for the right to vote.

   D. Like African Americans and women in the United States, they fought for the right to vote.

22 Sentences

L.7.1.b

Getting the Idea

Not every sentence has the same structure. However, all sentences fall into four basic types. Sentence variety makes writing more interesting.

A **simple sentence** is made up of one independent clause. The sentence below is a simple sentence.

> Lia and Sheree visited their aunt last summer.

A **compound sentence** is made up of two or more independent clauses joined by a **coordinating conjunction**: *and*, *but*, *for*, *so*, *or*, *nor*, *yet*. An **independent clause** is a group of words that can stand alone as a sentence. You can spot independent clauses on either side of the conjunction, *but*, in the example below.

> Brett's car is old, but it is still in good condition.

A **complex sentence** has at least one dependent clause connected to an independent clause. A **dependent clause** cannot stand alone. It needs the rest of the sentence to complete its meaning. The dependent clause may be at the beginning or end of the sentence. Complex sentences usually include **subordinating conjunctions**, such as *because*, *when*, *if*, *although*, *after*, *before*, and *since*. The sentences below are complex sentences.

> Because mice love cheese, it is commonly used as bait.
> I spent two hours in the department store before it closed.

If a sentence contains more than one independent clause joined to a dependent clause, it is a **compound-complex sentence**. Here is an example.

> After I finish my research paper, I'm going to read it carefully,
> so I can make any necessary revisions.

Thinking It Through 1

Read the following sentences. Write "simple," "compound," "complex," or "compound-complex" below each sentence on the lines provided.

1. Gina ran down the block and caught the bus just in time.

_____

HINT Compound sentences have independent clauses on both sides of the conjunction.

2. You're not going to the park until you clean up your room.

_____

HINT The word *until* is a subordinating conjunction.

3. Whenever I ride in cars, I get nauseous and dizzy.

_____

4. Stephanie works long hours, yet she always has time for her family.

_____

5. Although the test was hard, T.J. had studied for it, so he did very well.

_____

6. Pandas are known for their distinctive black and white fur.

_____

7. Ernesto has one hour to find the tickets, or he will miss the concert.

_____

8. Since the game is expensive, we'll pool our money, and we'll share it.

_____

Some types of sentences require the use of the **comma**, so their meaning is clear. Keep the following comma rules in mind when you write.

Use a comma <u>before</u> coordinating conjunctions in compound sentences.

> Amy had no reason lie, nor was it in her nature.

> Fire drills are important, for they could save one's life.

> The new skating rink is enormous, and it is open year-round.

Use a comma to separate a dependent clause that leads into an independent clause in a complex or compound-complex sentence.

> Before I go to the beach, I need to find my suntan lotion.

> Unless they feel threatened, most bears will not attack humans.

> While the pasta cooks, Jerry will stir the sauce, and Raven will prepare the salad.

> When Zelda plays the drums, her parents leave the house, and her neighbors shut their windows.

Use a comma after introductory phrases, including transitional expressions, such as *therefore*, *however*, *in addition*, and *in contrast*.

> Beginning next week, I will be working part-time.

> To prevent cavities, brush your teeth and floss regularly.

> Later that year, Frederic Chopin had his first piano lesson.

> Furthermore, the mall will bring too much traffic to our town.

> However, the campgrounds will re-open on May 25.

> Therefore, the theater deserves to be a historic landmark.

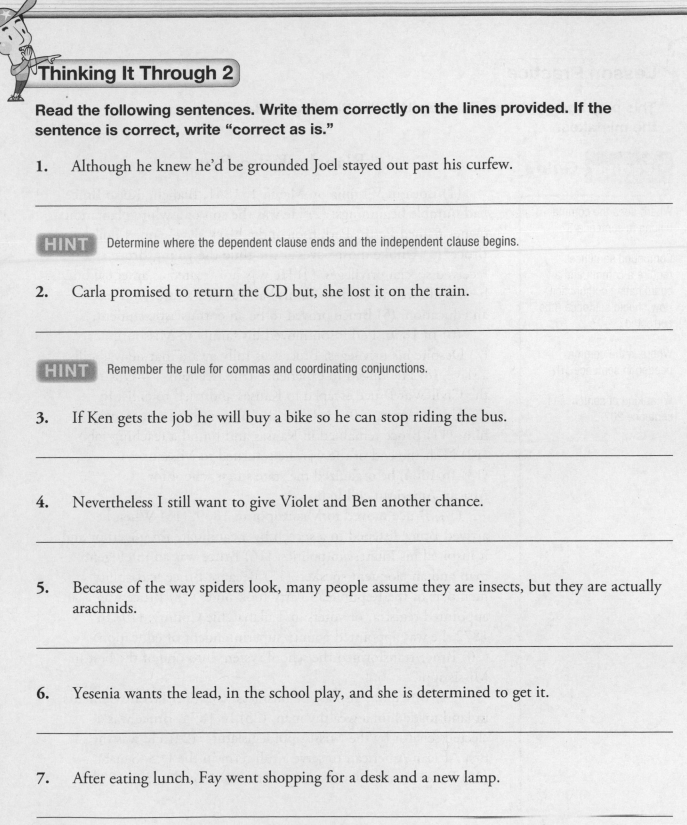

Thinking It Through 2

Read the following sentences. Write them correctly on the lines provided. If the sentence is correct, write "correct as is."

1. Although he knew he'd be grounded Joel stayed out past his curfew.

_____

HINT Determine where the dependent clause ends and the independent clause begins.

2. Carla promised to return the CD but, she lost it on the train.

_____

HINT Remember the rule for commas and coordinating conjunctions.

3. If Ken gets the job he will buy a bike so he can stop riding the bus.

_____

4. Nevertheless I still want to give Violet and Ben another chance.

_____

5. Because of the way spiders look, many people assume they are insects, but they are actually arachnids.

_____

6. Yesenia wants the lead, in the school play, and she is determined to get it.

_____

7. After eating lunch, Fay went shopping for a desk and a new lamp.

_____

8. Due to, bad weather we can't go to the park but we can make other plans.

_____

Lesson Practice

This passage contains mistakes. Use the Reading Guide to help you find the mistakes.

Reading Guide

Where does the comma belong in sentence 3?

Compound sentences require a comma and a coordinating conjunction. How should sentence 4 be corrected?

Where is the comma needed in sentence 10?

What kind of sentence is sentence 20?

Blanche Kelso Bruce

(1) Born in Virginia on March 1, 1841, Blanche Kelso Bruce had humble beginnings. (2) He was the son of a white plantation owner named Pettus Perkinson and a black slave named Polly Bruce. (3) Unlike most slaves at the time the young Bruce received special privileges. (4) He was not treated as an equal but he was allowed to study with his half-brother's tutor and receive an education. (5) Bruce proved to be an enthusiastic student.

(6) In 1850, Perkinson moved his family to Missouri. (7) Despite his privileges, Bruce was fully aware that he was still a slave. (8) He longed to experience true freedom. (9) During the Civil War Bruce escaped to Kansas and tried to enlist in the Union Army. (10) However the army refused to accept him. (11) Bruce remained in Kansas and found a teaching job. (12) Near the end of the war, he returned to Missouri. (13) In 1864, he organized the state's first school for African American children.

(14) Bruce moved to Mississippi in 1869. (15) When he arrived Bruce listened to a speech by a candidate for governor and it inspired his interest in politics. (16) Bruce was an intelligent man and an eloquent speaker. (17) Because Bruce had ability, members of the Republican Party took note. (18) Bruce was appointed registrar of voters in Tallahatchie County. (19) In 1872, he was appointed county superintendent of education. (20) Bruce transformed the school system into one of the best in Mississippi.

(21) Bruce was also a wise businessman. (22) His investments in land made him a wealthy man. (23) In 1874, Bruce was elected senator by the Mississippi legislature. (24) He was the first African American to serve a full term in the U.S. Senate. (25) Bruce remained active in politics until his death in 1898.

Answer the following questions.

1. Which version of sentence 4 is correct?

    A. He was not treated as an equal but he was allowed to study with his half-brother's tutor, and receive an education.

    B. He was not treated as an equal but, he was allowed to study with his half-brother's tutor, and receive an education.

    C. He was not treated as an equal, but he was allowed to study with his half-brother's tutor, and receive an education.

    D. He was not treated as an equal, but he was allowed to study with his half-brother's tutor and receive an education.

2. Read this sentence from the passage.

    During the Civil War Bruce escaped to Kansas and tried to enlist in the Union Army.

    Where should the comma go?

    A. after *War*

    B. after *Bruce*

    C. after *Kansas*

    D. after *War* and *Kansas*

3. Which of the following is a complex sentence?

    A. He was the son of a white plantation owner named Pettus Perkinson and a black slave named Polly Bruce.

    B. Bruce was appointed registrar of voters in Tallahatchie County.

    C. In 1864, he organized the state's first school for African American children.

    D. Because Bruce had ability, members of the Republican Party took note.

4. What is the correct way to write sentence 15?

    A. When he arrived Bruce, listened to a speech by a candidate for governor, and it inspired his interest in politics.

    B. When he arrived Bruce listened to a speech by a candidate for governor, and it inspired his interest in politics.

    C. When he arrived, Bruce listened to a speech by a candidate for governor, and it inspired his interest in politics.

    D. When he arrived, Bruce listened to a speech by a candidate, for governor and it inspired his interest in politics.

23 Punctuation, Capitalization, and Spelling

L.7.2.a, L.7.2.b

Getting the Idea

Punctuation is the set of standard marks used to clarify meaning in writing. Follow the rules below to punctuate your sentences correctly.

Use a **comma** to separate coordinate adjectives. **Coordinate adjectives** are two or more adjectives that modify a noun equally. Adjectives are coordinate if they pass either of these tests: 1) You can insert the word *and* between them. 2) You can switch the order of the adjectives without changing the meaning or creating a nonsensical statement.

Read this sentence: *The **tired, hungry** players walked off the field*. These adjectives pass both tests and are coordinate. Now read this sentence: *Emily admired the **fancy silver** watch*. These adjectives do not pass the tests. They are not coordinate and are not separated by a comma.

Use a **colon** to introduce a list when you lead into the list with an independent clause (complete sentence). For example:

>*Correct:* I got everything I needed: a shirt, new shoes, and a belt.

>*Incorrect:* I went: hiking, fishing, and swimming all summer.

Use a **semicolon** to separate two or more independent clauses that are closely related. For example:

>I'll let you know tomorrow; right now I can't decide.

Use **quotation marks** around someone else's exact words.

>"You never listen to me," Trey complained.

Use a **dash** to set off nonessential information in a sentence.

>The cheetah—the fastest land animal—can run up to 60 mph.

In this example, the information about the cheetah is set off with dashes. It would also be correct to use commas around this phrase.

Thinking It Through 1

Read the following sentences. Write them correctly on the lines provided. If the sentence is correct, write "correct as is."

1. All that was in the box was: an ugly, red shirt, a pair of socks, and a hat.

    _____

    HINT Ask yourself, does the colon introduce a complete sentence? Also, test for coordinate adjectives.

2. Dante laughed and said "I can't believe you slipped on a banana".

    _____

    HINT Review quotation marks on the previous page. Do you see any missing or misplaced punctuation in this sentence?

3. Mammals are vertebrates, this means they have a spinal column.

    _____

4. Olivia to no one's surprise—was carrying her favorite, leather bag.

    _____

5. The following: items are missing, my earrings, my wallet, and my phone.

    _____

6. "I've been writing for hours I wish I could go to sleep" Tanisha cried.

    _____

7. Tarsiers are known for their enormous, creepy eyes and long tails.

    _____

8. I'm not eating that nasty, foul-smelling soup!

    _____

Capitalization is the use of capital, or uppercase, letters in certain circumstances and situations. Follow these rules for capitalization.

Rule	Examples
proper names and titles	Neil Armstrong, Mrs. Chen, Aunt Ruthie, Dr. Callas, President Obama
geographical names	Grove Street, Pacific Ocean, Mount McKinley, Lake Superior, Poland
names of organizations	Children's Aid Society, Salvation Army, U.S. Forest Service
days of the week, months, and holidays	Monday, December, Memorial Day
major words in titles	*A Wrinkle in Time*, "The Gift of the Magi" (Do not capitalize a word like *a, the, and*, *in*, *of*, and *for* unless it is the first word in a title.)
abbreviations and acronyms	NAFTA, NASA, DNA, FBI, NBA
languages	English, Italian, Swahili, Spanish

Correct spelling is an essential part of a well-written composition. There are specific rules for spelling. For instance, put *i* before *e*, except after *c*. Like many spelling rules, there are exceptions. The best way to improve your spelling is to read often and check your spelling in a dictionary. Below is a list of words that are frequently misspelled because they are confused with words that look or sound alike.

accept, except	forth, fourth	stationery, stationary
advice, advise	hear, here	there, their, they're
affect, effect	it's, its	then, than
all ready, already	know, no	through, threw, thorough
assistants, assistance	moral, morale	two, too, to
board, bored	patience, patients	weak, week
coarse, course	personnel, personal	where, were
compliment, complement	presents, presence	whether, weather
conscience, conscious	principal, principle	whose, who's
desert, dessert	right, write	you're, your

Thinking It Through 2

Read the following sentences. Write them correctly on the lines provided. If the sentence is correct, write "correct as is."

1. Mark twain's expereinces on the Mississippi river influenced his writing.

_____

HINT Reading each word carefully can help you find spelling errors.

2. On Arbor day, our School planted a tree on franklin street.

_____

HINT Proper names should be capitalized.

3. Principle Kavanagh told students too dress warmly four the whether.

_____

4. Their are only two patience in dr. Medina's wading room write now.

_____

5. You're book report on *My Side of The Mountain* is do on friday.

_____

6. Will the students whose parents are here tonight raise their hands?

_____

7. This terible headache effects my abiliety to get thorough this book.

_____

8. The EPA is an agency that enforces pollution-control standards in the United States.

_____

This passage contains mistakes. Use the Reading Guide to help you find the mistakes.

Reading Guide

Correct the spelling and capitalization errors in sentence 5.

Rewrite sentence 10 to correct the errors.

What is wrong with sentence 18?

Rewrite sentence 22 using correct punctuation.

Mastering the Pulley

(1) The pulley is a simple machine that we use often in everyday life; for example, pulleys are used in blinds and on flagpoles. (2) Pulleys have been used for centuries to help humans survive and prosper.

(3) We know that plants need three main things to grow into healthy organisms soil, water, and sunlight. (4) However, rainfall is not allways dependable. (5) If the Spring and Summer are two dry, droughts cause crops too develop poorly. (6) Less food is harvested, and people go hungry.

(7) Watering crops is a serious problem in lands with arid climates. (8) Despite the dryness of the great sahara desert and the desserts of the Middle east, the early egyptians developed a successful irrigation system. (9) It worked so well that the kingdom became a great civilization.

(10) Little rain falls in the area, but the Nile—the world's longest River flows through Egypt. (11) Its waters fed the crops that fed the nation. (12) Moving the water from the river to the fields required great physical labor. (13) Ditches dug from the earth channeled water into the fields. (14) The system included simple, wooden doors—that acted as dams. (15) When the doors were raised, water flowed out over the fields. (16) When they were shut, work was done for the day.

(17) But what about the very hot periods when the level of the Nile dropped? (18) How did the people irrigate there fields than? (19) They used a simple pulley system that involved a lever, a leather bag, and a large stone or other heavy object. (20) By pulling and pushing on the weighted end, a worker could direct water from the river into an irrigation canal. (21) Egypt grew enough food to sell to neighboring kingdoms. (22) As one historian states Egypt was the envy of the ancient world."

Answer the following questions.

1. Which version of sentence 3 is correct?

   A. We know that plants need three main things to grow into healthy organisms: soil, water, and sunlight.

   B. We know that plants need three main things to grow into healthy organisms; soil, water, and sunlight.

   C. We know that plants need three main things to grow into healthy organisms, soil, water, and sunlight.

   D. We know that plants need three main things to grow into healthy organisms: soil; water; and sunlight.

2. Read this sentence from the passage.

   Less food is harvested, and people go hungry.

   How can this sentence be rewritten using the semicolon?

   A. Less food is harvested; and people go hungry.

   B. Less food is harvested; people go hungry.

   C. Less food is harvested; and, people go hungry.

   D. Less food is; harvested; people go hungry.

3. Which version of sentence 8 is correct?

   A. Despite the dryness of the great Sahara Desert and the Deserts of the Middle east, the early Egyptians developed a successful irrigation system.

   B. Despite the dryness of the great Sahara desert and the desserts of the Middle East, the Early Egyptians developed a successful irrigation system.

   C. Despite the dryness of the great sahara desert and the deserts of the middle East, the early Egyptians developed a successful irrigation system.

   D. Despite the dryness of the great Sahara Desert and the deserts of the Middle East, the early Egyptians developed a successful irrigation system.

4. Read this sentence from the passage.

   The system included simple, wooden doors—that acted as dams.

   How can this sentence be corrected?

   A. Change the comma to a colon.

   B. Delete the comma and the dash.

   C. Delete the dash.

   D. Delete the comma.

24 Writing Concisely

L.7.3.a, L.7.6

Getting the Idea

Choosing your words carefully is essential to good writing. Another key aspect of good writing is **conciseness**. Concise writing is direct and to the point. The opposite of conciseness is wordiness. As its name suggests, *wordiness* is the use of too many words to express an idea. You will write more concisely if you avoid words and phrases that do not contribute to the essential meaning of a sentence. Examples of these "empty" expressions are in the chart below.

at any rate	in the case of	as a matter of fact
in a very real sense	in the event that	in the process of
due to the fact that	in light of the fact that	exist

These phrases are often overused. See how the sentences below are improved when you eliminate the empty phrases.

Wordy: The water pollution that exists is out of control.
Concise: Water pollution is out of control.

Wordy: I'm angry due to the fact that you lied to me.
Concise: I'm angry because you lied to me.

Another way to be more concise is to avoid redundancies. A **redundancy** is a repetition of words or ideas. Phrases like *final completion*, *circled around*, and *join together* say the same thing twice. Read this example.

Nadia and Pam have nothing in common with each other.

The phrase *with each other* is redundant. It repeats the idea of *in common*. Rewrite it to say:

Nadia and Pam have nothing in common.

Here is another example.

Redundant: Our <u>main</u> and <u>central</u> goal is to raise students' grades.
Concise: Our central goal is to raise students' grades.

Thinking It Through 1

Read the following sentences. Write them correctly on the lines provided. If the sentence is correct, write "correct as is."

1. I'm in the process of eating right now, so I'll have to play later.

_____

HINT   The empty phrase adds nothing to the meaning of the sentence.

2. My favorite actor is writing the autobiography of his life.

_____

HINT   Think about the meaning of *autobiography*. Eliminate the redundancy.

3. I'll take a break when I'm done and finished painting my room.

_____

4. As a bonus, our company will send new subscribers a free gift.

_____

5. Due to his past history with the shop, Dean refused to take his bike there.

_____

6. Leah took her umbrella, so she would be ready if it rained.

_____

7. Marilyn's house is surrounded on all sides by huge, giant trees.

_____

8. The birthday party was an unexpected surprise for the two twin sisters.

_____

Another way to write more concise statements is to use the active voice—let the subject do the action. With **passive voice**, the subject is acted upon. Passive voice often leads to wordiness.

> *Passive:* The art work was created by Jacqueline.
> *Active:* Jacqueline <u>created</u> the artwork.

The **active voice** makes the sentence shorter and more direct. You can write more concisely by choosing strong verbs, as well. Read the sentences below.

> *Wordy:* The recipe <u>involves the use of</u> a fresh lemon.
> *Concise:* The recipe <u>requires</u> a fresh lemon.

> *Wordy:* The article <u>has to do with</u> the American Civil War.
> *Concise:* The article <u>discusses</u> the American Civil War.

Note that the revised sentences use more precise verbs. Wordiness also occurs when ideas are repeated from one sentence to the next. Combine sentences to be more concise.

> Penguins are flightless seabirds. There are seventeen species of penguins. Penguins live mainly in the southern hemisphere.

Notice the constant repetition of *penguins*. Here's one way to revise.

> There are seventeen species of penguins, flightless seabirds that live mainly in the southern hemisphere.

Another way to eliminate wordiness is to reduce clauses that begin with *who*, *which*, or *that* when these are unnecessary. Read these sentences.

> *Wordy:* Mount Rushmore, <u>which is</u> a national monument, is located in South Dakota.
> *Concise:* Mount Rushmore, a national monument, is located in South Dakota.

> *Wordy:* The store threw a party for the people <u>who had won</u> the contest.
> *Concise:* The store threw a party for the contest winners.

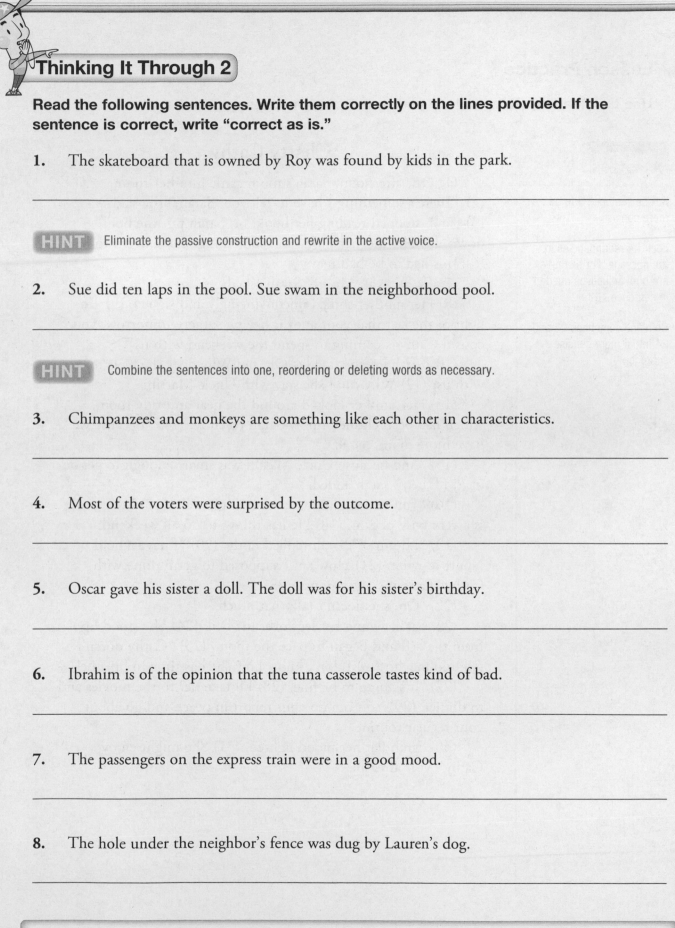

Thinking It Through 2

Read the following sentences. Write them correctly on the lines provided. If the sentence is correct, write "correct as is."

1. The skateboard that is owned by Roy was found by kids in the park.

    _____

    HINT Eliminate the passive construction and rewrite in the active voice.

2. Sue did ten laps in the pool. Sue swam in the neighborhood pool.

    _____

    HINT Combine the sentences into one, reordering or deleting words as necessary.

3. Chimpanzees and monkeys are something like each other in characteristics.

    _____

4. Most of the voters were surprised by the outcome.

    _____

5. Oscar gave his sister a doll. The doll was for his sister's birthday.

    _____

6. Ibrahim is of the opinion that the tuna casserole tastes kind of bad.

    _____

7. The passengers on the express train were in a good mood.

    _____

8. The hole under the neighbor's fence was dug by Lauren's dog.

    _____

Use the Reading Guide to help you understand the passage.

Chatty Cathy

Reading Guide

Revise sentence 5 to be more concise.

Look for redundancies in the passage. For example, are both adjectives needed in sentence 16?

Combine sentences 23 and 24 into a more concise sentence.

(1) One afternoon, Sarah's mom came into her room. (2) "There's something I have to tell you, Sarah," she said. (3) Sarah stopped reading her book. (4) Sarah put the book down. (5) Her mother's tone was something of a concern to her. (6) This had to be bad news.

(7) "What is it, Mom?" Sarah asked.

(8) Her mother smiled unconvincingly and sighed. (9) "In light of the fact that your aunt is having surgery tomorrow, your cousin Cathy is coming to spend the weekend with us."

(10) Sarah groaned. (11) "Oh, no! Why does she have to stay with us? (12) Why can't she stay with Uncle Martin?"

(13) Her mother looked around the neat and tidy room, which had been cleaned up by Sarah recently. (14) "Because we have more room, Sarah."

(15) "And because Uncle Martin was smart enough to get out of it, I'll bet," Sarah added.

(16) "You're being unjust and unfair, Sarah. (17) Your uncle is a very busy person. (18) He has things to do all weekend."

(19) "I do, too!" Sarah replied hotly. (20) "I have a book report to write. (21) How am I supposed to get it done with Cathy chattering away nonstop?"

(22) "Oh, she doesn't talk that much."

(23) Sarah swung her legs over the bed. (24) She stood up from the bed and began to pace the room. (25) "Cathy doesn't talk too much? (26) I don't know how she has time to breathe!"

(27) "It's going to be fine. (28) I'll take her to the movies and to dinner. (29) You can do your report in peace and go about your regular routine."

(30) Sarah felt her mood lighten. (31) She might enjoy Cathy's visit after all.

Answer the following questions.

1. Which is the BEST way to combine sentences 3 and 4?

    A. After she stopped reading, Sarah put the book down.

    B. Sarah stopped the book she was reading and put it down.

    C. Sarah stopped reading and put her book down.

    D. Sarah stopped reading her book, and she put it down.

2. Which is the BEST way to make sentence 9 more concise?

    A. "Because your aunt is having surgery tomorrow, your cousin Cathy is spending the weekend with us."

    B. "Since your aunt is having surgery tomorrow, your cousin is coming to spend the weekend with us."

    C. "Because of the fact that your aunt is having surgery, your cousin Cathy is spending the weekend with us."

    D. "Due to the fact that your aunt is having surgery tomorrow, cousin Cathy is coming to spend the weekend."

3. Read this sentence from the passage.

    Her mother looked around the neat and tidy room, which had been cleaned up by Sarah recently.

    Which is the BEST way to revise this sentence?

    A. Her mother looked around the clean room, which Sarah had recently made neat and tidy.

    B. Her mother looked around the tidy room Sarah had recently cleaned.

    C. Her mother looked around the neat room, which had been cleaned up by Sarah recently.

    D. Her mother looked around the tidy room, cleaned up neatly by Sarah recently.

4. Which phrase from the passage is redundant?

    A. pace the room

    B. time to breathe

    C. mood lighten

    D. regular routine

25 Finding Word Meanings

L.7.4.a, L.7.4.c, L7.4.d, L.7.6, RH.7.4, RST.7.4

Getting the Idea

When you read, you often come across unfamiliar words. One of the simplest ways to learn their meanings is to use a dictionary. However, you may not always have one at hand. An effective strategy for figuring out the meaning of a word is to use context. **Context** is the words and sentences surrounding a particular word in a text. Read the sentence below.

> You have to stop being so <u>impetuous</u> and start thinking things through before you act.

Suppose you do not know what *impetuous* means. The context suggests that someone who is impetuous does not think things through before acting. You figure out that *impetuous* means "to act rashly or hastily."

Many words in the English language have more than one meaning. Context can help you determine how a multiple-meaning word is being used in a sentence. Read the sentence below.

> Liam could not <u>recall</u> where he had last seen his helmet.

The word *recall* can be a noun, as in a company's *recall* of an unsafe product. In this sentence, though, it is used as a verb. The verb *recall* has several meanings, including "restore," "take back or revoke," or "remember." Try each meaning in the sentence. As you see, only the meaning "remember" makes sense. The word's function in the sentence helped you figure out the meaning.

Using context can help you determine the meaning of words in historical and scientific texts. Read this sentence from a history book.

> Tired of being <u>disenfranchised</u>, women fought a long battle to win the right to vote.

Based on the second half of the sentence, you might guess that *disenfranchised* means "deprived of the right to vote." But what if your guess is wrong? Perhaps *disenfranchised* means "disrespected" or "ignored." Key words in textbooks are usually listed in a **glossary** at the back of the book. First, check the glossary to see if *disenfranchised* is defined. If the word is not in the glossary, use a dictionary to verify the meaning. In fact, *disenfranchised* does mean "deprived of the right to vote."

A **dictionary** is an essential tool for finding word meanings. Read this sample entry.

---

ag•gra•vate \á-grə-vāt\ *v.***1.** to make worse or more troublesome **2.** to rouse to exasperation or anger [Latin *aggravāre*, *aggravāt-* : *ad-* + *gravāre*, to burden (from *gravis*, heavy)]

The entry tells you the word's pronunciation, part of speech (verb), definitions, and origin (the information in brackets).

Thinking It Through

Read the following paragraph, and then answer the question that follows.

An ectotherm is an animal whose body temperature depends on external sources, such as sunlight. Thus, it changes depending on the temperature of the environment. In this way, ectotherms are different from endotherms. Ectotherms are sometimes called "cold-blooded" and include amphibians and reptiles. Examples of endotherms are birds and mammals.

What is an endotherm?

_____

_____

_____

 HINT   Use context clues to figure out the meaning of this scientific term.

Read the passage and answer the questions.

Cartography, or mapmaking, has been practiced for many centuries. Ptolemy, a Greek man skilled in the sciences and mathematics, created maps around 150 CE. During the Renaissance, a period from around the 14th through 16th century, cartographers created maps from Ptolemy's writings. None of Ptolemy's actual maps were <u>extant</u> during the Renaissance. Cartographers created maps based on reconstructions of Ptolemy's writings. These early maps look very different from modern maps of the world. The land formations are much larger. Bodies of water are different. The words are written in Latin. Limited knowledge of Earth was an <u>impediment</u> for early mapmakers. They did not know all of the world's features. In modern times, satellites allow people to make very accurate maps. Cartography has advanced greatly over thousands of years. Maps give us pictures of the world we live in and our place in it.

1. The word <u>extant</u> MOST LIKELY means

   A. still in existence.

   B. in bad shape.

   C. exaggerated.

   D. missing.

    Read the surrounding sentences and use context to figure out the meaning.

2. What does the word <u>impediment</u> MOST LIKELY mean?

   A. an obstacle

   B. an advantage

   C. a surprise

   D. an impossibility

    Replace *impediment* with each answer choice. Choose the one that best fits the meaning of the sentence.

Lesson Practice

Use the Reading Guide to help you understand the passage.

Reading Guide

Several unfamiliar words are underlined in the passage. Use the context clues surrounding each of the words to figure out its meaning.

Read paragraph 7 carefully. Based on the context, what do you think the word *exorbitant* means?

The Game

Roberto was walking home from school when he felt a tap on his shoulder. He turned around to find Christopher standing behind him with a friendly smile on his face.

Christopher was in eighth grade. Roberto was only in seventh. Everyone in school knew Christopher. He wore the coolest clothes and played on the football team. When Christopher talked, people listened; when he laughed, people laughed with him. He had never spoken to Roberto before. So, Roberto was <u>flabbergasted</u> that Christopher actually wanted to talk to him. He couldn't help wondering if Christopher had confused him with someone else.

"Oh, hi, Christopher."

"Hey, Roberto," Christopher said, never losing the smile.

Roberto could not believe that Christopher even knew his name. "What's up?" he asked, trying to appear <u>nonchalant</u>. He didn't want Christopher to realize that this was a big deal for him.

"I heard a rumor that you just got Secret Mission 2. Is that true? The first Secret Mission is my favorite game."

Roberto nodded. Secret Mission had set video game sales <u>records</u> two years ago. It had been so popular that the company had created a sequel. When it had gone on sale last week, people had stood outside video game stores for hours looking for the chance to buy the game. It had sold out almost immediately in most stores. Now it was practically impossible to get, unless someone was willing to pay an <u>exorbitant</u> price. Luckily for Roberto, his father worked in a video game store and had set a copy aside for him.

"I do have it. It's awesome!"

"Man!" Christopher exclaimed. "I would love to try it out." He paused. "Listen, I know we don't normally hang out or anything, but do you think I could come by your house later, maybe around five o'clock, and play it for a while? If you're not going to be too busy, that is."

What does the word *commenced* in paragraph 15 most likely mean? Use the rest of the sentence to help you figure it out.

In paragraph 15, the phrase *barely acknowledged* him gives you a clue to the meaning of the word *halfhearted*.

Other kinds of context clues include antonyms and synonyms. For example, in the last paragraph, the word *forceful* is a synonym of *assertive*. Look up the word *assertive* in a dictionary to verify its meaning.

Roberto's face lit up. Christopher Johnson hanging out at his house? Roberto was <u>elated</u> at the thought. Wait until everybody found out! "Sure!" Roberto answered. Then, forcing himself to appear less enthusiastic, he added, "If you want."

"Great," Christopher responded. "You live in Anthony's building, right?" Anthony was on the football team.

"Yeah, apartment 3C."

"Okay, so I'll be there around five. Thanks, Rob."

Roberto said goodbye and hurried home, where he spent the next hour tidying up his room. He pulled down the poster of his favorite cartoon character, rolled it up, and threw it in the back of the closet. He looked at the comforter on his bed and frowned. It was a dark-blue space-rocket print. The comforter screamed "baby!" at anyone who came into the room. Did his mother think he was 9 years old? Hastily, he yanked the comforter off the bed and threw that into the closet, too.

When Christopher arrived, he was not alone. Anthony and three other boys that Roberto did not know were with him. They quickly settled in and <u>commenced</u> playing the game. Roberto tried to make conversation, but except for a few <u>halfhearted</u> nods, they barely acknowledged him. They took turns playing, never even asking Roberto if he wanted to play.

"Hey, Christopher," one of the boys said. "Is there any food around here?"

"Yeah, I'm <u>famished</u>," said another.

"Roberto," Christopher said as his fingers moved rapidly over the control pad. "You got any popcorn?"

Just then, the phone on Roberto's desk rang. Roberto glanced glumly at the invaders in his room then picked up the phone. "Hello? Oh, hi Nate!" Nate Taylor was Roberto's best friend. He listened to Nate a moment, then said loudly, "Sure, Nate, come right over. I'm not doing anything right now. We can play Secret Mission 2!"

Roberto hung up the phone then turned to Christopher. "The party's over," he said in a forceful, <u>assertive</u> voice. "You can all leave now."

Answer the following questions.

1. Read this sentence from the passage.

   So, Roberto was <u>flabbergasted</u> that Christopher actually wanted to talk to him.

   The context clues in the paragraph suggest that <u>flabbergasted</u> MOST LIKELY means

   A. dismayed.

   B. embarrassed.

   C. astonished.

   D. frustrated.

2. What is the MOST LIKELY definition of <u>nonchalant</u>?

   A. nervous

   B. casual

   C. confused

   D. excited

3. Read this sentence from the passage.

   Secret Mission had set video game sales <u>records</u> two years ago.

   Which dictionary meaning of <u>records</u> does the author use in this sentence?

   A. an account of information or facts

   B. the known history of a performance or an activity

   C. an unsurpassed, or unmatched, measurement

   D. a disk designed to be played on a phonograph

4. The word <u>elated</u> MOST LIKELY means

   A. overjoyed.

   B. disturbed.

   C. frightened.

   D. relaxed.

5. What does the word <u>famished</u> mean? Explain how context helps you figure it out.

   _____

   _____

   _____

   _____

   _____

   _____

26 Roots and Affixes

L.7.4.b

Getting the Idea

Understanding the parts of a word can help you figure out its meaning. The **root** is the main part of a word. For example, consider the word *invisible*. In this word, the root is *vis*. It comes from the Latin verb *video,* which means "to see." The root has additional parts attached to it. An **affix** is one or more letters attached to the beginning or end of a root. Affixes change the meaning of the root. A **prefix** is an affix added to the beginning of a word. The prefix in *invisible* is *in-*, which means "not." A **suffix** is an affix added to the end of a word. The suffix in *invisible* is *-ible*, which means "capable of." When you put all of the parts together, you figure out that *invisible* means "not capable of being seen."

Many of the roots and affixes found in English words come from Greek and Latin. The charts below list commonly used Greek and Latin roots.

Greek Roots

Root	Meaning	Examples
bene	good, well	benefit, benevolent
demos	people	demographics, democracy
gen	birth	generation, genetics
graph	write	graphics, graphite
hydr	water	dehydrate, hydrant
meter	measure	thermometer, diameter
phon	sound	phonics, symphony

Latin Roots

Root	Meaning	Examples
corp/corpus	body	corporation, corpuscle
cred	believe	incredible, credulous
frater	brother	fraternity, fraternize
magna/magni	great, large	magnificent, magnitude
mater/matri	mother	maternal, matrimony
omni	all	omniscient, omnivore
tempo	time	temporary, temporal

The charts below list prefixes and suffixes and show how they change the meaning of root words.

Prefixes

Prefix	Meaning	Examples
ambi-	both	ambidextrous, ambiguity
anti-	against	antibacterial, antifreeze
ex-	out	expel, exhale
mono-	single, one	monopoly, monologue
multi-	many	multigrain, multitask
peri-	around	perimeter, periscope
pseudo-	false	pseudonym, pseudopod

Suffixes

Suffix	Meaning	Examples
-able, -ible	worthy, capable of	laughable, flexible
-cian	having a skill	mathematician, magician
-fy	to make	fortify, liquefy
-ic	relating to	poetic, historic
-ity	state of, quality	clarity, equality
-ness	state of, quality	coarseness, forgiveness
-ure	act or process	exposure, legislature

Thinking It Through

Read the following paragraph, and then answer the questions that follow.

An oxide is a chemical compound in which oxygen is combined with another element. Some oxides are humanmade, but some occur naturally, such as carbon dioxide. Oxides are also found in water, sand, and quartz. They are also a part of carbon <u>monoxide</u>, a poisonous gas that is produced when certain fuels are not completely burned.

What is the prefix in the word <u>monoxide</u>? Based on that, how many atoms of oxygen are MOST LIKELY in each molecule of carbon monoxide?

 HINT   Look back at the chart of prefixes. What does the prefix *mono* mean?

Coached Example

Read the passage and answer the questions.

Throughout history, most cultures have traced their roots through the father's line of descendants. A person's lineage would follow the path of the father, the grandfather, the great-grandfather, and so on. Often, the mother's line of descendants was completely ignored. Today, it is still common for brides to take the surnames of their husbands.

Interestingly, some Native American tribes were <u>matrilineal</u> societies. Iroquois women played important roles in their tribes. They performed traditional duties, including making clothing and taking care of the children. However, they also organized agricultural labor. Colonial women were <u>excluded</u> from political meetings. Iroquois women not only attended meetings, they also selected the men who would represent each tribe at village councils. The women also had the power to remove the men from their position if they did not fulfill their duties. The Iroquois mother was the head of her family. She ran the household and arranged her children's marriages. When a couple was married, the man came to live in the longhouse of his wife's family.

---

1. What does the word <u>matrilineal</u> mean?

   A. managed by women

   B. resembling a woman

   C. traced through the mother's line

   D. traced through the father's line

   HINT Use your knowledge of the root *matri* and the information in the passage to figure out the meaning of the word.

2. The word <u>exclude</u> means to

   A. involve.

   B. request.

   C. invite.

   D. keep out.

   HINT Think about the meaning of the prefix *ex-*.

Lesson Practice

Use the Reading Guide to help you understand the passage.

Reading Guide

Prefixes are attached to the beginnings of root words. Suffixes are attached to the ends of root words. Both affixes change the meaning of the root words.

In paragraph 1, how does the prefix change the meaning of the word *impossible*?

Identify the suffix in the word *climatic* in paragraph 2. What does the suffix mean? Based on the root word, *climate*, what does *climatic* mean?

excerpted and adapted from

Rip Van Winkle

by Washington Irving

The great error in Rip's character was an intense dislike of all kinds of <u>profitable</u> labor. It could not be from the lack of trying or determination; for he would sit on a wet rock and fish all day without a murmur, even though he should not be encouraged by a single nibble. He would carry a fowling-piece on his shoulder for hours, trudging through woods and swamps, and up hill and down dale, to shoot a few squirrels or wild pigeons. He would never refuse to assist a neighbor even in the roughest toil, and was a foremost man at all country frolics for husking Indian corn or building stone-fences. The women of the village, too, used to employ him to run a multitude of errands, and to do such little odd jobs as their less obliging husbands would not do for them. In a word, Rip was ready to attend to anybody's business but his own; but as to doing family duty, and keeping his farm in order, he found it <u>impossible</u>.

In fact, he declared it was of no use to work on his farm; it was the most troublesome little piece of ground in the whole country; everything about it went wrong, and would go wrong, in spite of him. His fences were continually falling to pieces; his cow would either go astray, or get among the cabbages; weeds were sure to grow quicker in his fields than anywhere else; the rain always made a point of setting in just as he had some outdoor work to do. Even under the ideal <u>climatic</u> conditions, something was bound to go wrong. Thus, his estate had dwindled away under his management until there was little more left than a mere patch of Indian corn and potatoes.

His children, too, were as ragged and wild as if they belonged to nobody. His son Rip, who bore a striking resemblance to his father, promised to inherit the habits, with the old clothes of his father. He was generally seen trooping like a colt at his mother's heels, giggling instead of doing chores, and equipped in a pair of his father's cast-off breeches, which he had much ado to hold up with one hand.

Find the word *adversity* in paragraph 4. The word *adverse* is an adjective that means "difficult." The addition of the suffix *-ity* makes the word a noun, meaning "state of being difficult."

Find two words with the suffix *-ness* in paragraph 4? What do the words mean?

Find the word *console* in the last paragraph. If you add the suffix *-able* to the word, what does the new word mean?

Which two words in the last sentence of the passage contain a suffix that means "without"? What is the root of each word?

Rip Van Winkle, however, was one of those happy mortals who takes the world easy, eats white bread or brown, whichever can be got with least thought or trouble, and would rather starve on a penny than work for a pound. He faced <u>adversity</u> with a carefree heart. If left to himself, he would have whistled life away in perfect contentment; but his wife kept continually dinning in his ears about his <u>idleness</u>, his carelessness, and the ruin he was bringing on his family. She would <u>magnify</u> even the most trivial of matters many times over.

Morning, noon, and night, her tongue was constantly going, and everything he said or did was sure to earn him a thorough scolding. Rip knew that nothing could <u>pacify</u> his wife, so he had but one way of replying to all lectures of the kind, and that had grown into a habit. He shrugged his shoulders, shook his head, cast up his eyes, but said nothing. This, however, always stirred up a fresh volley from his wife; so that he was glad to draw off his forces, and take to the outside of the house after dinner—the only side which, in truth, belongs to a hen-pecked husband.

Times grew worse and worse with Rip Van Winkle as years of matrimony rolled on; a tart temper never mellows with age, and a sharp tongue is the only edged tool that grows keener by constant use. For a long while he used to <u>console</u> himself, when driven from home, by <u>fraternizing</u> with a group of men from the village. They would sit in the shade, on a long lazy summer's day, talking carelessly over village gossip, or telling endless, sleepy stories about nothing.

Answer the following questions.

1. What is the root word in <u>profitable</u>?

   A. pro

   B. fit

   C. able

   D. profit

2. Which of these words has the same suffix as <u>idleness</u>?

   A. kindness

   B. impress

   C. idyllic

   D. address

3. In the word <u>pacify</u>, the suffix means

   A. to make.

   B. against.

   C. relating to.

   D. state of.

4. Based on the root of the word <u>fraternizing</u>, Rip treated the men in the group as

   A. friends.

   B. brothers.

   C. neighbors.

   D. strangers.

5. Identify the root and the suffix in the word <u>magnify</u>, and tell what each means. Explain what <u>magnify</u> means.

   _____

   _____

   _____

   _____

   _____

   _____

   _____

   _____

27 Denotation and Connotation

L.7.5.b, L.7.5.c

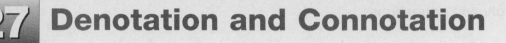

Getting the Idea

Denotation is what a word literally means, or how it would be defined in a dictionary. **Connotation** is the emotional weight a word carries, or the set of associations implied by the word. Read these sentences.

> Russell is a very careful editor. He is known in the company for being <u>thorough</u>.

Based on the word *thorough*, you probably have a positive image of Russell. Now, substitute the word *fastidious* in this sentence. Both words have a similar denotation. They describe a person who is very careful and pays attention to small details. However, *fastidious* also means "someone who is excessively careful to the point of fussiness."

If you were to look up the word *thorough* in a thesaurus, you would see the word *fastidious* listed as a **synonym**. But words with similar denotations can have different connotations. This is why it is important to consider not only what a word literally means, but the ideas it implies. Words are said to have neutral, positive, and negative connotations. The words below all have the denotation of "to converse," but think about their associated meanings as you read these sentences.

> Audra <u>talked</u> with her neighbors outside her building.
> Audra <u>chatted</u> with her neighbors outside her building.
> Audra <u>gossiped</u> with her neighbors outside her building.

The word *talked* is neutral. It has neither positive nor negative connotations. The word *chatted* is positive. It connotes a sense of ease and familiarity. The word *gossiped* is negative. It is associated with spreading rumors about personal matters.

If you think about the connotation of words as you read, you will have a more precise idea of what authors are trying to tell you. Authors choose their words carefully, and when they choose one word over another, it is because they are trying to convey a particular idea. For instance, an author describes a candidate's speech as *drawn-out*. He could have chosen the synonym *long*. Both words have a similar denotation: going on for an extended period of time. By choosing *drawn-out*, the author suggests to the reader that the speech was tiresome and boring.

The chart below contains more examples of the denotations and connotations of words.

Denotation (literal meaning)	Positive Connotations	Negative Connotations
a well-developed ability to think	intelligent, brilliant, clever, bright, smart	cunning, crafty, calculating, sly
truthful in speech	candid, frank, direct, straightforward	blunt, brusque, abrupt, insensitive
firmness of purpose	strong-minded, determined, persistent	stubborn, willful, inflexible

Thinking It Through

Read the following paragraph, and then answer the question that follows.

The aardwolf is a member of the hyena family. Although it is similar in appearance to the hyena, the aardwolf is more of a runt. Also, it has weaker teeth and jaws than the hyena. The aardwolf is found primarily in eastern and southern Africa. Its diet consists of small animals and insects.

Choose a word from the paragraph that has a negative connotation. What other word or phrase could you use to change this connotation?

_____

_____

_____

HINT Think about the meaning of the word and its associations.

Read the passage and answer the questions.

excerpted and adapted from

Heroes Every Child Should Know

by Hamilton Wright Mabie

If there had been no real heroes, <u>imaginary</u> ones would have been created, for people cannot live without them. The hero is just as necessary as the farmer, the carpenter, and the doctor; society could not get on without the hero. There have been a great many different kinds of heroes. In every age and among every people, the hero has stood for the qualities that were most admired and sought after by the bravest and best.

If you want to know what the men and women of a country care for most, you must study their heroes. To the child, the hero stands for the highest success; to the grown man and woman, he or she stands for the deepest and richest life. Courage and achievement are the two signs of the hero; heroes may possess or lack many other qualities, but they must be daring and must do things, not just <u>dream</u> or talk about them.

---

1. Which synonym for <u>imaginary</u> has a negative connotation?

   A. fantasy

   B. fake

   C. pretend

   D. make-believe

   HINT Choose the word that is most closely associated with something that is false and misleading.

2. The author uses the word <u>dream</u> to connote

   A. sleep deeply.

   B. lose touch with reality.

   C. make plans without fulfilling them.

   D. let the imagination go wild.

   HINT Reread the sentence in which the word *dream* appears. Test each answer choice in the sentence.

Lesson Practice

Use the Reading Guide to help you understand the passage.

Reading Guide

Notice the author's use of the words *plant herself* in the first sentence. In this context, the phrase means that Theresa intends to work at her desk to the exclusion of all other activities.

Why does the author use the word *groans* in paragraph 3?

Think of the denotation of the word *urged*. Explain why it is the right word to use paragraph 9.

Never Say Never

Theresa's plan was to come straight home from school, close the door to her bedroom, and plant herself at her desk for at least four hours. She wouldn't get up or take any phone calls and certainly wouldn't turn on the television. She'd have to eat dinner. But Theresa <u>vowed</u> to herself that it would be a quick dinner.

When the school bell rang, Theresa's math teacher said, "Don't forget to study for the test tomorrow. It's worth 20 percent of your grade."

The teacher's announcement was met by <u>groans</u> from the students. The test could cover everything they had learned in class so far. Mr. Klein refused to narrow down the types of questions that would actually be on the test.

"Oh, come on, Mr. Klein! Don't you have any hints or tips?" Josh asked.

"Sure. Study." Mr. Klein answered with a smile.

A few of the kids laughed, but Theresa maintained a <u>stony</u> expression on her face. She was more <u>resolved</u> than ever to pass the test with flying colors.

Theresa put her plan into action as soon as she left the school. She hurried home and got out her books and notebooks. "Okay," she said to herself. "It's now or never."

Just as she started looking through her notes, the phone rang. She remembered that no one was home, but she would not allow herself to get distracted. She let the answering machine pick up. After the long beep, she heard the muffled voice of her mother.

"Theresa, are you there? Please, Theresa, if you're there, pick up the phone. I have to speak to you," the voice <u>urged</u>.

Theresa frowned. She was annoyed by the interruption, but she knew she couldn't ignore her mom.

"I'd better see what she wants," Theresa said under her breath. "I'm here," she <u>snapped</u> as she picked up the receiver.

"Theresa, listen to me carefully."

Suddenly, Theresa felt a sense of unease as she <u>recognized</u> the seriousness in her mother's voice.

What is the meaning of the word *engrossed* in paragraph 15? What does the word tell you about the level of Theresa's involvement in her work?

What is the denotation of *frantic* in paragraph 16? How does this word add to the mood at this point in the story?

Does the word *cramming* in paragraph 19 have a positive or negative connotation? Compare its connotation with that of related words such as *studying, preparing,* and *prepping.*

In the last paragraph, what feeling does the author create by using the word *sprinted*? Would the words *walked* or ran be as effective?

"You need to get to the hospital. It's your brother," she said tearfully.

"What happened?" Theresa asked, forgetting all about the Pythagorean Theorem that had so <u>engrossed</u> her a few minutes ago.

"Reggie's broken his leg. It happened at soccer practice," her mother sobbed, her voice becoming <u>frantic</u>.

"Is he going to be okay?" Theresa asked, feeling emotions she didn't think she could feel for her pesky brother.

"We spoke to the doctor. He says it's too early to tell. You know your father's out of town on a business trip. And I can't get to the hospital for another hour. Your brother needs you, Theresa. The hospital is only ten minutes away from our house. Please go to him and stay there until I can get there."

For a split second Theresa contemplated her test the next day. All she had thought about for the past week was <u>cramming</u> enough information into her head to do well on the test. And now on the eve of the test, she would likely spend hours at the hospital.

Then she recalled her father's words. "Family comes first," he always said. So she might not ace the test. She had studied long and hard for it already. She pictured her brother lying in a hospital bed, frightened and alone. How could she leave him by himself while she stayed in her room, her face buried in books?

"Of course, Mom. I'll leave right away. I'll call you when I get to the hospital."

"Thanks, sweetheart," her mother said. Her voice reflected the weight that had been lifted off her shoulders.

Theresa hung up the phone and grabbed her house keys. Then she had an idea. She went into her brother's room. Quickly, she rummaged through his desk until she found two of his favorite comic books. With these in hand, she <u>sprinted</u> out the front door.

Answer the following questions.

1. The author uses the word <u>vowed</u> in paragraph 1 to connote

   A. the difficulty of studying for tests.

   B. the problem with skipping meals.

   C. Theresa's lack of interest in dinner.

   D. the seriousness of Theresa's attitude.

2. Read this sentence from the passage.

   "I'm here," she <u>snapped</u> as she picked up the receiver.

   In the sentence, the word <u>snapped</u> adds a feeling of

   A. fear.

   B. surprise.

   C. impatience.

   D. sadness.

3. The denotation of <u>resolved</u> is

   A. reminded.

   B. determined.

   C. frightened.

   D. uncertain.

4. Read this sentence from the passage.

   Suddenly, Theresa felt a sense of unease as she <u>recognized</u> the seriousness in her mother's voice.

   What is the denotation of <u>recognized</u> in this sentence?

   A. became aware of

   B. failed to notice

   C. was familiar with

   D. accepted officially

5. What does the author suggest by describing Theresa's expression as <u>stony</u>?

   _____

   _____

   _____

   _____

   _____

   _____

4 Cumulative Assessment for Lessons 21–27

The following passage contains mistakes. Read the passage and answer the questions that follow.

First Day

(1) Holly stood at the cash register, ringing up an order for a customer. (2) "Excuse me, sir," she asked reluctantly. (3) "I'm sorry, but if you wouldn't mind, uh…umm…"

(4) "Yes, what is it, young lady?" the man snapped impatiently. (5) He glanced conspicuously at his watch.

(6) "What kind of vegetable is this?" Holly finally managed to ask. (7) She didn't have a clue what it was.

(8) "Why, it's okra of course," the man answered, visibly annoyed. (9) He violently zipped up his sweatshirt, as if he thought that preparing to go back outside would speed up the process.

(10) "Thank you, sir. I mean, I'm sorry, sir," Holly stammered. (11) "It's just that it's my first day on the job, and I'm still learning." (12) Her voice faded as she looked back at the man, whose expresion was anything but sympathetic.

(13) Holly's first day as a cashier at the Fresh meadows grocery store wasn't going too well so far. (14) The okra incident was simply one in a series of botched checkout attempts. (15) First, she had miscounted some change, and the customer—thank goodness she was honest pointed out that Holly had given her an extra five dollars. (16) Then as she was bagging an order, the plastic bag slit down the middle, sending a large jar of pickles crashing to the floor.

(17) "How's it going, Holly?" she heard a voice say behind her. (18) She turned to see her friend Connor start bagging the order she was ringing up.

(19) "Oh, hi, Connor," she said distractedly, searching desperately through her laminated handbook for the code for broccoli.

(20) "Looks like you're a little stressed," he said with a smile. (21) "You're doing great for your first day."

(22) "Um, right, thanks," Holly answered, still trying to find the elusive code.

(23) "Miss!" an elderly lady shouted as she tapped Holly on the shoulder. (24) "I know it's $1.99 a pound. (25) Does that help you?"

(26) "Thank you, but I need to input the code," Holly answered with a thin smile. (27) She kept scanning the book and finally found it: 6040. (28) Her fingers couldn't type the numbers into the register fast enough. (29) She shot a look down the line at her register and saw three more customers who looked irritated and annoyed.

(30) "Just relax," she heard Connor say as he moved to the register next to hers to bag the groceries. (31) Although she appreciated Connor's support, Holly was frustrated.

(32) "Easy for him to say," she thought to herself. (33) Taking a deep breath, a big smile was plastered across her face to greet the next customer. (34) Holly was determined to try her best. (35) She was sure of one thing: it was going to be a long shift.

---

1. Read this sentence from the passage.

   Her voice faded as she looked back at the man, whose expresion was anything but sympathetic.

   Which word is spelled incorrectly?

   A. faded

   B. expresion

   C. anything

   D. sympathetic

2. Which version of sentence 13 is correct?

   A. Holly's first day as a cashier at the Fresh meadows Grocery Store wasn't going too well so far.

   B. Holly's first day as a Cashier at the fresh Meadows grocery store wasn't going too well so far.

   C. Holly's first day as a cashier at the fresh meadows grocery store wasn't going too well so far.

   D. Holly's first day as a cashier at the Fresh Meadows Grocery Store wasn't going too well so far.

3. Read this sentence from the passage.

   First, she had miscounted some change, and the customer— thank goodness she was honest pointed out that Holly had given her an extra five dollars.

   What is wrong with this sentence?

   A. It is missing a semicolon.

   B. It is missing a dash.

   C. It does not need a dash.

   D. The commas are in the wrong place.

4. Which is the BEST way to revise sentence 29?

   A. She shot a look down the line at her register and saw three more irritated customers.

   B. She shot a look down the line at her register and saw three more customers looking irritated and annoyed.

   C. She shot a look down the register and saw three more customers, irritated and annoyed.

   D. She shot a look down the line and saw three more irritated, annoyed customers.

5. Which sentence from the passage is a complex sentence?

   A. The okra incident was simply one in a series of botched checkout attempts.

   B. Holly stood at the cash register, ringing up an order for a customer.

   C. Although she appreciated Connor's support, Holly was frustrated.

   D. She kept scanning the book and finally found it: 6040.

6. Which sentence corrects the dangling modifier in sentence 33?

   A. Taking a deep breath and plastering a big smile on her face, ready to greet the next customer.

   B. Taking a deep breath, her face had a big smile plastered across it to greet the next customer.

   C. Taking a deep breath, Holly plastered a big smile across her face to greet the next customer.

   D. Taking a deep breath, the next customer plastered a big smile across Holly's face.

Read the passage and answer the questions that follow.

Music Videos from the 1920s?

Music videos are part of daily life in the 21st century. There are numerous networks whose primary programming is dedicated to music videos. Music videos began in the early part of the 20th century. Granted, MTV came on the air in the 1980s, but the roots of music videos started at least fifty years earlier in the form of movies made to promote record releases. Music videos began as a marketing <u>strategy</u> to sell music, and though there have been many changes in the content and the number of videos, their primary purpose is still to sell music.

A man named Oskar Fischinger is often credited with inspiring the art form that would evolve into music videos. Fischinger was born in Germany in 1900. As a teenager, Fischinger developed an interest in incorporating animation into interpretations of music and verse. In 1920, he began creating his first short films. By the end of the year, he was creating short animated films to help sell new released records. In the late 1920s, Fischinger created special effects for a feature film called *The Woman in the Moon*, a science fiction silent film.

By the end of the decade, short films were completely set to music. Music was an important component of silent movies. The actors did not speak; their dialogue appeared in print on the screen. Music helped create the mood of the scene. For example, sad violin music played in the background as a man bid farewell to his beloved wife. Dance music accompanied a scene set in a ballroom. In 1930–31, Fischinger produced a black-and-white film titled *Study No. 7*. This three-minute film was set to composer Johannes Brahms's *Hungarian Dance No. 5*. In 1936, Fischinger's short film *Allegretto* showed colorful oval and diamond shapes performing ballet moves to the music of composer Ralph Rainger.

Over time, music and movies became <u>inseparable</u>. This did not change when sound was added to movies and the audience could hear what the actors were saying. In the 1930s, performers were taped singing and playing their songs. Sometimes a bouncing ball appeared over the words of the song on the movie screen. Movie theater audiences sang along, much like modern-day karaoke. Even before there was a television in every home, music videos were being produced.

However, it wasn't until the Beatles that modern music videos began to take shape. The Beatles were a tremendously popular 1960s band who made feature-length movies based on their albums. The movie *Yellow Submarine*, for example, was an animated feature film that showcased the band's music. The songs appeared in the soundtrack of the same name. The hit film helped promote the band and boosted sales of the album. The Beatles also made short videos of their songs to be played like commercials on television. This idea helped to create record-setting album sales and even inspired a television show called *The Monkees*. This television show featured segments set to songs by the band. These musical segments were the <u>prototypes</u> of modern videos.

In June of 1981, the USA network aired the first television show dedicated to music videos. At this time, the artists and performers were starting to use more than just taped live performances. The videos had plots, themes, and ideas that were <u>independent</u> from the group performing the song. Two months later, MTV was launched and videos took their place in music history. Music videos are their own art form, yet they typically remain secondary to the song. However, some music videos actually manage to <u>surpass</u> the song because of a creative story line, computer graphics, or other hook that is particular to the video but not the song. Many contemporary artists owe their success to the popularity of their music videos. Additionally, some people have made very successful careers out of writing, producing, and directing music videos.

Today, there are many television channels that play music videos, including channels dedicated to specific genres, like heavy metal, blues, pop, rock, or country. These channels may also carry television shows aimed at the most likely audience for that type of music. Music videos appeal to both our visual and auditory senses, thus providing double the entertainment. They are an exciting part of the music industry, but their roots go back to an earlier era in which people may not have <u>envisioned</u> that music videos would become such an important part of pop culture.

7. Which word related to <u>strategy</u> has a negative connotation?

    A. approach

    B. scheme

    C. method

    D. plan

8. What is the root word in <u>inseparable</u>?

    A. in

    B. able

    C. parable

    D. separate

9. What does the word <u>surpass</u> MOST LIKELY mean?

    A. resemble

    B. ruin

    C. outshine

    D. surprise

10. Based on context, the word <u>envisioned</u> MOST LIKELY means

    A. imagined.

    B. doubted.

    C. wished.

    D. cared.

11. If the prefix <u>proto</u> means "first" or "earliest," explain how musical segments of the 1960s were the "prototypes of modern videos."

_____

_____

_____

_____

_____

_____

12. Read this sentence from the passage.

> **The videos had plots, themes, and ideas that were <u>independent</u> from the group performing the song.**

Explain the denotation of <u>independent</u> as it is used in this sentence.

_____

_____

_____

_____

_____

_____

_____

**Crosswalk Coach for the
Common Core State Standards,
English Language Arts, Grade 7**

SUMMATIVE ASSESSMENT
FOR CHAPTERS 1–4

Name: _____

Session 1

Read the passage and answer the questions that follow.

The Emperor's New Clothes
adapted from the original by Hans Christian Andersen

Many, many years ago lived an emperor who thought so much of new clothes that he spent all his money in order to obtain them. He changed his clothes almost every hour and loved to show them off to his people.

One day, two swindlers came to his city. They told the people that they were weavers, and declared they could manufacture the finest cloth to be imagined. Their colors and patterns, they claimed, were not only exceptionally beautiful, but the clothes made of their material possessed the wonderful quality of being invisible to any man who was unfit for his office or incredibly stupid.

"If I were to be dressed in a suit made of this cloth," thought the emperor, "I should be able to find out which men in my empire were clever or stupid. I must have this cloth woven for me without delay." He gave a large sum of money to the swindlers, in advance. They set up two looms and pretended to be very hard at work, but they did nothing whatsoever on the looms. They asked for the finest silk and the most precious gold-cloth; all they received they kept for themselves. They worked at the empty looms until late at night.

Soon the emperor wished to check on the weavers' progress. But he felt rather uneasy when he remembered that he who was not fit for his office could not see it. "I shall send my honest old minister to the weavers," thought the emperor. "He can judge best how the suit looks, for he is intelligent, and nobody understands his office better than he."

The good old minister visited the swindlers as they sat before the empty looms. He tried his very best, but he could see nothing, for there was nothing to be seen. "Oh dear," he thought, "can I be so stupid? Is it possible that I am not fit for my office? No, no, I cannot say that I was unable to see the cloth."

"Oh, it is exceedingly beautiful," the old minister told the weavers. "What a beautiful pattern, what brilliant colors! I shall tell the emperor that I like the cloth very much."

Now the swindlers asked for more money, silk, and gold-cloth, which they required for weaving. They kept everything for themselves, and not a thread came near the loom.

Soon afterward, the emperor sent another honest courtier to the weavers to see how they were progressing. Like the old minister, he looked and looked but could see nothing, as there was nothing to be seen. "I am not stupid," said the man. "Therefore, I must not be fit for my appointment. It is very strange, but I must not let anyone know it." He praised the cloth to the emperor.

Everybody in the whole town talked about the precious cloth. At last the emperor wished to see it himself. With a number of courtiers, including the two who had already been there, he went to see the two clever swindlers.

"Is it not magnificent?" said the two old statesmen who had been there before. "Your Majesty must admire the colors and the pattern." Then they pointed to the empty looms, for they imagined the others could see the cloth.

"What is this?" thought the emperor. "I do not see anything at all. That is terrible! Am I stupid? Am I unfit to be emperor?"

"Your cloth has our most gracious approval," he said, turning to the weavers. Nodding contentedly, he looked at the empty loom, for he did not like to say that he saw nothing. All his attendants, who were with him, looked and looked, and although they could not see anything more than the others, they said, like the emperor, "It is very beautiful." And all advised him to wear the new magnificent clothes at a great procession which was soon to take place.

On the night before the procession, the swindlers pretended to work and burned more than sixteen candles. At last they cried, "The emperor's new suit is ready now." The swindlers held their arms up as if they held something in their hands and said: "These are the trousers!" "This is the coat!" and "Here is the cloak!" and so on. "They are all as light as a cobweb, and one must feel as if one had nothing at all upon the body. But that is just the beauty of them."

The emperor undressed, and the swindlers pretended to put the new suit upon him, one piece after another; and the emperor looked at himself in the looking-glass from every side. "How well they look! How well they fit!" they all said. "What a beautiful pattern! What fine colors! That is a magnificent suit of clothes!"

"I am ready," said the emperor. "Does not my suit fit me marvelously?" Then he turned once more to the looking-glass, that people should think he admired his garments.

The emperor marched in the procession under a beautiful canopy, and all who saw him in the street and out of the windows exclaimed, "Indeed, the emperor's new suit is incomparable! What a long train he has! How well it fits him!" Nobody wished to let others know he saw nothing, for then he would have been unfit for his office or too stupid. Never were an emperor's clothes more admired.

"But he has nothing on at all!" said a little child at last. "Good heavens! Listen to the voice of an innocent child," said the father, and one whispered to the other what the child had said. "But he has nothing on at all!" cried everyone. That made a deep impression upon the emperor, for it seemed to him that they were right; but he thought to himself, "Now I must follow this through to the end." And the chamberlains walked with still greater dignity, as if they carried the train which did not exist.

1. People do not want to admit that they cannot see the emperor's suit because they

   A. secretly want to help the swindlers succeed.

   B. want the emperor to make a fool of himself.

   C. are worried about appearing stupid or unfit.

   D. do not want to offend the emperor.

2. What is the theme of the passage?

   A. No one should wear invisible clothes.

   B. Do not trust strangers who are new in town.

   C. Emperors should not spend so much money on extravagant clothes.

   D. People who are too vain to admit the truth make fools of themselves.

3. Which sentence from the passage contains a simile?

   A. "They set up two looms and pretended to be very hard at work, but they did nothing whatsoever on the looms."

   B. "'They are all as light as a cobweb, and one must feel as if one had nothing at all upon the body.'"

   C. "'Is it not magnificent?' said the two old statesmen who had been there before."

   D. "Soon afterward, the emperor sent another honest courtier to the weavers to see how they were progressing."

4. Why is the child important to the plot?

   A. He reveals the swindlers' deception.

   B. He is the only one who actually sees the clothes.

   C. He makes everyone realize how smart they really are.

   D. He teaches the emperor that clothes are not important.

5. This passage can BEST be described as

A. a myth.

B. a short story.

C. historical fiction.

D. contemporary fiction.

6. The minister and courtiers' reaction to the emperor's suit is important because it

A. makes the emperor distrust the swindlers.

B. shows that they are smarter than the emperor.

C. proves to the emperor that the suit must be real.

D. reveals the truth about the emperor's new suit.

7. Write a brief summary of this passage.

_____

_____

_____

_____

_____

_____

_____

_____

_____

In A Connecticut Yankee in King Arthur's Court, *Mark Twain tells the story of Hank Morgan, from 19th-century Hartford, Connecticut. One day, Hank gets hit on the head and wakes up in medieval England, at the court of the legendary King Arthur. An expert in machinery and a strong believer in the benefits of technology, Hank uses his skills and wit to survive in the 6th-century society that is very different from his own. Early in the novel, a page at the court, named Clarence, tells Hank that he is to be burned at the stake the next day.*

excerpted and adapted from

A Connecticut Yankee in King Arthur's Court

by Mark Twain

The shock that went through me was distressing. My situation was in the last degree serious, dream or no dream. I knew from past experience of the lifelike intensity of dreams, that to be burned to death, even in a dream, would be very far from being a jest, and was a thing to be avoided, by any means. So I said beseechingly:

"Ah, Clarence, good boy, only friend I've got, don't fail me; help me to devise some way of escaping from this place!"

"Why, poor lad, what is the matter? Why do you turn pale? Why do you tremble so?"

He hesitated, pulled one way by desire, the other way by fear. Then he stole to the door and peeped out, listening. Finally he crept close to me and put his mouth to my ear and told me his fearful news in a whisper.

"Merlin, in his malice, has woven a spell about this dungeon. No man in this kingdom would be desperate enough to attempt to cross its lines to help you!"

I laughed the only really refreshing laugh I had had for some time. Then I shouted: "Merlin has wrought a spell! *Merlin*, forsooth! That cheap old humbug, that maundering old fool? Bosh, pure bosh, the silliest nonsense in the world! Why, it does seem to me that of all the childish, idiotic, chuckle-headed, chicken-livered superstitions that I ever heard—oh, what nonsense!"

But Clarence had slumped to his knees before I had half finished, about to go out of his mind with fright. "Oh, beware! These are awful words! Any moment these walls may crumble upon us if you say such things. Oh, call them back before it is too late!"

Now this strange exhibition gave me a good idea and set me to thinking. If everybody about here was so sincerely afraid of Merlin's pretended magic as Clarence was, certainly a superior man like me ought to be able to take advantage of such a state of things. I went on thinking, and worked out a plan. Then I said:

"Get up. Pull yourself together; look me in the eye. Do you know why I laughed? Because I'm a magician myself."

You see, I knew of a famous eclipse that had occurred on the very day and time I was to be burned at the stake. It came into my mind in the nick of time, how Columbus, or Cortez, or one of those people, once used an eclipse to fool some natives, and I saw my chance.

"Go back and tell the king that if he persists on having me burned, I will smother the whole world in the dead blackness of midnight. I will blot out the sun, and it shall never shine again. The fruits of the earth shall rot for lack of light and warmth. The peoples of Earth shall famish and die, to the last man!"

The terrified lad delivered the message. But Merlin wanted to prevent my magic of the next day by executing me one day early. He had me dragged out of my cell immediately.

As the soldiers assisted me across the court, the stillness was profound. If I had been blindfolded, I should have supposed I was alone instead of walled in by four thousand people. There was not a movement perceptible in those masses of humanity; they were as rigid as stone images, and as pale. Dread sat upon every countenance. This hush continued while I was being chained to the stake and wood was piled about my body. When the torch was lit, the multitude strained forward.

Then, with a common impulse, the multitude rose slowly up and stared into the sky. I followed their eyes. My eclipse was beginning! The lad must have told me the wrong date when I asked him. The life went boiling through my veins. I was a new man! The rim of black spread slowly into the yellow sun's disk. My heart beat higher and higher. Still, the assemblage stared into the darkening sky, motionless. I knew that this gaze would be turned upon me next. When it was, I was ready. I was in one of the grandest attitudes I ever struck. My arm was stretched up pointing to the sun. It was a noble effect. You could see the shudder sweep the mass like a wave. Two shouts rang out, one close upon the heels of the other:

"Apply the torch!"

"I forbid it!"

The first was from Merlin, the other from the king. Merlin started from his place to apply the torch himself. I said: "Stay where you are. If any man moves—even the king—before I give him leave, I will blast him with thunder. I will consume him with lightning!"

The multitude sank meekly into their seats, just like I was expecting they would.

"For a lesson, I will let this darkness proceed and spread night in the world. But whether I blot out the sun for good, or restore it, shall rest with you. These are the terms, to wit: You shall remain king over all your dominions, and receive all the glories and honors that belong to the kingship. But you shall appoint me your perpetual minister and executive. Is it satisfactory?"

There was a prodigious roar of applause. Out of the midst of it the king's voice rose, saying: "Away with his bonds, and set him free!"

"If I might ask that my clothes be brought again—"

"They are not suitable," the king broke in. "Get him the proper clothing. Clothe him like a prince!"

8. How does Hank's opinion of Merlin differ from Clarence's?

   A. Hank believes Merlin will help him escape, but Clarence does not.

   B. Hank thinks Merlin is powerful, but Clarence thinks he is weak.

   C. Hank believes Merlin is dangerous, but Clarence thinks he is harmless.

   D. Hank thinks Merlin is a fool, but Clarence is in awe of him.

9. Based on this excerpt, which of the following is MOST LIKELY a theme of "A Connecticut Yankee in King Arthur's Court"?

   A. Magic really is possible.

   B. Life was better in the past than it is today.

   C. A good friend is hard to find and worth keeping.

   D. A knowledge of science can end superstitions.

10. Which element of the story was MOST LIKELY the author's own addition to the medieval legend?

   A. Merlin the magician

   B. the dialogue

   C. the setting

   D. the type of punishment

11. Read these sentences from the passage.

    The rim of black spread slowly into the yellow sun's disk. My heart beat higher and higher. Still, the assemblage stared into the darkening sky, motionless.

    This sentence is an example of

    A. personification.

    B. metaphor.

    C. imagery.

    D. simile.

12. How is the setting important to the plot?

    A. It helps readers understand why Hank does not want to die.

    B. It sets up events that would not likely happen in modern times.

    C. It enables readers to sympathize with Hank Morgan.

    D. It explains why Merlin wants to end Hank's life.

Use "The Emperor's New Clothes" and "A Connecticut Yankee in King Arthur's Court" to answer questions 13–14.

13. How are the swindlers in "The Emperor's New Clothes" and Hank Morgan alike?

    A. They learn how difficult it is to be strangers in a new city.

    B. They see a weakness in people and use it to their advantage.

    C. They use their wits in order to save themselves.

    D. They get the punishment they truly deserve.

14. Based on the actions of the characters, what similar statement do both passages make about human nature?

    _____

    _____

    _____

    _____

    _____

    _____

    _____

    _____

    _____

The Path that Leads to Nowhere
by Corinne Roosevelt Robinson

There's a path that leads to Nowhere
    In a meadow that I know,
Where an inland island rises
    And the stream is still and slow;
There it wanders under willows
    And beneath the silver green
Of the birches' silent shadows
    Where the early violets lean.

Other pathways lead to Somewhere,
    But the one I love so well
Had no end and no beginning—
    Just the beauty of the dell,
Just the windflowers and the lilies
    Yellow striped as adder's tongue,
Seem to satisfy my pathway
    As it winds their sweets among.

There I go to meet the Springtime,
    When the meadow is aglow,
Marigolds amid the marshes,
    And the stream is still and slow.
There I find my fair oasis,
    And with care-free feet I tread
For the pathway leads to Nowhere,
    And the blue is overhead!

All the ways that lead to Somewhere
    Echo with the hurrying feet
Of the Struggling and the Striving,
    But the way I find so sweet
Bids me dream and bids me linger,
    Joy and Beauty are its goal,
On the path that leads to Nowhere
    I have sometimes found my soul!

15. What is the rhyme scheme of the last four lines of stanza 3?

A. AABB

B. ABCA

C. ABBA

D. ABCB

16. Which line from the poem contains alliteration?

A. "And the stream is still and slow"

B. "Echo with the hurrying feet"

C. "As it winds their sweets among"

D. "And beneath the silver green"

17. Read these lines from the poem.

**Just the wildflowers and the lilies
Yellow striped as adder's tongue,**

These lines contain an example of

A. simile.

B. alliteration.

C. metaphor.

D. personification.

18. Which details from the poem indicate that the speaker probably likes to spend time alone?

_____

_____

_____

_____

_____

_____

_____

_____

_____

_____

To Climb a Mountain

For people who dream of climbing to the top of the world, there is only one place to go. At 29,035 feet above sea level, Mount Everest is the highest mountain on Earth.

Mount Everest is located on the border between Sagarmatha Zone, Nepal, and Tibet (a region of China). It is part of the Himalayas, a mountain chain in Asia that includes nine of the world's ten highest peaks. In English, it is called Everest after Sir George Everest, a British surveyor who in the 1900s spent over thirty-five years conducting a geographical survey of India. In Nepal, they call the mountain Sagarmatha, or Goddess of the Sky. In Tibet, it is known as Chomolungma, or Mother Goddess of the Universe.

In 1852, the height of the mountain was first recorded at 29,002 feet by Radhanath Sickdhar, a mathematician analyzing data from the survey. He conveyed the news to the Surveyor-General, exclaiming, "Sir, I have discovered the highest mountain in the world." The news generated a great deal of excitement worldwide. But rushing out to explore the mountain was quite another matter. The weather on Mount Everest is forbidding. June through September is monsoon season, and the mountain is subjected to violent snowstorms. In the winter, winds on the mountain reach over 175 miles per hour, or hurricane force. Temperatures can reach 76 degrees below zero. Windstorms can happen at any time, hurling stones, sand, ice, and snow through the air. The extreme climate led many to label Mount Everest as unclimbable. Nonetheless, some fearless adventurers were determined to reach the top.

Unfortunately, there were political barriers that banned or greatly limited access to the mountain. Westerners were not allowed to enter the region. In the early 1920s, the British finally obtained permission and began to explore the mountain in earnest. At first, local people would not help them because they considered the peaks sacred and would not climb them. However, foreign expeditions brought money into the region, as well as new ideas. A group of people of Tibetan descent, called Sherpas, found work as porters and guides for the explorers.

The British organized preliminary expeditions to survey the region and determine the best route to the top. One of the men on these early expeditions was George Mallory. Asked why he wanted to climb Everest, George Mallory famously replied, "Because it is there." After participating in two unsuccessful climbs, Mallory made a third attempt in 1924, accompanied by Andrew Irvine. It was not a successful endeavor, for both climbers disappeared in bad weather. It was not until 1999 that an American climber found Mallory's body, frozen at about 27,000 feet. Whether Mallory reached the summit or not may never be known.

On May 29, 1953, Edmund Hillary of New Zealand and his Sherpa guide Tenzing Norgay made history. They became the first climbers to reach the summit. Since then, thousands of climbers have tried to duplicate this impressive feat, but only less than half have done so. In 1963, James Whittaker became the first American to reach the summit. In 1975, Japanese climber Junko Tabei became the first woman to accomplish it.

Many of these famous, and not so famous, climbs might not have been successful had it not been for the Sherpa guides. Sherpas are excellent climbers known for their expertise and stamina. They function extremely well at high altitudes, an important quality since high altitude can result in mountain sickness and lead to death. Even before the earliest attempts to climb Mount Everest, Sherpas were being hired for all climbing expeditions in the Himalayas. However, for decades these invaluable guides received very little public recognition and none of the glory they deserved. Over time, their invaluable contributions to Mount Everest expeditions have been acknowledged.

For the Sherpas, being part of expeditions is much more than just a way to earn money. Tenzing Norgay once said, "You cannot be a good mountaineer, however great your ability, unless you are cheerful and have the spirit of comradeship. Friends are as important as achievement. Another is that teamwork is the one key to success and that selfishness only makes a man small. Still another is that no man, on a mountain or elsewhere, gets more out of anything than he puts into it." Norgay's sentiments are shared by many of his fellow climbers, some of whom know each other personally. There is a kinship and mutual respect among those who brave the climb up Mount Everest.

Today, Mount Everest climbers use the latest gear and equipment. When George Mallory attempted his fateful climb, he wore a tweed jacket and knickers, loose pants cut just below the knee. By today's standards, this clothing is considered highly <u>unsuitable</u> for the extreme weather conditions on Everest. Unlike today's climbers, Mallory had no satellite telephone, GPS unit, high-tech boots, or tent. Nonetheless, he, like the others who would follow, looked at the colossal mountain and thought "Why not?" For some, reaching the summit of Mount Everest is not an impossible quest, but the greatest challenge on Earth.

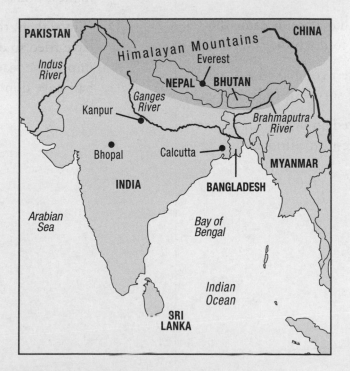

19. The last paragraph in the passage is mainly arranged according to

A. sequence.

B. procedure.

C. cause and effect.

D. comparison and contrast.

20. According to the map, Mount Everest is closest to

A. the Arabian Sea.

B. Bay of Bengal.

C. Bhutan.

D. Bhopal.

21. What is a central idea in the passage?

A. George Mallory said he wanted to climb the mountain "because it is there."

B. In 1975, Junko Tabei became the first woman to reach the summit.

C. George Everest conducted a geographical survey of India.

D. Sherpas played an important role in Mount Everest expeditions.

22. Which of these words has the same suffix as <u>unsuitable</u>?

A. manageable

B. scribble

C. tablet

D. unstable

23. Which sentence from the passage BEST supports the idea that the climb to Mount Everest is dangerous?

A. "Unfortunately, there were political barriers that banned or greatly limited access to the mountain."

B. "Windstorms can happen at any time, hurling stones, sand, ice, and snow through the air."

C. "It is part of the Himalayas, a mountain chain in Asia that includes nine of the world's ten highest peaks."

D. "Since then, thousands of climbers have tried to duplicate this impressive feat, but only less than half have done so."

Because It Is There: The Story of George Mallory

Of the relatively few who have tried to climb Mount Everest, even fewer have succeeded. One of the most famous attempts to climb the tallest mountain in the world was made by George Mallory. His quest to the top of Mount Everest made him a legendary figure in mountaineering history.

Early Life

George Mallory was born in England on June 18, 1886. He lived in a rural village, where his father was a wealthy clergyman. Mallory and his siblings spent a great deal of time outdoors, where Mallory displayed an early affinity for climbing. He would climb trees, roofs, poles, and any other object that piqued his interest. He seemed to enjoy taking risks, as if the danger excited him.

When Mallory was 14, he won a scholarship to Winchester College. It was here that Mallory made an acquaintance that would greatly influence his future career. The headmaster of the school, Graham Irving, was a mountain climber. He, too, was willing to take risks that some considered <u>needless</u>. Not only did Irving climb without local guides, he also climbed alone. If Irving were ever in distress on a climb, he would have no one to assist him. Still, as far as Mallory was concerned, Irving was living the kind of life he had dreamed of. Irving formed the Winchester Ice Club, a climbing group that Mallory eagerly joined.

Climbing the Alps

In 1904, the Winchester Ice Club traveled to the Alps to do some mountain climbing. Their goal was to climb a 12,000-foot mountain. Although this was a fairly modest mountain, Mallory and another young climber developed mountain sickness as a result of the diminished oxygen pressure at higher elevations. They had to turn back 600 feet from the summit. However, Mallory did not give up. He returned to the mountain with Irving and reached the summit twice. Mallory was hooked on mountain climbing. He spent the following summer in the Alps.

Major Life Changes

The Alps are a mountain system in south-central Europe. Mallory had some important decisions to make after finishing school. After considering various options, he took a job teaching. He passed on his love of climbing to his students, taking them along on climbing trips. Some even became lifelong friends with him. In 1914, Mallory married Ruth Turner, and they had three children. During World War I, Mallory had a short stint as a second lieutenant until an old ankle injury got him sent home. In some ways, Mallory's life had taken a turn for the ordinary. He had a job, a wife, and children. But he needed more to feel truly fulfilled. He needed to climb and to reach new heights. In 1921, Percy Farrar asked him to join the first expedition to Mount Everest. Farrar, who had been introduced to Mallory years before, was a respected mountaineer. Everest had been closed to European exploration for decades. The opportunity to be part of a historic expedition to the highest mountain on Earth was exactly what Mallory needed. As he put it, "to refuse the adventure is to run the risk of drying up like a pea in its shell."

The Quest Begins

In September of 1921, the members of the expedition set off to explore uncharted territory. Their goal was to survey the area and figure out a way to the top. They marched through the region, taking photographs and recording what they saw. It was <u>arduous</u> physical work. For weeks, the men climbed peaks and tramped through valleys and over glaciers. They determined that certain paths to the top of Everest were more dangerous than others. The weather and avalanches posed the greatest threats. Finally, the men concluded that the North Col, the low point on one of the three ridges that extend from the mountain's summit, was the key to finding the route. However, when the group tried to reach the Col, they were turned back by violent wind. The weather conditions made another attempt in that year unfeasible. Still, Mallory was certain that they could find a clear route to the summit. The following year, another expedition, of which Mallory was also a part, was more successful. The group reached 27,000 feet, but the peak remained an elusive goal. During that expedition, Mallory climbed up the slopes of the North Col too soon after a fresh snowfall. A huge avalanche killed seven Sherpas, leaving Mallory devastated by guilt.

The Final Attempt

In 1924, plans were made for a third attempt to reach the peak. Mallory had doubts about joining this expedition. He had recently begun a new job at a university in England, and he wanted to spend more time with his family. But the call of the mountain was too great, and after having made such laborious efforts to conquer it, he could not bear the thought of being left out if the others made it to the peak without him. So, he joined the expedition.

When they were at around the 23,000-foot mark on the mountainside, Mallory and fellow climber Andrew "Sandy" Irvine continued up on their own to the next camp, a particularly treacherous part of the climb. They began their ascent on June 6. Two days later, they were seen climbing by another member of the group. A snowstorm followed soon after, and Mallory and Irvine disappeared. Although the other climbers searched and waited for them, they could not find their friends.

In 1999, Mallory's frozen body was found at about 27,000 feet up the mountain. Evidence at the scene suggested he had fallen. To this day, it is unknown whether Mallory and Irvine ever reached the top, or reached it and died during their descent.

Once, Mallory was asked why he felt the need to climb Mount Everest. He replied, "Because it is there." Mallory's body was buried on Mount Everest by the men who found him, perhaps fitting for someone who literally gave his life to the mountain.

24. Read these sentences from the passage.

> **It was <u>arduous</u> physical work. For weeks, the men climbed peaks and tramped through valleys and over glaciers.**

What does the word <u>arduous</u> MOST LIKELY mean?

A. reasonable

B. outstanding

C. hard to determine

D. demanding great effort

25. Which sentence from the passage is an opinion?

A. "Although the other climbers searched and waited for them, they could not find their friends."

B. "He seemed to enjoy taking risks, as if the danger excited him."

C. "In 1904, the Winchester Ice Club traveled to the Alps to do some mountain climbing."

D. "During World War I, Mallory had a short stint as a second lieutenant until an old ankle injury got him sent home."

26. To improve organization, which sentence should be moved from the section called "Major Life Changes"?

A. "In 1921, Percy Farrar asked him to join the first expedition to Mount Everest."

B. "In some ways, Mallory's life had taken a turn for the ordinary."

C. "The Alps are a mountain system in south-central Europe."

D. "After considering various options, he took a job teaching."

27. Which question would be MOST relevant to do further investigation on the topic of the passage?

A. What other evidence did climbers find when they discovered Mallory's body?

B. Have climbers measured the height of Mount Everest in recent times?

C. How much do Sherpas get paid for going on expeditions?

D. Did any of Mallory's siblings become climbers, too?

28. In which section should more details about the initial search for Mallory and Irvine be added?

A. "Climbing the Alps"

B. "Major Life Changes"

C. "The Quest Begins"

D. "The Final Attempt"

29. Read this sentence from the passage.

He, too, was willing to take risks that some considered <u>needless</u>.

Which possible replacement for the word <u>needless</u> has the LEAST negative connotation?

A. extreme

B. excessive

C. unjustified

D. unnecessary

Use "To Climb a Mountain" and "Because It Is There: The Story of George Mallory" to answer questions 30–31.

30. Write three key details you learn about George Mallory in this passage that you did NOT learn from "To Climb a Mountain."

_____

_____

_____

_____

_____

_____

31. How does the author of this passage present Mallory in a more sympathetic light than the author of "To Climb a Mountain" does?

_____

_____

_____

_____

_____

_____

excerpted from

The Story of My Life
by Helen Keller

It was in the spring of 1890 that I learned to speak. The impulse to utter audible sounds had always been strong within me. I used to make noises, keeping one hand on my throat while the other hand felt the movements of my lips. I was pleased with anything that made a noise and liked to feel the cat purr and the dog bark. I also liked to keep my hand on a singer's throat, or on a piano when it was being played. Before I lost my sight and hearing, I was fast learning to talk, but after my illness it was found that I had ceased to speak because I could not hear. I used to sit in my mother's lap all day long and keep my hands on her face because it amused me to feel the motions of her lips; and I moved my lips, too, although I had forgotten what talking was. My friends say that I laughed and cried naturally, and for a while I made many sounds and word-elements, not because they were a means of communication, but because the need of exercising my vocal organs was imperative. There was, however, one word the meaning of which I still remembered, *water*. I pronounced it "wa-wa." Even this became less and less intelligible until the time when Miss Sullivan began to teach me. I stopped using it only after I had learned to spell the word on my fingers.

I had known for a long time that the people about me used a method of communication different from mine; and even before I knew that a deaf child could be taught to speak, I was conscious of dissatisfaction with the means of communication I already possessed. One who is entirely dependent upon the manual alphabet has always a sense of restraint, of narrowness. This feeling began to <u>agitate</u> me with a vexing, forward-reaching sense of a lack that should be filled. My thoughts would often rise and beat up like birds against the wind; and I persisted in using my lips and voice. Friends tried to discourage this tendency, fearing lest it would lead to disappointment. But I persisted, and an accident soon occurred which resulted in the breaking down of this great barrier—I heard the story of Ragnhild Kaata.

In 1890 Mrs. Lamson, who had been one of Laura Bridgman's teachers, and who had just returned from a visit to Norway and Sweden, came to see me, and told me of Ragnhild Kaata, a deaf and blind girl in Norway who had actually been taught to speak. Mrs. Lamson had scarcely finished telling me about this girl's success before I was on fire with eagerness. I resolved that I, too, would learn to speak. I would not rest satisfied until my teacher took me, for advice and assistance, to Miss Sarah Fuller, principal of the Horace Mann School. This lovely, sweet-natured lady offered to teach me herself, and we began the twenty-sixth of March, 1890.

Miss Fuller's method was this: she passed my hand lightly over her face, and let me feel the position of her tongue and lips when she made a sound. I was eager to imitate every motion and in an hour had learned six elements of speech: M, P, A, S, T, I. Miss Fuller gave me eleven lessons in all. I shall never forget the surprise and delight I felt when I uttered my first connected sentence, "It is warm." True, they were broken and stammering syllables; but they were human speech. My soul, conscious of new strength, came out of bondage, and was reaching through those broken symbols of speech to all knowledge and all faith.

No deaf child who has earnestly tried to speak the words which he has never heard—to come out of the prison of silence, where no tone of love, no song of bird, no strain of music ever pierces the stillness—can forget the thrill of surprise, the joy of discovery which came over him when he uttered his first word. Only such a one can appreciate the eagerness with which I talked to my toys, to stones, trees, birds and dumb animals, or the delight I felt when at my call Mildred ran to me or my dogs obeyed my commands. It is an unspeakable boon to me to be able to speak in winged words that need no interpretation. As I talked, happy thoughts fluttered up out of my words that might perhaps have struggled in vain to escape my fingers.

32. Helen Keller writes that she was "on fire with eagerness" to show that

A. she was angry.

B. her feelings were intense.

C. she felt unusually nervous.

D. her temperature was rising.

33. Read this sentence from the passage.

This feeling began to agitate me with a vexing, forward-reaching sense of a lack that should be filled.

What does the word agitate MOST LIKELY mean?

A. to push

B. to soothe

C. to upset

D. to surprise

34. Which sentence BEST summarizes the central idea of this passage?

    A. For a deaf person, the joys of speaking are immense.

    B. A deaf-blind girl from Norway learned to speak.

    C. Laughing and crying are means of communication.

    D. Speaking and hearing are two very different abilities.

35. Read this sentence from the passage.

> **I was pleased with anything that made a noise and liked to feel the cat purr and the dog bark.**

What is the correct way to quote this sentence in a research paper?

    A. As Keller writes: I was happy with anything that made a sound and "liked to feel the cat purr and the dog bark."

    B. As Keller writes, "I was pleased with anything that made a noise and liked to feel the purring of cats and dogs."

    C. "As Keller writes, I was pleased with anything that made a noise and liked to feel the cat purr and the dog bark."

    D. As Keller writes, "I was pleased with anything that made a noise and liked to feel the cat purr and the dog bark."

36. Which phrase from the passage BEST illustrates Helen Keller's frustration?

    A. laughed and cried naturally

    B. different from mine

    C. prison of silence

    D. joy of discovery

Read the passage and answer the questions that follow.

A Meaningful Life

Helen Keller was born in the rural town of Tuscumbia, Alabama, on June 27, 1880. Her father owned a cotton plantation and edited the local newspaper. Her mother worked on the plantation and lived as independently as possible, even making the family's butter and bacon. They lived in a simple house built by Helen's grandfather.

When Helen was 19 months old, she became gravely ill. At the time, doctors diagnosed her illness as brain fever. However, many doctors now think that it may have been meningitis or scarlet fever. For days, Helen clung to life, until, finally, she recovered, and her parents thought that she was healed. As Helen's mother soon discovered, something was not right with her daughter. Helen no longer responded when the dinner bell rang or to visual cues, like a hand passing in front of her eyes. Helen had lost her hearing and sight.

Over the next few years, Helen became unmanageable. She threw terrible temper tantrums, screaming and breaking dishes and other items. Some family members advised that Helen be institutionalized, but Helen's parents held out hope that she would change. Desperate, the Kellers took her to Baltimore to see a specialist. Although the doctor confirmed that Helen would never recover her sight or hearing, he believed that Helen could be helped. He referred them to a teacher of deaf children named Alexander Graham Bell. Bell was familiar with the Perkins Institution and Massachusetts Asylum for the Blind. He suggested that the Kellers contact the school and hire a teacher for Helen. The institution recommended a woman who had once been a pupil there. Her name was Anne Sullivan.

Twenty-year-old Anne had something in common with Helen. When Anne was 5 years old, she had lost most of her sight. Anne had been educated at Perkins and undergone an operation that restored her sight enough to allow her to read for short periods of time. Still, she had struggled since graduating from the institution, so she was thrilled to find work as a teacher. On March 3, 1887, Anne Sullivan arrived at Helen's house. Helen was almost 7 years old. She would later describe that day as "the most important day I can remember in my life."

Anne's education of Helen began simply but effectively. The children at Perkins had given Anne a doll to take to Helen. Anne gave the doll to Helen and spelled *d-o-l-l* into Helen's hand with her finger. Helen was able to trace the letters herself correctly, but she couldn't manage to make the connection between the object and the word. She did not understand the concept of words, much less how to spell them. Then, one day Anne held Helen's hand under the running water from the outdoor pump. As the water flowed over Helen's hand, Anne spelled *w-a-t-e-r* into the other hand. Suddenly, it clicked. Helen understood that the letters traced into her hand identified the water running over her other hand. She immediately began touching other objects, demanding to know their letter names. By the end of the night, she had learned thirty words.

After that <u>momentous</u> day, Helen's education progressed rapidly. She learned the alphabet and began to read and write. Anne taught her how to read Braille and write with both regular and Braille typewriters. Helen was a quick learner, devouring knowledge with an insatiable hunger. But learning how to read and write was not enough. When Helen was 10, she discovered that a deaf-blind girl in Norway had learned how to speak. Helen wanted to learn as well. Her first teacher was Sarah Fuller at the Horace Mann School. Despite some success over the years, Helen was never able to fully master the power of speech.

In 1896, Helen entered the Cambridge School for Young Ladies. Four years later, she enrolled in Radcliffe College. Anne, who by now was inseparable from Helen, continued to help her with her studies. While in college, Helen wrote her autobiography, *The Story of My Life*. It was the beginning of Helen's writing career. Helen earned her Bachelor's Degree and graduated with honors in 1904. She was the first deaf-blind person to graduate from college. Even after her formal education was over, Helen continued to read and learn about the events and social issues of her day. She was outspoken about her views and wrote many articles for magazines and newspapers.

Anne and Helen went on lecture tours, and Helen continued to gain worldwide fame. She became a social activist and had the ear of powerful people, including a succession of U.S. presidents. Helen passed away on June 1, 1968. In his eulogy, Senator Lister Hill said, "She will live on, one of the few, the immortal names not born to die." He may have been right. Helen Keller's autobiography is still in print and has been published in over fifty languages.

Timeline of Hellen Keller's Early Life

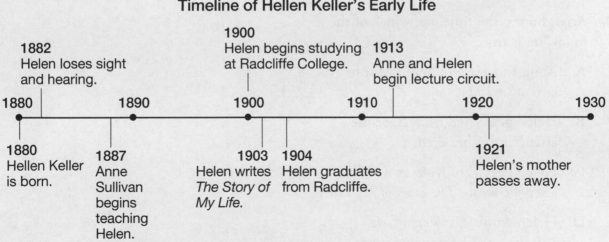

37. The suffix ous in momentous means the same as the suffix in

    A. momentary.

    B. poisonous.

    C. raucous.

    D. mindless.

38. Which detail from the passage suggests that Helen had emotional trouble coping with her physical challenges?

    A. She did not react when a hand passed in front of her eyes.

    B. She demanded to know the names of objects.

    C. She threw violent temper tantrums.

    D. She did not respond to the dinner bell.

39. According to the timeline, which of the following is true?

    A. Anne and Helen began a lecture circuit in 1921.

    B. Helen graduated from Radcliffe after her mother died.

    C. Helen began studying at Radcliffe after she wrote *The Story of My Life*.

    D. Helen wrote *The Story of My Life* before she graduated from Radcliffe.

40. Which of the following BEST describes the organizational structure of this passage?

    A. sequence

    B. process

    C. cause and effect

    D. comparison and contrast

41. Which would be the BEST resource to find more information on Helen Keller?

    A. an educational Web site with articles on Helen Keller

    B. an online encyclopedia entry on blindness

    C. a newspaper review of a movie about Helen Keller's life

    D. a blog by a person who read *The Story of My Life*

Use "The Story of My Life" and "A Meaningful Life" to answer questions 42–43.

42. Explain how both passages show the influence that other people had on Helen Keller's life.

_____

_____

_____

_____

_____

_____

_____

_____

_____

_____

43. How do both passages illustrate Helen Keller's passion for learning?

_____

_____

_____

_____

_____

_____

_____

_____

_____

The Debate Over Spelling Reform

For many students throughout this country, spelling is the bane of their existence. Even some of the smartest, most accomplished students have trouble spelling. It's understandable. English can be a tricky language. For one thing, the pronunciation of many words does not match how they are spelled on paper. For instance, the word *station* is pronounced *stayshun*. In some languages, such as Italian and Spanish, words are usually written phonetically. So, if a word is spelled with a *t*, it will be pronounced with a *t* sound, not a *sh* sound. Furthermore, in the English language, the same letters or combinations of letters can be pronounced in different ways. For example, think of the words *cough, soup*, and *shout*. These words all have the same vowel combination—*ou*—but they are pronounced in three different ways. Not surprisingly, some people believe that the spelling of English should be reformed to make it more logical and simpler. This is hardly a new idea. Benjamin Franklin made this argument long ago. Despite some admittedly good reasons to support spelling reform, it is not a feasible plan. We should not change the way we spell English words.

One of the reasons for variant pronunciations and spellings is that English is derived from Germanic and Latin languages. Additionally, English has borrowed countless words from other languages, such as *marriage, immediate*, and *question* from French. Furthermore, the pronunciation of vowels has changed over the centuries, but the spelling has remained the same. Although these factors play a role in the complexities of English spelling, contributions from other languages have enriched our own. No one is sure exactly how many words are in the English language. Some say 500,000; some say one million, if you count scientific and medical terms. We have so many words because English has a long and rich cultural history. If spelling were reformed, much of that history would be lost.

Supporters of reform point out that there are too many spelling rules. For example, if you want to add a suffix to a word that ends in *-y*, look at the letter that comes just before the *y*. If it is a consonant, change the *y* to an *i* unless the suffix begins with *i*. If a word ends in *-e*, drop the *e* to add a suffix that begins with a vowel. Put *i* before *e*, except after *c* and when it sounds like *a*, as in *neighbor* and *weigh*. People also complain that most spelling rules have exceptions, which only complicates things further. It's true that spelling rules are often too complex and inconsistent. However, most people spell correctly because they memorize the spelling of thousands of words. Does anyone really stop to think of a rule when he or she is writing a letter or a book report? Suppose one doesn't remember how to spell the word *millennium*. What is one to do? How about looking up the word in the dictionary? It's really not that much of an effort. After a while, people naturally start memorizing the spelling of any words they frequently write.

Of course, some people argue that we ask too much of children when we expect them to memorize so many words with illogical spellings. The problem is not whether children spell correctly. The problem is how big a deal we want to make of their spelling. These people argue that we don't need to reform English spelling entirely. We can just relax our attitude toward small variations in commonly misspelled words. Let's view these as alternative spellings instead of misspellings. If the meaning is clear, does it really matter if a student writes *cogh* instead of *cough*? But this line of thinking ignores the simple truth that correct spelling benefits any piece of writing, whether a school composition or a business memo.

Reforming English spelling would be impossible to achieve for another reason. Who is going to decide on the new spellings of words? France has the *Académie Française*, or French Academy. The forty members of the Academy act as the official authority on the language. They make decisions on vocabulary and grammar. They work to prevent the Anglicization of French. In other words, they advise against borrowing words from English, in the fear that these words will gradually be adapted into the French language. For instance, when the word *e-mail* began creeping into French conversation and writing, the Academy recommended the use of *courriel* instead. But we have no such organization in the United States. Who will be the authority? We also need to take into account other English-speaking countries. Should only one country be in charge of spelling reform? The debate within our own shores will be heated enough. Imagine what it will be like on an international scale. No English-speaking nation is going to go along with the spelling reforms <u>dictated</u> by another country.

It would be easier to learn English and spell correctly if words sounded like they are spelled, and we eliminated the need for complicated spelling rules. Nonetheless, it is much too late for any sort of comprehensive reform. The only acceptable compromise is to allow for spelling variations. However, even this seems unnecessary. Countless generations have managed to learn how to spell correctly. Current and future generations will do just fine.

44. Which sentence from the passage is a fact?

A. "How about looking up the word in the dictionary?"

B. "Benjamin Franklin made this argument long ago."

C. "The only acceptable compromise is to allow for spelling variations."

D. "Nonetheless, it is much too late for any sort of comprehensive reform."

45. What is the author's main purpose for writing this passage?

A. to inform readers about the history of the English language

B. to explain how France feels about spelling reform

C. to persuade readers that spelling reform is not needed

D. to convince readers that spelling correctly is not important

46. Read this sentence.

> **No English-speaking nation is going to go along with the spelling reforms <u>dictated</u> by another country.**

The author uses the word <u>dictated</u> to suggest that other countries will feel

A. comfortable.

B. imposed upon.

C. suspicious.

D. left out.

47. Paragraph 1 of the passage is arranged to show

A. the causes of spelling trouble.

B. how spelling changed over time.

C. the process of reforming English spelling.

D. how English compares to Italian and Spanish.

48. The author brings up the French Academy as a way to argue against spelling reform. Is this a relevant and convincing point? Explain your answer.

_____

_____

_____

_____

_____

_____

_____

_____

_____

_____

This passage contains mistakes. Read the passage and answer the questions that follow.

Stars

(1) What is it about stars that has fascinated people for thousands of years? (2) Most people who look up toward the sky are not interested in the science of stars. (3) They look skyward for the same reason that poets and songwriters have done so for centuries; they want to absorb the lovely silent beauty of a starry night. (4) However, for others, studying celestial objects offers the opportunity to understand the universe we live in. (5) As early as 3,000 BCE, the ancient Babylonians studied the night sky and identified various constellations. (6) Other early civilizations created star maps and tracked the positions of the stars for navigation and timekeeping purposes. (7) Over the centuries, advancements in science and technology has unlocked many mysteries of stars.

(8) In the 16th century, galileo, an italian astronomer and mathematician, built the first high-powered telescope. (9) It was an improvement over earlier telescopes but it had limitations. (10) For one thing, it distorted the image. (11) Around 1670, Isaac Newton used mirrors to invent a reflecting telescope. (12) By the close of the 1600s, a bunch of observatories were using reflecting telescopes. (13) During the next two centuries, hundreds of stars were watched and observed. (14) In 1838, Friedrich Bessel of Germany computed the distance to a star for the first time. (15) In 1849, the first photos of stars were taken at an observatory in Boston.

(16) Using modern methods, new facts and theories about stars have been developed by astronomers. (17) What is a star, exactly? (18) Stars are formed from dust and gas in space. (19) A cloud of dust and gas is called a nebula. (20) Over time, turbulence and gravitey cause the cloud to collapse. (21) As the cloud collapses, the material at its center begins to heat up. (22) This hot core at the center of the collapsing cloud will one day become a star. (23) At this stage, this hot, condensed material is called a protostar. (24) If the protostar's temperature rises high enough, it will become a true star. (25) At this point, a star is classified as a main-sequence star.

(26) A main-sequence star is basically a huge ball of glowing gas with a lifespan of about 10 billion years. (27) It is fueled by hydrogen. (28) Earth's sun is a main-sequence star. (29) Astronomers have come up with the idea that it took about 50 million years from its origins as a collapsing cloud to reach its current phase. (30) Main-sequence stars can vary widely in size, color, and brightness. (31) The smallest main-sequence stars are called red dwarfs and make up the majority of stars in the universe. (32) Red dwarfs may be as little as one-tenth the size of the sun.

49. Which of the following is a compound sentence?

A. The smallest main-sequence stars are called red dwarfs, and they make up the majority of stars in the universe.

B. What is it about stars that has fascinated people for thousands of years?

C. Around 1670, Isaac Newton used mirrors to invent a reflecting telescope.

D. A main-sequence star is basically a huge ball of glowing gas with a lifespan of about 10 billion years.

50. Read this sentence from the passage.

As the cloud collapses, the gases and other material at its center begin to heat up.

Which is the dependent clause in this sentence?

A. As the cloud

B. As the cloud collapses, the gases and other material

C. As the cloud collapses

D. the gases and other material at its center begin to heat up

51. Which version of sentence 3 is correct?

A. They look skyward for the same reason that poets and songwriters have done so for centuries. To absorb the lovely, silent beauty of a starry night.

B. They look skyward for the same reason that poets and songwriters have done so for centuries, they want to absorb the lovely silent beauty of a starry night.

C. They look skyward for the same reason that poets and songwriters have done so for centuries, they want to absorb the lovely, silent beauty of a starry night.

D. They look skyward for the same reason that poets and songwriters have done so for centuries; they want to absorb the lovely, silent beauty of a starry night.

52. What is the correct way to revise sentence 7?.

A. Over the centuries, advancements in science, and technology have unlocked many mysteries of stars.

B. Over the centuries, advancement in science and technology have unlocked many mysteries of stars.

C. Over the centuries advancements in science and technology had unlocked many mysteries of stars.

D. Over the centuries, advancements in science and technology have unlocked many mysteries of stars.

53. What is the correct way to write sentence 8?

A. In the 16th century, Galileo, an Italian astronomer and mathematician, built the first high-powered telescope.

B. In the 16th century, Galileo, an italian astronomer and mathematician, built the first high-powered telescope.

C. In the 16th century, galileo, an Italian astronomer and mathematician, built the first high-powered telescope.

D. In the 16th century, Galileo, an Italian Astronomer and Mathematician, built the first high-powered telescope.

54. Read this sentence from the passage.

It was an improvement over earlier telescopes but it had limitations.

Where should the comma go in this sentence?

A. after *earlier*

B. after *improvement*

C. after *telescopes*

D. after *but*

55. Which sentence from the passage uses language inappropriate for the purpose and audience?

A. sentence 6

B. sentence 12

C. sentence 14

D. sentence 18

56. What is the BEST way to revise sentence 13?

A. Stars were watched by astronomers during the next two centuries.

B. During the next two centuries, astronomers observed hundreds of stars.

C. Hundreds of stars were watched and observed during the next two centuries.

D. During the next two centuries, astronomers watched and observed hundreds of stars.

57. Read this sentence from the passage.

> **Over time, turbulence and gravitey cause the cloud to collapse.**

Which word is spelled incorrectly?

A. turbulence

B. gravitey

C. cloud

D. collapse

58. Read this sentence from the passage.

> **If the protostar's temperature rises high enough, it will become a true star.**

What kind of sentence is this?

A. simple

B. compound

C. complex

D. compound-complex

59. What is the BEST way to revise sentence 29?

A. Astronomers have concluded that it took about 50 million years from its origins as a collapsing cloud to reach its current phase.

B. Astronomers have been thinking that it took about 50 million years from its origins as a collapsing cloud to reach its current phase.

C. Astronomers have an existing idea that it took about 50 million years from its beginning as a collapsing cloud to reach its current phase.

D. Astronomers have an idea that it took about 50 million years from its origins as a collapsing cloud to reach its current phase.

60. Read this sentence from the passage.

Using modern methods, new facts and theories about stars have been developed by astronomers.

Revise this sentence to correct the dangling modifier.

_____

_____

_____

STOP

Session 2

Persuasive Prompt

Studies have shown that eating too many snack foods such as candy, cupcakes, and potato chips, as well as soft drinks, can lead to serious health problems. As a solution, some states have suggested placing a tax on processed foods high in fat, sugar, and salt, so that people would be less inclined to buy them. Companies in the food industry are against this idea, claiming the tax would threaten their profits. Opponents also argue that the tax will have little impact on people's food choices. What do you think? Should a tax be imposed on unhealthy foods? Be sure to organize your essay and support your argument with reasons and evidence.

Use the checklist to help you do your best writing.

Does your essay

❑ have a clear topic?

❑ show a point of view about that topic?

❑ have a logical structure?

❑ support reasons with details?

❑ connect reasons and details with the right words or phrases?

❑ use a style and vocabulary that is correct for the audience and purpose?

❑ have a solid conclusion?

❑ have good spelling, capitalization, and punctuation?

❑ follow the rules for good grammar?

Write your response on the page provided. You may use your own paper if you need more space.

Glossary

act a major division of a play (Lesson 2)

active voice the form of a verb in which the subject does the action in a sentence (Lesson 24)

affix one or more letters attached to the beginning or end of a root word to change its meaning (Lesson 26)

alliteration the repetition of consonant sounds at the beginning of words (Lesson 3)

audio something that relates to sound, such as music or the spoken word (Lesson 20)

allusion an indirect reference to a well-known person, place, event, or object in history or in a literary work (Lesson 7)

argument a persuasive attempt to convince others to think or act in a certain way (Lessons 10, 16)

bibliography an organized list of all the sources used in a research paper (Lesson 20)

capitalization the use of capital, or uppercase letters, in certain circumstances and situations (Lesson 23)

cause the reason something happens, such as an event or action (Lesson 13)

cause and effect a text structure in which causes (reasons) for events and the results (effects) of those causes are examined (Lesson 13)

CD-ROM a compact disk containing electronic information (Lesson 20)

character a person, animal, or other creature in a fictional text (Lessons 5, 18)

chart a graphic organizer that presents information arranged into columns and rows in a box (Lesson 14)

citation a specific reference within a research paper to a source of information (Lesson 20)

claim a statement of an author's point of view in an argument, which the author must prove (Lessons 10, 16)

clause a group of words that contains a subject and a predicate (Lesson 21)

climax the turning point in a story, usually the most exciting part (Lesson 4)

colon a punctuation mark used to introduce a list or an example (Lesson 23)

comma a punctuation mark used to separate elements in a sentence (Lesson 23)

compare to examine the similarities between two or more things (Lesson 12)

comparison and contrast a text structure in which the similarities and differences between two or more things are examined (Lesson 13)

complex sentence a sentence containing one independent clause and one dependent clause (Lesson 22)

compound sentence a sentence containing two or more independent clauses joined by a coordinating conjunction (Lesson 22)

compound-complex sentence a sentence containing more than one independent clause and at least one dependent clause (Lesson 22)

conciseness clear and direct expression of ideas (Lesson 24)

conclusion the last paragraph in a composition (Lessons 16, 17)

conflict a problem that a character must solve (Lessons 4, 18)

connotation the emotional weight a word carries, or the set of associations implied by the word (Lesson 27)

contemporary fiction a narrative set in modern times (Lesson 1)

context the background or circumstances in which events occur; the words and sentences surrounding a particular word in a text (Lessons 18, 25)

contrast to examine the differences between two or more things (Lesson 12)

coordinate adjectives two or more adjectives that equally modify a noun (Lesson 23)

coordinating conjunction a word such as *and, but,* or *so* that joins two independent clauses (Lessons 22, 23)

dangling modifier a phrase that describes or limits a word or word group that does not appear in the sentence, or is associated with a word or word group other than the one intended (Lesson 21)

dash a punctuation mark used to set off nonessential information in a sentence (Lesson 23)

database a collection of information stored on a computer, such as an online library catalog (Lesson 20)

denotation a word's dictionary definition, or what it literally means (Lesson 27)

dependent clause a clause that cannot stand alone as a complete sentence (Lessons 21, 22)

detail descriptive information that expands upon the main idea in a text (Lesson 17)

diagram an illustration with labels that describes something or shows how it works (Lesson 14)

dialogue the words spoken by characters to each other (Lessons 2, 18)

dictionary an alphabetical listing of words that provides their meanings, pronunciations, parts of speech, and origins (Lesson 25)

digital source a resource that is accessed through a computer or other electronic device (Lesson 20)

drama a literary work intended to be performed by actors for an audience (Lesson 2)

edit to correct errors in content, grammar, and style (Lesson 19)

effect what happens as a result of a cause (Lesson 13)

example something that represents a group or type (Lessons 9, 17)

exposition the beginning of a story, when the setting and characters are established (Lesson 4)

fact a statement that can be verified independently and objectively (Lessons 9, 15, 17)

fable a short story with a moral or lesson; often has animal characters (Lesson 1)

falling action the events leading to the solving of the problem (Lesson 4)

fiction a literary work produced from a writer's imagination (Lesson 1)

figurative language the use of words to create an image in the reader's mind (Lesson 7)

flowchart a graphic that shows the sequence of events in a story or steps in a process (Lesson 18)

genre a category, or type, of literature (Lesson 1)

glossary a list of key or specialized words and their definitions, found at the back of a book (Lesson 25)

graph a diagram that shows relationships between sets of data, such as a bar graph or line graph (Lesson 14)

graphics visual representations of information and ideas (Lesson 14)

heading a title over a section of text; usually in larger and darker print (Lesson 17)

historical fiction a narrative that is set in the past and gives a fictional account of historical figures or events (Lesson 1)

imagery language that appeals to the five senses (sight, sound, touch, taste, and smell) (Lesson 7)

independent clause a clause that can stand alone as a complete sentence (Lessons 21, 22)

inference an educated guess based on information and evidence in a text, and your own prior experience (Lesson 8)

informative text a text that informs the reader or explains something (Lesson 17)

introduction the first paragraph in a text (Lessons 16, 17)

main idea the central message of a text (Lesson 9)

map a graphic representation of regions on Earth and their geographical features (Lesson 14)

metaphor a comparison of two unlike things, without using the word *like* or the word *as* (Lesson 7)

meter the pattern of stressed and unstressed syllables in a line of poetry (Lesson 3)

misplaced modifier a modifier that is positioned incorrectly in a sentence (Lesson 21)

modifier a word or group of words that describes or limits another word or word group (Lesson 21)

motivation the reason a character acts a certain way (Lesson 5)

myth a traditional story that tells about a culture's heroes, ancestors, or gods and goddesses; may explain how the natural world was created or how it works (Lesson 1)

narrative writing that tells a story (Lesson 18)

nonfiction writing that conveys information using facts and other details. Nonfiction tells about actual people, events, or other real-life subjects. (Lesson 9)

novel a long narrative, usually divided into chapters (Lesson 1)

opinion a personal belief that cannot be proven true and with which others may disagree (Lesson 15)

outline a graphic organizer that establishes the sequence of ideas and arranges information into topics and subtopics (Lesson 16)

pacing the rate of speed in which events are described in a narrative (Lesson 18)

paraphrase a restatement of someone else's words in your own words (Lesson 20)

passive voice the form of a verb in which the subject is acted upon in the sentence (Lesson 24)

personification giving human qualities to an animal, object, or abstract idea (Lesson 7)

phrase a group of words that contains a subject or a predicate but not both (Lesson 21)

plagiarism using someone else's words as your own and failing to use quotation marks or give credit to the source (Lesson 20)

playwright the author of a play (Lesson 2)

plot the sequence of events in fiction or drama (Lessons 4, 18)

poetry a literary work written in verse, or in short lines (Lesson 3)

point of view the perspective of a character or narrator in a fictional text; an author's perspective, or position, in an argument (Lessons 5, 10, 18)

predicate the part of a sentence that contains the verb (Lesson 21)

prefix an affix added to the beginning of a word to change the meaning of the word (Lesson 26)

primary source material that is created by an eyewitness or a participant in an event (Lesson 11)

print source a source that is printed on paper, such as a book or journal (Lesson 20)

procedure an organizational pattern that explains how to do something in a series of steps (Lesson 13)

process an organizational pattern that explains how a series of actions or functions bring about a result (Lesson 13)

publish to produce writing for others to read (Lesson 19)

punctuation the set of standard marks used to clarify meaning in writing (Lesson 23)

purpose the reason an author writes a text; for example, to persuade (Lessons 10, 16, 17)

quotation the exact words of someone other than the writer (Lessons 9, 17)

quotation marks punctuation marks placed around someone's exact words (Lesson 23)

quote to copy the exact words from a source, enclosing them in quotation marks (Lessons 9, 20)

reason something that supports the central idea of an essay (Lesson 9)

reasoned judgment a statement based on an issue for which there is more than one standard of judgment (Lesson 15)

redundancy a repetition of words or ideas (Lesson 24)

research a scholarly or scientific investigation of a specific topic (Lesson 20)

resolution the ending of the story, when the conflict is resolved (Lesson 4)

resource a text, audio, or video used to gather information (Lesson 20)

revise to check that a paper is well-organized and to make any needed changes (Lesson 19)

rhyme the repetition of sounds at the ends of lines (Lesson 3)

rhythm the repeated pattern of sounds used in poetry (Lesson 3)

rising action the bulk of the story, during which the character works to resolve the problem (Lesson 4)

root the main part of a word (Lesson 26)

run-on sentence two or more independent clauses joined without the proper punctuation (Lesson 19)

scene a subdivision of an act with a fixed setting (Lesson 2)

secondary source material by someone who studied an event, but was not present for it (Lesson 11)

semicolon a punctuation mark used to separate two or more independent clauses that are closely related (Lesson 23)

sensory language language that appeals to the five senses (sight, sound, touch, taste, and smell) (Lesson 18)

sentence fragment a sentence missing either a subject or a verb (Lessons 19, 22)

sentence structure the grammatical arrangement of words in a sentence (Lessons 19, 22)

sequence the ordering of information or events in the order that they happen (Lessons 13, 18)

setting where and when a story takes place (Lessons 4, 18)

short story a short narrative with a plot and characters (Lesson 1)

simile a direct comparison of two unlike things, using the word *like* or the word *as* (Lesson 7)

simple sentence a sentence made up of one independent clause (Lesson 22)

soliloquy a speech in a play delivered by one character while he or she is alone onstage (Lesson 2)

sonnet a fourteen-line poem with a precise rhyme scheme and meter (Lesson 3)

source something that provides information, such as a printed text, an electronic text, or a video (Lessons 11, 16)

stage directions instructions in a drama that tell actors what to do and how to speak their lines (Lesson 2)

stanza a group of lines within a poem (Lesson 3)

statistic a piece of information stated numerically (Lesson 9)

subject the word that performs the action in a sentence (Lesson 21)

subject-verb agreement when the subject and verb agree in number (Lesson 19)

subordinating conjunction a word or phrase that introduces a dependent clause (Lessons 21, 22)

suffix an affix added to the end of a word to change the meaning of the word (Lesson 26)

summary a short restatement of a text in the reader's own words (Lesson 6)

supporting detail a fact, example, reason, or other detail that backs up the main idea (Lesson 9)

supporting paragraph a paragraph in the body of a composition that includes facts, examples, and other details to support the main idea (Lessons 16, 17)

synonym a word that has the same meaning as another word (Lesson 27)

tense the form of a verb used to indicate time in a sentence (Lesson 19)

text structure the organizational pattern of a text (Lessons 13, 17)

theme the central message or lesson of a literary text (Lesson 6)

timeline a graphic representation of events in chronological order (Lesson 14)

tone an author's attitude toward a subject (Lesson 7)

topic sentence the main idea of a paragraph (Lesson 16)

trait a quality that defines a character (Lesson 5)

transitions words that show relationships among ideas and help writing to flow (Lessons 17, 18)

verb a word that shows action or describes a state of being (Lesson 21)

video a visual electronic recording, such as a documentary (Lessons 14, 20)

Web site electronic pages of information (Lesson 20)

word choice the author's careful selection of words in a text (Lesson 17)

Mechanics Toolbox

▷ **Pronouns**

A **pronoun** is a word that takes the place of a noun. The form of a pronoun shows both person and number.

Person refers to the point of view expressed by the pronoun: first person (the person speaking, or *I*), second person (the person spoken to, or *you*), or third person (the person or thing spoken of, or *he, she,* or *it*).

Number refers to how many people or things the pronoun represents. A **singular** pronoun represents one person or thing. A **plural** pronoun represents more than one person or thing.

This chart features the personal pronouns.

	Singular	Plural
First Person	I, me	we, us
Second Person	you	you
Third Person	he, him; she, her; it	they, them

An **antecedent** is the word that a pronoun replaces. Pronouns and antecedents need to agree in person and number. Third-person singular pronouns and antecedents also need to agree in gender. The antecedent for a pronoun may appear in a previous sentence. It may also appear earlier within the same sentence as the pronoun.

Examples:
My class organized a fundraiser. We raised nearly $10,000! (correct)
After Susan and Elfranko finished the laundry, they went swimming. (correct)
When a person does well on this exam, they should be congratulated. (incorrect)

In the fourth example, the plural pronoun, *they,* does not agree with the singular antecedent, *person*. The correct sentence is:

When people do well on this exam, they should be congratulated.

It also needs to be clear which noun is the antecedent of a pronoun. Consider this example:

We piled tall stacks of books on the tables until they fell over.

The antecedent of *they* is not clear. Did the stacks of books fall over, or did the tables? It is best not to use a pronoun in this sentence. The correct possibilities are:

We piled tall stacks of books on the tables until the books fell over.
We piled tall stacks of books on the tables until the tables fell over.

 ## Sentence Pattern

A sentence is a group of words that tells a complete thought. It can stand alone. It can include various combinations of clauses and phrases, but it has at least one subject and predicate. The **subject** tells who or what the sentence is about. The **predicate** tells what the subject does.

> Example:
> They left.

They is the subject of this sentence. The predicate is *left*. It tells what they did.

Phrases and Clauses

A **phrase** is a group of related words that does not include its own subject and verb. A comma should follow an introductory phrase. For example:

> Examples:
> From the very first day, Tabitha liked her new school. (prepositional phrase)
> Walking on tiptoe, James creeped behind his little sister. (participial phrase)
> To tell you the truth, I did not like that movie at all. (infinitive phrase)
> A sleepy town next to nowhere, Riverdale was beautiful. (appositive phrase)

A **clause** is a group of words that includes a subject and verb. There are two types of clauses: independent clauses and dependent clauses.

An **independent clause** can stand alone as a sentence. It tells a complete thought. In the following examples, each subject is underlined once, and each verb is underlined twice.

> We argued.
> George agreed to walk his neighbor's retriever.
> They practiced hard that entire year.

Although it includes both a subject and verb, a **dependent clause** cannot stand alone. It is not complete. Some dependent clauses begin with a relative pronoun, such as *who, whom, which,* or *that.* The relative pronoun may serve as the subject of the dependent clause. Other dependent clauses begin with a subordinating conjunction, such as *after, although, because, however, if, until,* and *when.* In the following examples, each subject is underlined once, and each verb is underlined twice.

> Until we started to laugh.
> Although he dislikes dogs.
> Which ended with their first championship.

On its own, none of these clauses expresses a complete thought. It needs to be joined to an independent clause.

Examples:
We argued until we started to laugh.
Although he dislikes dogs, George agreed to walk his neighbor's retriever.
They practiced hard that entire year, which ended with their first championship.

Compound Subjects and Predicates

A sentence can include more than one subject. For example:

Yolanda enjoys reading. Ursula enjoys reading, too.

These sentences can be combined into one sentence with a compound subject.

Example:
Yolanda and Ursula enjoy reading.

Notice the change in the verb when the sentences are combined. The compound subject, *Yolanda and Ursula*, needs a plural verb, *enjoy*.

A sentence can also include more than one predicate. For example:

Yolanda enjoyed that book. She did not like the movie based on it.

These sentences can be combined into one sentence with a compound verb.

Example:
Yolanda enjoyed that book but did not like the movie based on it.

Yolanda is the subject of both predicates, *enjoyed that book* and *did not like the movie based on it*.

A sentence can have both a compound subject and a compound verb. For example:

Yolanda and Ursula enjoyed that book and are looking forward to reading the sequel.

Both subjects, *Yolanda* and *Ursula*, are the subject of both predicates, *enjoyed that book* and *are looking forward to reading the sequel*.

Types of Sentences

Different combinations of independent and dependent clauses form different types of sentences. There are four basic sentence patterns.

1. A **simple sentence** includes one independent clause and no dependent clauses.

   Examples:
   The lilies bloomed.
   The violinist amazed the audience with her skill.
   When did you return home?

2. A **compound sentence** includes two or more independent clauses. In the following examples, each independent clause is underlined.

   Michael lost his wallet, but a stranger soon returned it to him.
   We could get the books at the library, or my sister will lend us her copies.
   I wrote the lead article, Amy did the interviews, and Jimmy designed the layout.

3. A **complex sentence** includes one independent clause and one or more dependent clauses. In the following examples, each independent clause is underlined once, and each dependent clause is underlined twice.

   Our basement floods whenever it rains.
   The dress that my mother made is my favorite.
   Because Lisa usually visits him on Saturday, her grandfather worried when he did not see her that weekend.

Notice that the dependent clause *that my mother made* appears between the subject and verb of the independent clause *The dress is my favorite.*

4. A **compound-complex sentence** includes two or more independent clauses and at least one dependent clause. In the following examples, each independent clause is underlined once, and each dependent clause is underlined twice.

   Although they had never taken care of a garden before, their flowers were healthy and their vegetables were delicious.
   Whenever Allison practices the clarinet, her dog starts barking and the stray cats that live in the empty lot behind her house start yowling.

Notice that the dependent clause *that live in the empty lot behind her house* appears between the subject and verb of the independent clause *the stray cats start yowling.*

Concise Words and Phrases

Good writers choose their words carefully. They use vivid words that appeal to the senses. They also use words that convey precise meanings. Consider these examples:

> I was hot. (general word choice)
> Sweat poured into my eyes. (vivid word choice)

The second sentence is more vivid. It helps the reader feel the speaker's discomfort in the heat. Using the verb *poured,* it is more active. It is best to avoid overusing forms of the verb *be,* such as *was* in the first sentence.

Consider these other examples:

> Swimming in the <u>water</u> <u>made me feel better</u>. (vague word choice)
> Swimming in the <u>lake</u> <u>cooled me off</u>. (precise word choice)

In fewer words, the second sentence conveys much more detail than the first. It tells precisely where the speaker went swimming: in a lake. It also tells precisely how the speaker felt better: he or she cooled off.

It is usually better to use a vivid verb or precise noun than add an adjective or adverb. Here are examples:

> Holly <u>walked quickly</u> across the parking lot. (verb and adverb)
> Holly <u>hurried</u> across the parking lot. (vivid verb)

Also avoid adjectives or adverbs that repeat ideas already conveyed through other words. For example:

> Neil Gaiman, my favorite writer, has written a wide variety of different books.

It is not necessary to use both *variety* and *different* in this sentence. The word *variety* on its own conveys the idea of difference. This sentence is better:

> Neil Gaiman, my favorite writer, has written a wide variety of books.

Verb Voice and Mood

In a sentence that reflects the **active voice**, the actor is the subject. In a sentence that reflects the **passive voice**, the object of an action is the subject. Compare these examples:

> My aunt donated the costumes for the performance. (active voice)
> The costumes for the performance were donated by my aunt. (passive voice)

My aunt is the subject of the first sentence. She is doing the donating. *The costumes* is the subject of the second sentence. They are the object of the donating.

The active voice is generally preferred. However, there may be times when the passive voice is acceptable or even necessary. For example, you might use the passive voice in a letter of complaint if you do not want to write a direct accusation:

> We have learned that some children were prevented from seeing the performance.

You might need to use the passive voice if the actor is unknown. For example:

> The flowers for the performance were also donated. We have no idea who sent them.

Conditional sentences tell about events that are dependent on a condition that may or may not occur. The condition is given in a dependent clause beginning with *if*. The possible consequence of the condition is given in the independent clause.

The tense and mood of the verbs in a conditional sentence depend on the truth of the condition given in the sentence. The condition may be true, possibly true, or untrue.

> If we <u>have</u> ice cream, we <u>are</u> happy. (true about the present)
> If we <u>have</u> ice cream, we <u>will be</u> happy. (true about the future)
> If we <u>have</u> ice cream, we <u>should be</u> happy. (possibly true about the future)
> If we <u>had</u> ice cream, we <u>would be</u> happy. (untrue about the present)

Notice the verbs in the independent clauses of the sentences about possibly true or untrue conditions. They are in the **conditional mood** and include the helping verbs *should* and *would*. The conditional mood expresses possible but uncertain events. The helping verbs *could* or *might* can also be used in the conditional mood.

Also notice the past-tense verb (*had*) in the dependent clause that expresses an untrue condition. This verb is in the **subjunctive mood**. The subjunctive mood expresses untrue or hypothetical events. It is often used in clauses beginning with *if* or to express wishes. For example:

> If I <u>were</u> you, I would give up now.
> I wish I <u>were</u> in charge.

Notes

Notes

Notes

Notes

Notes

Notes

Notes

Notes

Notes

Notes

Notes

Notes